STANLEY®

Plumbing

Steve Cory

The Taunton Press

The Taunton Press
Inspiration for hands-on living®

The Taunton Press, Inc.
63 South Main Street
PO Box 5506
Newtown, CT 06470-5506

Email: tp@taunton.com

Editor: Peter Chapman
Copy Editor: Seth Reichgott
Indexer: Jay Kreider
Jacket/Cover design: Stacy Wakefield Forte
Interior design: Stacy Wakefield Forte
Layout: Alison Wilkes
Photographers: Steve Cory and Diane Slavik (except where noted)

The following names/manufacturers appearing in *Plumbing* are trademarks: American Standard™, Chicago Faucets®, Craigslist®, Crane®, DeWALT®, IKEASM, Kohler®, SharkBite®, Speakman™, Speed® Square, STANLEY®, STANLEY FATMAX®, Teflon®, Vikrell®, Vintage Tub & BathSM, WaterSense®, Zip-It®

Library of Congress Cataloging-in-Publication Data

Names: Cory, Steve, author. | Stanley Black & Decker Inc., issuing body.
Title: Stanley plumbing : a homeowner's guide / Steve Cory.
Other titles: Plumbing
Description: Newtown, CT : The Taunton Press, Inc., [2016] | Includes index.
Identifiers: LCCN 2016023105 | ISBN 9781631861628
Subjects: LCSH: Plumbing--Amateurs' manuals. | Dwellings--Maintenance and
   repair--Amateurs' manuals.
Classification: LCC TH6124 .C675 2016 | DDC 644/.6--dc23
LC record available at https://lccn.loc.gov/2016023105

Printed in the United States of America
10 9 8 7 6 5 4 3 2 1

MANY THANKS to Danny Campana for his plumbing expertise and aplomb, not to mention his excellent qualities as a photo model; and his singing was often tolerable. Joe Hansa contributed sage advice, Mike Fish of Vogon Construction set me straight on a number of issues, and William Shuman was essential as a model and setup guy.

A special thank you to the companies that generously donated products for use in step-by-step photos. The beautiful sinks, bathtubs, faucets, and showerheads featured in installation photos came from American Standard™, the Kohler® Company, IKEA℠, Vintage Tub & Bath℠ (Mountain Top, Pennsylvania), and Speakman™ (Wilmington, Delaware). It was a pleasure working with these companies. And, of course, Stanley Black & Decker supplied a good number of high-quality tools.

CONTENTS

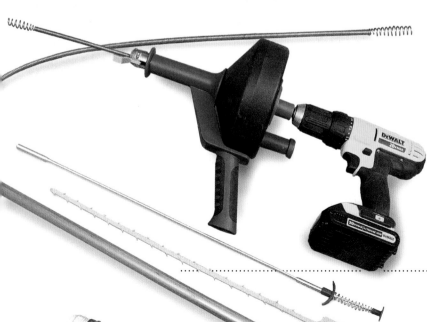

STANLEY

Introduction

A home plumbing system can seem like a mystifying tangle of different sizes and types of pipes, not to mention all those valves, connections, and fixtures. Many people automatically call a professional plumber at the first sign of a leak, a balky faucet, or a clogged sink or toilet, or when they want to replace a toilet or faucet. This book will demystify your plumbing system and enable you to make repairs and replacements with confidence.

What You Should and Should Not Do

If you are reasonably handy, ready to work carefully and systematically, and have the time to learn and perform a job, you can tackle most of the projects in this book. That includes almost every type of repair and upgrade to your existing system. This book will show you how.

A homeowner who is doing plumbing work for the first—or even the second or third—time will certainly work more slowly than a professional plumber. And a pro may have all the needed tools and materials on hand, whereas you may have to buy or assemble them. But plumbers charge plenty, so even taking into account the extra time and the expense of buying new tools, it is usually cost-effective to do the work yourself.

Make a serious attempt to anticipate the costs before tackling a job. Read through the instructions, gather the necessary tools, buy the right parts, and realistically assess the amount of time it will take. As a general rule of thumb, you can estimate the time you think it will take—and then multiply the time by two or three. On many plumbing projects you will spend more time traveling to the home center, hardware store, or plumbing supply store and buying supplies than you spend actually doing the work.

How This Book Is Organized

This book begins with an explanation of your plumbing system. This information will equip you to approach repairs and installations with confidence. Or it can help you speak knowledgeably with a pro if you decide to hire one.

Chapters 2 through 6—a bit more than half the book—describe projects of varying complexity, but all can be tackled with the small collection of inexpensive tools shown on pp. 26–29. That's because none of these projects requires changing supply or drain pipes. These are the most common homeowner repairs and upgrades: unclogging stopped-up sinks and toilets; repairing and replacing faucets; replacing sinks and toilets; and adding new plumbing features to a bathroom or kitchen.

The rest of the book deals with jobs that are more challenging because they usually require changing system pipes. We'll first show basic instructions for cutting and installing new pipes of various types. These procedures are less difficult than you may expect. You'll need more tools for these more advanced projects, but plumbing tools are less expensive than tools for other trades: Two hundred bucks or so will probably buy all you need.

Armed with pipe-assembly knowledge and a good set of tools, you can then dive into replacing a bathtub or shower unit; repairs and replacements for basement (or utility room) fixtures; and pipe repairs.

The final chapter introduces the most challenging projects of all: remodeling a kitchen or bathroom. Although no book can cover all the possibilities, this chapter will enable you to understand most of what a hired professional remodeler will do in your home, and can also enable you to approach some remodeling projects yourself.

Working Safely and Comfortably

Rule number one for most plumbing projects: *Before removing a fixture or unscrewing anything, shut the water off and test that the water is really off.* This doesn't apply to unclogging or other simple tasks, but it applies to many repairs and almost all replacements and upgrades.

Often plumbing is simple in principle, but the task is made difficult because you have to shoehorn your body into small spaces and uncomfortable positions. Take time to make the work site as cushy and well lit as possible.

Water can do plenty of damage to floors, walls, and ceilings, so have appropriately sized buckets and large thick towels or drop cloths on hand, because water often dribbles out even after the supply valves have been turned off.

When working with gas pipe, it is essential to shut off the gas and test to be sure there are no leaks before doing any work. After gas pipes and fixtures are installed, test carefully again.

Hiring a Pro

After reading this book, you may choose to hire a pro to do the "rough-in" work on a project—installing the supply and drain-waste-vent pipes. After the rough-in work is inspected and approved by a building inspector, you may choose to install the drywall, perhaps tile, and add other finish wall and ceiling materials, and then install the faucets, sinks, and other appliances yourself.

The plumber's quote for installing everything, including the finish fixtures, may be low enough that you'll decide to hire him or her for the work. This book will help you inspect the work all along the way for correct installation.

Develop a friendly relation with your contractor, but be firm in your determination to get the work done correctly and in a timely manner. The contract should stipulate a timetable and should have penalties for work that is not done on time. The final payment, which you will make once the work is completely done to your satisfaction, should be sizable enough to keep the contractor's eye on the prize.

A local building inspector should examine and sign off on the rough and finish plumbing. This ensures that the work is done correctly and safely. It may also be necessary when the time comes for you to sell your house.

CHAPTER ONE

GETTING READY

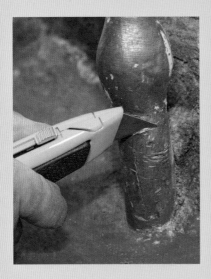

MANY PLUMBING JOBS CERTAINLY MERIT
calling in a pro, but the majority of plumbing
house calls are for things that could be accomplished by a motivated homeowner with a few
tools. Whether you know something about
plumbing or are a rank beginner, this chapter
will quickly point you in the right direction
to get started saving money while fixing
problems and upgrading your plumbing.

Begin with a general understanding of your system—or systems,
really, because the drain-waste-vent system works separately from the
water supply system. Know how to shut off water—either to the whole
house or to parts of your system—in case of emergency or in preparation
for repairs or replacements. Find out what type of pipes you have, their
sizes, and where they go. Learn the best places to access pipes when
needed for unclogging.

The last four pages of this chapter show the tools needed for all
the repairs and upgrades covered in Chapters 2 through 6. You may be
pleasantly surprised at how few and how inexpensive these tools are.

Shutting Off Water

Disconnecting a fixture, appliance, or pipe without shutting off the water will lead to a real disaster—high-pressure water shooting out so forcefully that you probably will not be able to push the fixture or pipe back into place. For most plumbing repairs and replacements, it's essential that you shut off the water—and test that the water is shut off—before you start disconnecting anything. (Exceptions to this rule include unclogging, removing drain traps, and replacing a garbage disposal.)

With the exception of a toilet, faucets and appliances are supplied with both cold and hot water, so you must turn off both hot and cold valves to stop all the water flow.

In many cases, shutting off the water is a simple matter of turning off nearby stop valves that control water leading to the individual faucet or fixture. In other cases, you may need to shut down partial-house valves that control pipes bringing water into an entire bathroom or a portion of a house's system. And there are times when you need to turn off water to the entire house by turning off the main shutoff valve.

THREE VALVE TYPES

An older globe valve must be turned multiple times in order to shut off. It has a rubber washer that will wear out in time. Both gate and ball valves shut off water with a quarter turn, but gates are not as reliable as balls.

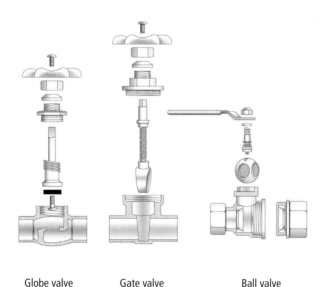

Globe valve   Gate valve   Ball valve

MAIN VALVE BY METER. In many homes the shutoff is inside, by the water meter. There may be a valve on each side of the meter.

SIMPLE MAIN. Here, a simple valve outside the house serves as the main shutoff. This house has a well, so there is no water meter. In areas where water is unmetered, a shutoff like this may be either inside or outside.

The main shutoff

Main shutoffs vary widely in type and placement. Yours may be a globe valve that has to be turned clockwise multiple times until you can feel it stopping. Or it may be an older gate or a newer ball valve, which shuts off when it is turned a quarter of the way around. Ball valves have proven to be the most reliable and durable type.

In some areas, the main is a simple valve located outside the house. Or it may be just inside your basement or utility room, near the water meter (if you have one). Some mains are located in an underground enclosure commonly called a Buffalo box (see the photos on p. 8). You may be able to turn it off by hand, or you may need to use a special "key" tool. Some houses have two main shutoffs, one in a Buffalo box and another near the water meter.

Partial-house shutoffs

If you see a pair of valves (one for hot and one for cold) in a basement, utility room, or in an access panel behind a bathtub (see p. 24), they may control more than one fixture or appliance. Shut them off, then test your faucets and toilets to see what they control. The illustration on p. 9 can help you figure out which part of the house they control.

Stop valves

A very old home may have pipes that run directly into faucets and toilets, with no stop valves. If that is your situation, you'll have to shut off partial-house or main valves

IN-FAUCET VALVES. Some tub-and-shower faucets, like this one, have integrated hot- and cold-water shutoffs. Use a large screwdriver or a wrench to turn the water off when making repairs.
Caution: Turning these shutoffs off does not turn off water in the pipes. If you need to replace the faucet, turn off the water prior to the faucet—at a partial-house or main shutoff.

PARTIAL-HOUSE VALVES. This pair of valves controls the water leading to one of the home's bathrooms. Other partial-house valves may be for a kitchen or for multiple bathrooms.

Saddle T Valves

A saddle T valve ties into a cold-water pipe to supply fixtures like an icemaker or a hot-water dispenser. *Caution: Be aware that turning this valve's handle does not turn off the water to the appliance it supplies.* If you need to turn the water off, do so at a partial-house or main shutoff downstream from the saddle T.

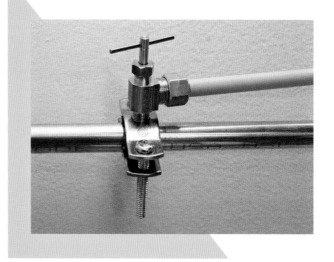

BUFFALO BOX. An in-ground service box, sometimes called a Buffalo box or a water bucket, may or may not contain the meter. Remove the cover to expose the valve. The main shutoff valve may be turned by hand, or you may need to use a special "key" tool. (In some areas, only the water company keeps a key.) The example here has both a handle and a key shutoff.

in order to change a toilet or faucet. When you do this, it's a good idea to install stop valves to make it easier to work on your system in the future.

Stop valves vary greatly in quality, and cheaper models are not completely reliable. See pp. 19–20 for more information.

The Supply System

For most homes, water is supplied by a public system. (If you live in a rural area, you may have your own well that supplies water.) Water enters the house through a single "service" pipe. It first passes through a water meter (if you have one), and may then pass through a water softener (again, if you have one), and then enters a water heater. From there, it branches out and travels in pairs of hot- and cold-water "distribution" pipes to provide water to all your appliances and fixtures. As discussed on pp. 6–7, various shutoff valves allow you to turn the water off at various points.

To determine the materials and sizes of your pipes, see pp. 16–18. These factors can affect your water pressure, and older materials such as galvanized steel or PVC— and maybe even copper—may develop leaks after some decades of service.

Testing for Lead

In some older cities and communities, the utility's main supply pipe may be made of lead, a toxic element. Also, many copper pipes installed before 1986 are joined with lead-based solder, which can also introduce lead into your water. However, nearly all of these municipalities now add a trace element of phosphate to the water, which effectively coats the pipe and solder so that virtually no lead leaches into the water. If you are concerned about possible lead contamination in your water, buy an inexpensive home testing kit, or contact your water utility to find out about testing facilities.

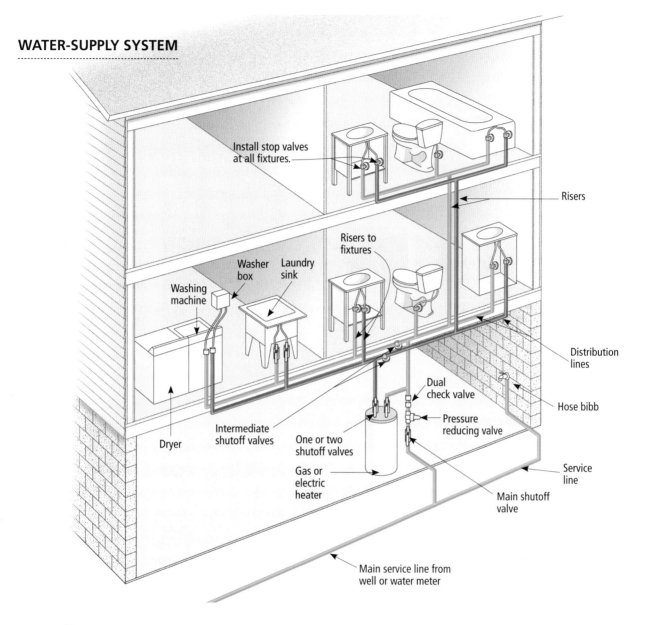

Install stop valves at all fixtures.

Risers

Risers to fixtures

Washer box

Washing machine

Laundry sink

Distribution lines

Dual check valve

Pressure reducing valve

Hose bibb

Intermediate shutoff valves

One or two shutoff valves

Gas or electric heater

Main shutoff valve

Service line

Dryer

Main service line from well or water meter

The Water Meter

In most (but certainly not all) areas, household water is metered. Your water usage should appear on your water bill in cubic feet. (If it does not, and if your bill is the same every month, you probably don't have a meter.) In some areas you are prohibited from reading the water meter, but in most locales you can access the meter. If the meter is not visible in your basement, utility room, or outside the house, you may have to pry off a Buffalo box lid to access it. Older meters have dials, some of which turn counterclockwise, whereas others turn clockwise. Newer meters are digital, so reading is easy.

Safe and tasty water

Water from a utility company should be tested regularly for safety. If you have a well, be sure to test it regularly for pathogens. If your water tastes bad, if it has a milky color, or if it stains your sinks and tubs, it likely is "hard," meaning it has a high mineral content. A water softener or a filter (pp. 156–157, 225) usually solves these problems.

A better system

A standard water distribution system, as shown in the drawing on p. 9, branches off at various points to save piping costs. The disadvantage: When one user, for example, a washing machine, faucet, or dishwasher, is using water, other "downstream" users will get lower water pressure. The most famous example is when you are taking a shower and someone flushes a toilet, and the shower suddenly becomes piping hot. (Or if a dishwasher starts up, shower water will suddenly become cold.)

A manifold system greatly reduces this problem, because each faucet, appliance, or fixture is supplied by a pair of dedicated pipes. That way, one water user does not affect another user. A manifold system would be prohibitively expensive with copper pipes, but it is reasonable in price when inexpensive PEX tubing (see p. 18) are used. If you have the opportunity to install a new plumbing system, consider a manifold.

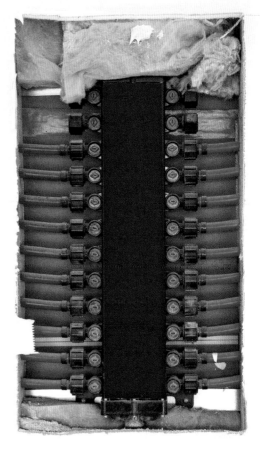

MANIFOLD SYSTEM. A manifold system sends water directly to each faucet or appliance.

Drain-Waste-Vent System

The drain-waste-vent (DWV) system has two jobs: to carry liquid and solid waste out of the house, and to prevent noxious sewer gasses from entering the house. Drain lines take care of the first task, and vent lines take care of the second—and also ensure that waste materials will flow smoothly through the drainpipes, without gurgling. A good number of very specific plumbing codes require

that both drains and vents be installed in certain ways, to ensure that everything works without problems.

The main stack

Most homes have one main stack, also called the main vent stack. This is a large-diameter vertical pipe that runs from the building drain at the bottom up through the house's roof. It serves to vent most of a home's drainpipes.

Drainpipes and vent pipes

The drainpipes are fairly straightforward, sloping downward so that water can run out of the house and toward a municipal sewer system or a septic system.

> **TIP** The difference (if any) between a "drain" line and a "waste" line is not entirely clear, so some people speak of the "drain/vent" system. However, it is more usual to speak of the system and its pipes using the term "DWV."

STANDARD DRAIN-WASTE-VENT SYSTEM

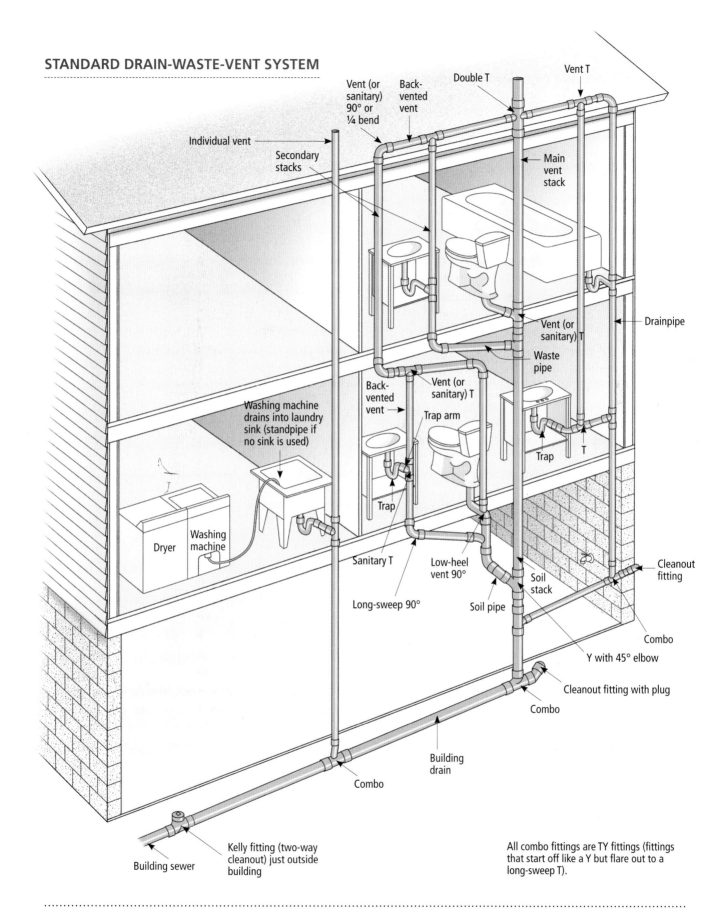

Individual vent

Vent (or sanitary) 90° or ¼ bend

Back-vented vent

Double T

Vent T

Secondary stacks

Main vent stack

Vent (or sanitary) T

Drainpipe

Waste pipe

Washing machine drains into laundry sink (standpipe if no sink is used)

Back-vented vent

Vent (or sanitary) T

Trap arm

Trap

Dryer

Washing machine

Trap

T

Trap

Sanitary T

Low-heel vent 90°

Soil stack

Cleanout fitting

Long-sweep 90°

Soil pipe

Combo

Y with 45° elbow

Cleanout fitting with plug

Combo

Building drain

Combo

Kelly fitting (two-way cleanout) just outside building

Building sewer

All combo fittings are TY fittings (fittings that start off like a Y but flare out to a long-sweep T).

Drainpipes either are straight (or nearly straight) verticals, or they slope at specified angles. Horizontal pipes should be sloped at a prescribed rate, usually ¼ in. per running foot. This horizontal sloping angle ensures both that liquids will flow and that solids will get washed away.

Traps, which are smaller-dimensioned pipes connecting sinks to the main drains, also have very specific requirements; see p. 19 for more information.

Various branch drain and vent pipes carry waste from fixtures and appliances to the main stack. These pipes are often 1½ in. or 2 in. in diameter. "Re-vent" pipes join to the stack in configurations that are strictly specified by plumbing codes, to ensure that there will always be air behind the draining liquid, even when multiple fixtures are in use. In most cases, a pipe should not serve double duty as a drain and a vent pipe—something called "wet venting"—unless the drainpipe is large enough in diameter that it will never get full.

Code considerations

Drain and vent pipes are joined with fittings made specifically for the purpose, so waste will not get stuck or back up into vent pipes; see pp. 228–231 for more information.

Codes limit how far drainpipes, as well as vent pipes, can travel to get to the main stack. For that reason, most homes also have one or two secondary stacks, typically 2 in. or 3 in. in diameter, that serve specific water users that are too far away from the main stack. Most often, a secondary stack serves a kitchen or a laundry, though it can also serve a bathroom.

Codes also require that drainpipes and stacks be accessible in order to clear blockages. Traps under sinks can be dismantled so that an auger or pressure-clearing tool can be used. Elsewhere you will find cleanouts, which have large plugs that can be removed so you can auger the pipe.

Pipe materials

Older homes may have cast-iron stacks, and perhaps galvanized steel for smaller drainpipes. Newer homes have plastic drain and vent pipes; see pp. 16–19 for more information.

In places where it is difficult to install a code-approved vent pipe, some building departments allow for the use of air admittance valves (AAVs); see the drawing on the facing page.

Air Keeps It from Gurgling

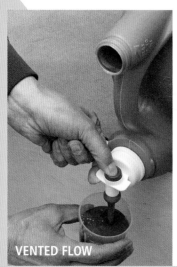
VENTED FLOW

FLOW WITH WIDE OPENING

A detergent dispenser, far left, illustrates how venting helps water move efficiently through a narrow opening. If the can's vent cap is closed, liquid will move sluggishly, and in gulps. But once you open the vent cap, air is admitted behind the liquid, and it can flow smoothly. In the same way, vent pipes provide air behind drainpipes, so liquid can flow easily even if the drainpipe is full.

A bottle with a wide mouth, left, shows how waste water can move smoothly even without venting, as long as the opening is large enough that the liquid does not fill it. Codes often call for drainpipes to be large in diameter, so they will rarely be filled.

AAVS CAN REPLACE SOME VENT PIPES

Air admittance valves (AAVs) open when needed to allow air behind the waste flow, and so perform the same task as vent pipes. They are designed to close after the pipe has drained, to prevent sewer gases from entering the house. Still, they are not allowed for toilets. AAVs are usually the exception rather than the rule in a home DWV system. They are most often used when adding new service during remodeling in situations where it may be difficult to run a vent pipe.

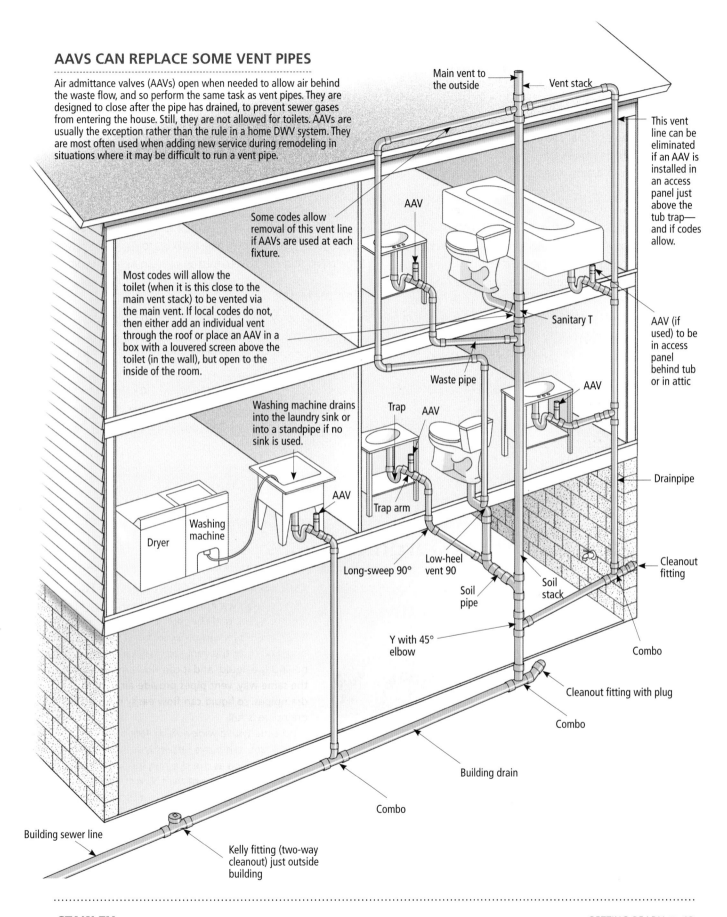

Main vent to the outside

Vent stack

This vent line can be eliminated if an AAV is installed in an access panel just above the tub trap—and if codes allow.

AAV

Some codes allow removal of this vent line if AAVs are used at each fixture.

Most codes will allow the toilet (when it is this close to the main vent stack) to be vented via the main vent. If local codes do not, then either add an individual vent through the roof or place an AAV in a box with a louvered screen above the toilet (in the wall), but open to the inside of the room.

Sanitary T

AAV (if used) to be in access panel behind tub or in attic

Waste pipe

AAV

Washing machine drains into the laundry sink or into a standpipe if no sink is used.

Trap   AAV

Drainpipe

Dryer   Washing machine

AAV

Trap arm

Long-sweep 90°

Low-heel vent 90

Soil pipe

Soil stack

Cleanout fitting

Combo

Y with 45° elbow

Cleanout fitting with plug

Combo

Building drain

Combo

Building sewer line

Kelly fitting (two-way cleanout) just outside building

A TRAP SEALS OUT GASES

A plumbing trap is shaped to hold water in such a way as to create a seal, so that fumes and gases cannot enter the house. Sinks typically have traps that can be dismantled in order to clear out clogging debris; the downside is that they may develop leaks if they get bumped. Some sinks have traps that are glued solidly together; they may have drains that can be removed for clearing out clogs. A toilet has a built-in trap, so it doesn't need to be connected to a piped trap. See p. 19 for more on traps.

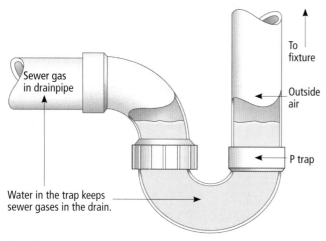

Sewer gas in drainpipe

To fixture

Outside air

P trap

Water in the trap keeps sewer gases in the drain.

Septic systems

If you live in a rural area, your waste may be directed to a septic system rather than a municipal system. Septic systems vary in design, but most of them have most of the elements shown in the drawing below.

How septic systems work Waste runs via a downward-sloping drainpipe into a concrete or plastic septic tank. There, solids sink to the bottom and a layer of scum floats on the top. Baffles and openings are positioned so that only liquids move from one tank compartment to the next, and then out the drainpipe. Bacteria in the tank slowly break down much of the scum and solids into liquids.

Not all the solids can be broken down, so you must hire a septic company to send a "honey dipper" to pump your tank from time to time. How often they come depends on the size of the tank and how much waste gets pumped into it.

From the tank, waste liquid flows through a large-diameter solid pipe and into a distribution box. From the box, two or more (usually more) perforated drainpipes carry waste into a leach field. The pipes are typically embedded in gravel, then loose soil. The liquid seeps into the soil through the pipes' perforations. Once in the soil, microbes continue to break down the waste liquid, which provides good fertilization for the lawn or plantings in the field.

In some systems, a solid pipe leads from the tank to a leaching pool, also called a cesspool. This acts much like the perforated pipes in the first system, sending waste water slowly outward underground. Cesspools may need to be pumped like the tank, though usually not as often.

TYPICAL SEPTIC SYSTEM

Water flows through a pipe to the tank, where solids are separated from liquids and bacteria break down much of the waste. From there, liquid waste flows into a distribution box, then out through perforated pipes into a leach field.

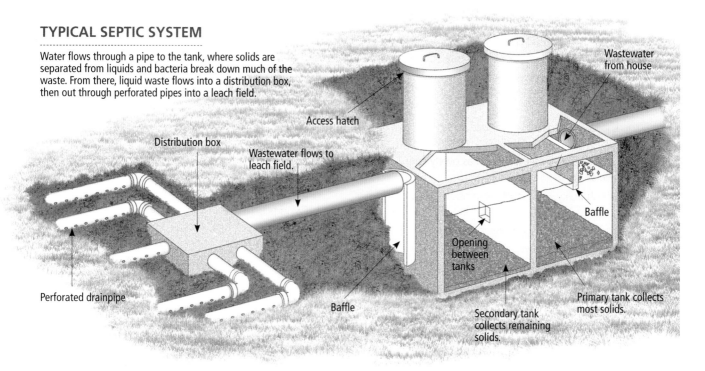

Distribution box

Wastewater flows to leach field.

Access hatch

Wastewater from house

Baffle

Perforated drainpipe

Baffle

Opening between tanks

Secondary tank collects remaining solids.

Primary tank collects most solids.

SEPTIC MAINTENANCE. Call a septic cleaning company to suck out all the gunk from your system. The cleaning company can also make repairs, clean out pipes, and add enzymes to keep your system healthy.

Maintaining a septic system Users of septic systems should:

- Avoid excessive water use, such as overly long showers.
- Not flush bulky items, such as tampons, down the toilet.
- Use only septic-approved toilet paper, which can break down quickly.
- Not flush or pour down sinks toxic products, such as solvents, oils, and even bleach and drain cleaners.

Some more maintenance tips:

- Take steps to ensure that the leach field stays as dry as possible, such as redirecting downspouts or digging drainage trenches.
- At least once a year, open the tanks and poke down a sludge pole to check the sludge's depth. Once the tank is half full, have it pumped.
- If you get a strong sewage smell and the tank is not overly full, the bacteria may have been killed. Buy an enzyme additive and pour it down a drain, as directed.
- If an enzyme does not solve the problem, call a septic company to check for clogs or other problems.

Understanding Pipes

It's a good idea to identify the materials and sizes of your home's pipes. This will help you understand your system, and may help you spot possible problems down the road.

Nowadays, most new residential plumbing installations call for DWV pipes (and fittings) that are made of PVC plastic, supply pipes made of either copper or PEX tubing, and gas pipes that are either black steel or CSST. However, older homes may have existing pipes and fittings of different materials.

DWV pipes

Nowadays, most DWV pipes are made of PVC plastic, but in an older home you may find two or more other materials.

Cast iron Homes built before World War II, and some built afterward, have stacks and some horizontal lines that are made of cast iron. These pipes often last for many decades, but some cast-iron pipes have surprising weak spots. Check yours for leaks, both at the fittings and along the pipe lengths. Older cast-iron pipes had a widened hub at one end, into which a succeeding piece could be inserted. The joint then was packed with a fiber called oakum, and molten lead was poured to make the final seal. In newer installations, rubber "no-hub" fittings, with hose clamps, are used instead.

Cast iron is quieter than plastic drainpipe, so it is still installed in a few locales. But almost everywhere else it has been replaced with plastic drainpipe. When remodel work is done, or when a cast-iron pipe develops a leak, it

DWV PIPES. From left to right: cast iron, copper, galvanized steel, PVC, and ABS.

DRAIN TRANSITION. In the course of remodeling an old home, PVC drainpipe is sometimes joined to an old cast-iron pipe using a rubber coupling with hose clamps.

COMMON PIPES. Here we see PVC drainpipes and copper supply pipes—probably the most common combination. The purple streaks at the drainpipe joints show that primer was applied before the pipes were glued together.

is common to attach a section of plastic drainpipe to the old cast-iron pipe using a neoprene connector (see the top right photo on the facing page).

Steel Older homes often have smaller drain lines—usually 2 in. or less—made of galvanized steel. This material can rust and can get clogged with mineral deposits, but it's not nearly the problem that it is with steel supply pipes.

Copper Copper drain pipes are found in some areas, though they are not common nationwide. Copper may be used for large or small drainpipes. Copper pipes used for drains may be labeled "DWV," indicating that the material is thinner than the "M" copper used for supply pipes. Copper is an improvement over steel, but it has lately become very expensive and has largely been replaced by plastic drainpipe.

ABS Black drainpipe is made of acrylonitrile-butadiene-styrene, mercifully shortened to ABS for us non-scientists. It was often used for post-WWII homes, but has fallen into disfavor in most locales. Its joints can sometimes loosen and leak, and so codes call for PVC instead. Much ABS has proved reliable for a long time, but check yours for leaks.

PVC White or ivory-colored polyvinyl-chloride pipe, or PVC, has clearly emerged as the DWV material of choice. It lasts about forever, and reliably watertight fittings can be easily joined with primer and glue. The most common type, "schedule 40," is inexpensive and reliable for almost all residential uses.

TIP At PVC fittings, you should see a purple line, indicating that primer was applied before the glue was applied. If there is no evidence of primer, the joint may come loose and leak.

Supply pipes

Supply pipes hold water under constant pressure, so they need to be strong and tightly joined in order to prevent leaks.

Galvanized Silver-colored galvanized steel pipes (sometimes called galvanized iron) are screwed together via threads. They were the only supply pipe used for many years, and in some areas they are still used when

SUPPLY PIPES. From left to right: CPVC, PVC, galvanized steel, copper, and two colors of PEX.

remodeling and connecting to existing galvanized pipe. They are also often used for a stub-out—the short length of pipe that pokes out of a wall, to be joined to a valve or a tub faucet.

Galvanized pipe is very strong, so you don't have to worry about nailing through it while remodeling. But its advantages end there. Old galvanized pipes, especially in areas with hard water, accumulate mineral deposits that clog the pipe, leading to low water pressure. And galvanized pipes can rust, especially at the threaded joints, causing leaks. For these reasons, it is generally recommended that you replace galvanized pipe that is 50 years old or older with copper pipe or PEX tubing. In many areas there are companies that specialize in such repiping.

Copper In most areas, copper supply pipe will last for several lifetimes. However, in areas with acidic water (that is, water with pH lower than 7.0), pinhole leaks may develop. In some locales, leaking copper pipe is a notorious problem, whereas in most of the country—where water has a pH of more than 7.0—copper lasts indefinitely. If you are concerned about water acidity and copper pipes, be sure to consult with a local plumber or your building department.

This pipe is "rigid," as opposed to flexible copper tubing sometimes used for icemakers and dishwashers. Copper pipe labeled "M" is made of the thinnest available material, but is considered strong enough for residential use. Pipes labeled "L" are stronger and are recommended in areas with somewhat acidic water. "K" pipes are often used for commercial installations or for underground piping.

Copper is most commonly joined to fittings by a process of soldering or "sweating" (see pp. 169–173). However, newer joining methods involve the use of crimping tools or special no-solder fittings.

As of this book's writing, copper has gotten quite expensive, and so many people choose PEX or CPVC instead.

PVC and CPVC For a short while, white PVC pipe, usually labeled "schedule 80," was used for supply lines. However, it has proved somewhat unreliable and is no longer approved by most codes. PVC pipe is particularly problematic when used for hot-water lines.

CPVC (chlorinated polyvinyl-chloride) pipe, which is ivory rather than white in color, is more reliable than PVC and is heat-resistant so there are no problems using it for hot-water lines. It has been supplanted by PEX tubing but is still a viable option in some areas, especially where copper pipe may be damaged by acidic water. Check to see if CPVC is allowed for use by your local codes.

PEX tubing Cross-linked polyethylene tubing, referred to as PEX, is the newest supply pipe material, but it has been available for long enough to gain the approval of most building departments. Still, some areas are holdouts, and it may not be allowed where you live.

PEX is not affected by hot water, and can even withstand freezing—something none of the other materials can say. Because it is flexible (it comes in 100-ft.-long rolls), it is quick and easy to install, and requires fewer fittings than other materials. It is far less expensive than copper and less costly to install than CPVC.

PEX comes in different colors, but the material is the same—you can use any color for either hot or cold water. Still, some installers color-code hot and cold lines, just to avoid confusion.

Gas pipe

Gas lines use special materials. You may see galvanized pipe used for gas lines, but it is disallowed by plumbing codes because the galvanizing can flake off and clog ports and openings in appliances. Copper has often been used

GAS PIPE Though copper is sometimes used, black steel and CSST pipe are most commonly used for gas.

for gas lines, but is disallowed in many areas because the sweated joints can develop leaks. However, this is a matter of debate; many claim that if properly sweated, copper is a good choice for gas lines.

Black steel Inside a home, black steel pipe is still the most common material used for natural gas lines. Black steel is threaded, and assembles by applying special gas-approved Teflon® tape to the threads and then tightening fittings with pipe wrenches.

CSST Corrugated stainless-steel tubing (CSST) has a plastic coating that is usually yellow but sometimes black. It is somewhat more expensive than black pipe, but because it is flexible and comes in long rolls, it is often a good deal easier to install.

Under the Sink: Traps, Tubes, and Stops

Plumbing supply and DWV pipes are often hidden in walls, so their fittings are joined in permanent ways. Under a sink, where you can access the plumbing, you'll find pipes, tubes, and valves that can be disconnected and replaced with relative ease.

Traps

The pipes that carry drain water are often referred to as "trap piping," or just "traps." They connect via special nuts and washers. Traps are almost always shaped like a sideways P, and so are called P traps. A trap collects water in such a way as to seal out sewer gases (see p. 14). Traps may be plastic or chrome-plated copper. Plastic traps are very inexpensive and are actually more durable than metal traps. (If you have an old chrome trap that has developed a leak, replace it with a plastic trap unless you need the trap to look good.) Many have large knurled nuts, so you can assemble them using hand-tightening only—no pliers or wrenches needed. A plastic trap joins together with rubber or plastic washers. The trap arm usually has one end shaped so that no washer is needed.

The only good reason to use a metal trap is for its looks; nowadays, they are most often installed under pedestal

TIP A common mistake is to get the wrong size of trap. Kitchen sinks connect to traps that are 1½ in. in diameter; bathroom sinks use 1¼-in. traps.

or console bathroom sinks, where they are on display and may even be a decorative element. The most common metal trap is copper or brass with chrome plating, but brushed nickel and other finishes are also available. Metal traps come in various thicknesses. Unsurprisingly, thin-gauge traps (often 22 gauge) cost less and deteriorate sooner than traps made with thicker material (perhaps as thick as 17 gauge).

Stop valves

Fixture-shutoff valves, often called stop valves, control water running to a single faucet or toilet. You'll find pairs

Plastic and Chrome Traps for Kitchen and Bathroom

Kitchen sink traps are 1½ in. in diameter; bathroom sink traps are 1¼ in. Either size is available in plastic and chrome. The main parts of a trap are the tailpiece, which has a flange that fits against a kitchen sink's basket strainer or threads to screw onto a bathroom sink's drain body; the trap itself; and a trap arm, which runs to the plumbing in the wall. In the case of a double-bowl kitchen sink, other parts are used (see p. 20).

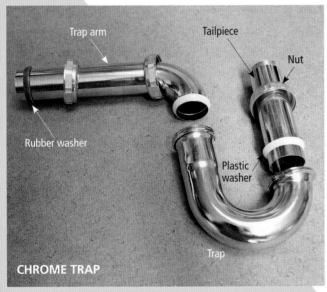

CHROME TRAP

Trap arm · Tailpiece · Nut · Rubber washer · Plastic washer · Trap

PLASTIC TRAP FITTING, NO WASHER. Where a plastic trap is flanged like this, no washer is used.

TAILPIECE WASHER. Whether plastic or chrome, a tailpiece for a kitchen sink uses this type of flanged plastic washer.

Angled ball-type
stop valve

Straight-run ball-type
stop valve

Gate-type
stop valve

STOP VALVES

A CHEAP STOP VALVE. Here, in a remodeling situation, an inexpensive gate-type stop valve fails to completely shut off the water.

of stop valves—for hot and cold lines—for faucets, and a single stop valve for a toilet. In an old house, stop valves may be missing—the water lines will simply run to the faucet or toilet. In that case, you will have to shut off water at an intermediate or whole-house valve in order to repair or replace a fixture. While you're making the repair, it's a very good idea to install a stop valve, so water can be more easily shut off in the future.

Not all stop valves are created equal. Very inexpensive gate valves, called multi-turn valves for obvious reasons, are notoriously unreliable. Often, after some years they will fail to completely shut water off, which can be very annoying when working on plumbing. Better-quality and more reliable valves are usually of the ball type, meaning that you make a quarter turn to shut water off or turn it on.

Supply lines

Supply lines, also called supply tubes, run from the stop valves to the faucet or toilet. They are flexible, or at least (in the case of chrome-plated copper lines) bendable, and can be disconnected easily. Today the most common supply line is made with braided stainless steel. Other types include braided plastic and simple plastic. Various sizes fit onto faucets or toilets at one end, and to the threads of a stop valve, which may be ⅜ in. or ½ in., at the other end. Braided valves have nuts that simply screw onto the threads of the faucet and the stop valve. Plastic and copper lines connect via a ferrule and a nut, or a nut and the shaped end of a plastic line (see the top right photos on the facing page).

Double-Bowl Arrangements

Where there is a double-bowl sink, various trap configurations have been used over the years. The arrangement shown here, favored by modern codes, has a separate P trap for each of the bowls. In many installations, only one P trap serves for both bowls.

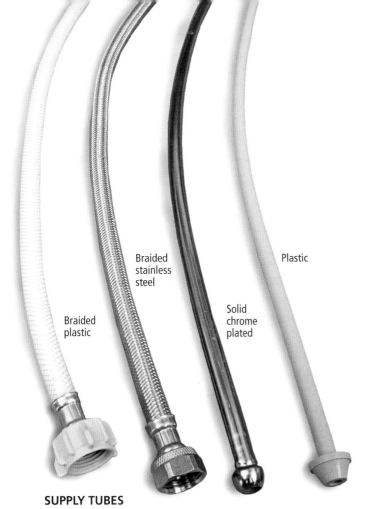

Braided
stainless
steel

Braided
plastic

Solid
chrome
plated

Plastic

SUPPLY TUBES

FERRULE AND NUT CONNECTIONS. Where tubing is inserted into a valve or faucet, a watertight joint is made with a brass or plastic ferrule, which expands when a nut tightens it against the inlet.

Under-the-Sink Complications

The plumbing under a kitchen sink can get very complicated, but it's usually not difficult to understand as long as you take the time to follow the different lines. In this example, there are two water filters, a large reverse-osmosis filter in the middle, and a two-stage filter to the left. The bowl on the right drains into a garbage disposal, and the trap piping—a combination of metal and plastic materials—has a single P trap. (Where there is a garbage disposal, a separate P trap for that bowl is not called for.)

INSPECTING YOUR SYSTEM

Plumbing codes and materials have changed a great deal over the last century, so the plumbing in an older home will look far different from that in a newer home. Older plumbing does not need to meet current codes, but it should be inspected for safety. If you are unhappy with your home's water pressure, or if your pipes have a tendency to leak, you may want to upgrade parts of your system.

CHECK DRAIN LINES (A). Drainpipes in a basement are often held in place with plastic or metal straps. The arrangement may look casual, but the pipes must all slope correctly at all points. Though it is a matter of debate, many inspectors demand that horizontal pipes slope at about ¼ in. per running foot; it is thought that an incorrect slope—either too flat or too steep—can cause solids to collect and not get washed away by flowing liquids. Others believe that the steeper the slope the better. For PVC pipes like these, the purple stripes at the joints are a good sign that primer was applied before they were glued together, ensuring a solid, tight fit.

DRAIN FITTINGS (B). Special drain fittings, which make gradual rather than sudden turns, ensure smooth flowing of waste. For more information on fitting types, see pp. 232–234.

Dealing with Low Water Pressure

The smaller a pipe's diameter, the lower the water pressure will be. The service pipe is usually 1 in. or 1¼ in. in diameter; this generally gets reduced to ¾ in. soon after entering the house. Horizontal distribution pipes often continue at the ¾-in. size; vertical "risers" are often only ½ in. If you have low water pressure, first try clearing aerators (pp. 32–34). If that doesn't solve the problem, you may need some new piping. If you have old galvanized supply pipes, they may have become encrusted with minerals, narrowing the pipes' capacity and lowering water pressure. There are companies that specialize in clearing out these pipes, but replacing with PEX or copper is a better solution.

CLEANOUTS (C). There should be easily accessible cleanouts at a number of locations, so an auger can be inserted to clear any clogs.

SUMP PUMP (D, E, F,). A sump pump in the basement works during heavy rainfalls to direct water out of the

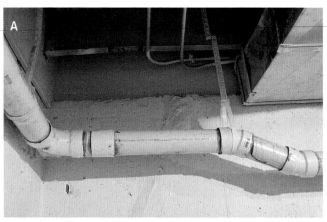

basement to prevent flooding. It is connected to drainpipes, called drain tiles, under the basement floor. Inside, there is typically a pipe reaching down through a cover, with an electric cord leading to a small pump (D). Outside, make sure there is a drain line that directs water well away from the house (E). If your basement gets wet, open the cover and inspect the sump pump (F), as described on p. 208.

WATER HEATER (G). Check that your water heater complies with local codes. Your building department should have a set of guidelines that can be seen at their online site. This water heater has an expansion tank (the gray cylindrical tank above and to the right), which is now required by many municipalities. If yours does not have an expansion tank, check with a plumber to see if you need one. If you have a gas water heater, check that the flue is working properly. See pp. 212–218 for more information on testing and maintaining a water heater.

continued on p. 24

continued from p. 23

TRANSITION FITTINGS (H). During remodeling, new pipes are often joined to old ones. Here, a PEX line is attached to a copper line, using a correct and safe fitting.

GAS PIPING (I, J). It's common for the wrong pipes to be used for gas lines. In (I), gray-colored galvanized pipe is used for a gas line leading to the water heater. This type of pipe can flake off on the inside and plug up the water heater's valve. It should be replaced with black pipe, like that seen in (J).

CRAWLSPACE (K). If your home has a crawlspace, some pipes may run through it. Check to be sure that drain lines are correctly sloped, and that any supply pipes are protected from freezing in the winter.

BE KIND TO PIPES (L). Supply pipes make handy rods for hanging clothes and other things, but it's probably not a good idea: A quick tug could dent a copper pipe.

ACCESS PANEL (M). In the adjoining room or closet behind a tub/shower's plumbing, there should be an access panel. This enables you to spot leaks, and may make it possible to turn off water for repairs or replacements.

CATCH BASIN (N). Old houses had separate drain lines that led to catch basins, where grease and oils could be trapped. Unless you use animal-based tallow soap or dump lots of grease down your kitchen sink, you don't need a catch basin any more. If the drain line works, you can leave it alone, but plumbers often bypass the catch basin when making repairs or remodeling.

LEAD PIPE (O). If you live in an older home and have gray pipes that bend like a snake, they may be made of

Listen for Gurgles

If you hear a strong gurgling noise at a nearby sink when you flush a toilet or drain another nearby sink, you may have a clogged vent line. In that case, water may get sucked out of the gurgling sink's vent, rendering it useless. If you smell sewer gas, then that is most certainly the problem. Call in a professional plumber; rodding the vent line from the roof may solve the problem, or you may need to install an AAV or a new vent line (see pp. 228–231).

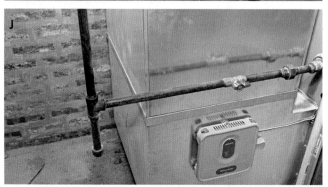

lead. The way to test is to press with a knife; a lead pipe will nick easily.

FLOOR DRAINS (P). It's easy to ignore floor drains like this, but they may be needed in times of heavy rain, so keep them cleared of debris. A floor drain often has a trap just below it, and a trap works only if it is full of water. So if you smell sewer gas in your basement, the solution may be to pour a quart of so of water into the drain to fill the trap.

STACKS (Q, R). Main stacks are usually 3 in. or 4 in. in diameter, whereas secondary stacks are narrower. The photo (Q) shows a main stack next to a secondary stack. (R) shows a copper secondary stack, which is a bit unusual but should work fine.

continued on p. 26

continued from p. 25

UNDERSTAND YOUR FITTINGS (S). This fitting, which is attached with U-clamps, is a saddle T drain fitting, which is sometimes used to tie a new fixture to an old drainpipe when installing a new toilet or faucet. Saddle T valves are not allowed by some new codes, but when installed properly they should drain well.

OLD RUSTY STUFF (T). If you have older pipes and funny-looking valves, don't panic. Quite often, the problems are only cosmetic, though in some cases you may need to call in a professional to figure things out. In this photo we see a rusty cleanout. The rust means that water is slowly leaking out. The solution is simply to remove the cleanout plug, wire-brush the opening, and install a new plug that seals well. The large valve on the right is another matter: It is part of an older setup for draining water out of the basement, and ties into the sump pump.

Tools for Replacements and Repairs

The tools shown on the next four pages will enable you to perform the installations and repairs described in the first six chapters of this book. None of these tasks involves cutting and installing new supply or DWV pipes (other than traps and flexible supply lines). Chapters 7 through 10 do call for new piping—and for additional tools, which are shown on pp. 166–168.

These tools are modestly priced, and if you've done some handyman work around the house you may already own many of them. Avoid bargain-bin tools and opt for quality tools that feel solid, operate smoothly, and are made of materials that will last.

Unclogging tools

To clear stopped-up drain lines in sinks, tubs, and pipes, and to clear a balky toilet, have on hand a good set of tools that can meet every challenge—with the possible

Cup or sink plunger

All-angle plunger

Toilet plunger

PLUNGERS

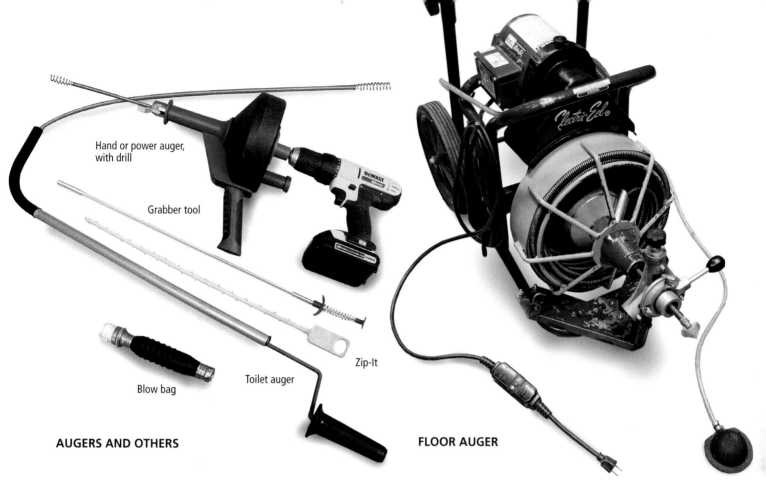

AUGERS AND OTHERS

Hand or power auger, with drill

Grabber tool

Zip-It

Blow bag

Toilet auger

FLOOR AUGER

exception of a floor auger, which you probably want to rent rather than buy.

Start with plungers (facing page). Here we show three types. A traditional cup plunger, also called a sink plunger, works well for small openings where the surrounding area is flat. A toilet plunger, also called a flange plunger, has a very flexible flange that can be popped out, making it fit snugly all around the large and curved opening of a toilet. An "all-angle" plunger works well in hard-to-reach areas, and creates a powerful whoosh of pressure; some people find it works well with low-flush toilets.

A Zip-It® drain-cleaning tool (photo above) is a simple strip of flexible plastic with back-facing barbs; slip it into a drain and pull back to remove hairballs and other clumps. A grabber tool opens and closes its claws to retrieve hard objects.

Next, augers (photo above). A hand-crank auger works slowly, and it can be laborious to use. An auger that attaches to a power drill generates a good deal of force and so works more quickly and gets at clogs that can't be reached with a hand tool. However, there is an advantage to hand cranking, because you can better feel an obstruction when you hit it. A good solution is to buy

a unit like the one shown here, which can be operated either by hand or with a drill. A floor auger (photo above) is used for clearing major clogs in large drainpipes. And a toilet auger is the only auger that works on a toilet.

Instead of augering, you may choose to blast the obstruction out. Use a blow bag attached to garden hose, or a pressurized drain opener, which shoots a blast of air.

PRESSURIZED DRAIN OPENER WITH ATTACHMENTS

WRENCHES

A Crescent or
   adjustable wrenches
B Slip-joint pliers
C Locking pliers
D Longnose locking pliers
E Strap wrench
F Basin wrench
G Spud wrench
H Strainer wrench
I Deep socket wrench

Pliers and wrenches

A pair of slip-joint pliers comes in handy for a variety of plumbing tasks. Newer types like the pair shown above have a button you can push for easy adjustment. Crescent or adjustable wrenches are the best tools for tightening nuts. Locking pliers grab and hold on, a useful quality, especially when you need to tighten two nuts at once. You'll occasionally need longnose pliers to get at hard-to-reach places. A strap wrench loosens and tightens tub spouts, shower arms, and other things without scratching.

Though you may not use it often, a basin wrench is indispensable when installing a faucet. A spud wrench, which may be adjustable or may have a variety of

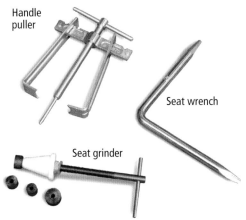

Handle
puller

Seat wrench

Seat grinder

FAUCET TOOLS

STANLEY

openings, grabs large nuts like those on a toilet or a basket strainer's nut. Use a strainer wrench to unscrew or tighten a basket strainer or a bathtub drain. You may need a deep socket wrench to work on a tub/shower faucet.

Faucet tools

Faucets often can be repaired or replaced using standard pliers, wrenches, and screwdrivers, but sometimes specialty tools are needed. If a handle is stuck, a handle puller will do what it says it will do. A seat wrench can remove seats, and a seat grinder can smooth the seats.

General tools

Handyman and carpentry tools that often are needed for plumbing jobs are shown above. Use these tools to cut trap pieces, test sinks for level, pry, scrape excess putty and caulk, measure, and tighten screws. A flashlight or two can be essential when working in a basement or inside a sink cabinet.

TIP SAFETY GEAR Wear protective eyewear when cutting pipes, and when operating a propane torch while soldering copper pipes. If you work at a site that is being extensively remodeled, wear a safety helmet. Most pipes can be handled barehanded, but wear heavy-duty work gloves when touching copper pipe that is being soldered and when working with cast-iron pipe.

CHAPTER TWO

UNCLOGGING

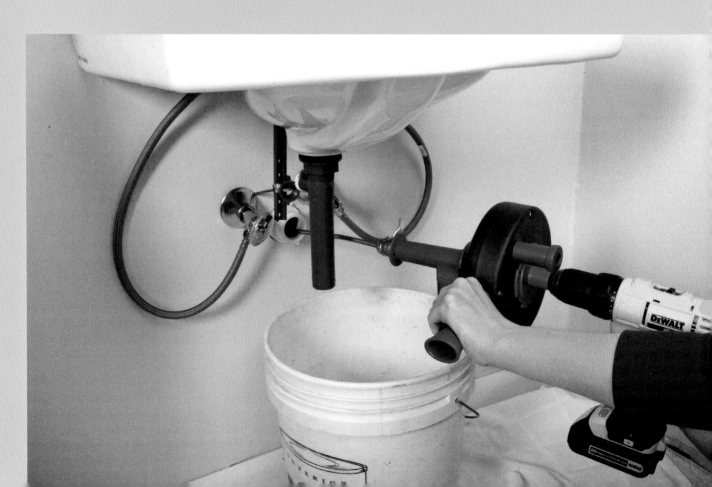

THE MOST COMMON HOUSEHOLD plumbing problem is sluggish movement in pipes. In most cases, this problem can be solved without calling in a plumber or taking drastic action.

A stopped-up or slow-moving drain line can usually be cleared by one of four basic methods: (1) Plunging employs a simple tool to produce both suction and forward motion to force blockages either forward or backward; (2) augering (or snaking) pushes a flexible line into a drain until it contacts the blockage, which it can either push forward or grab and pull out; (3) a blow bag or a pressurized drain opener uses air or water pressure to push the blockage through; (4) dismantling a trap allows you to remove solid blockages that collect in the bottom of the trap.

If only one sink, toilet, or other fixture has a slow-water problem, then taking one or more of these simple steps will probably solve the problem. But if sluggishness is more general, you may need to open a cleanout and auger a drainpipe or two. And if the whole house has slow-moving drainage, then it's time to break out the big guns and auger your main drain line.

When a faucet, showerhead, or other fixture's water pressure is weak, the problem can often be solved by disassembling the fixture and clearing out collected debris. Most fixtures are designed with screens that make the debris easily accessible.

Improving Water Pressure

If a showerhead or faucet has low pressure, erratic water flow, or a disorganized spatter of water spray, or if a washing machine fills slowly, it's time to do a little disassembling and cleaning.

TIP If you find that you need to clean out aerators every month or so, your water supply is less than pristine. Call your water utility to see if they can correct the problem. If you have old galvanized supply pipes, the only solution is probably to replace them with copper or PEX piping. If the problem is global and other people in your area have the same issues, you may need to install a whole-house water filter, as shown on pp. 225–227.

Cleaning aerators

An aerator has a mesh screen that mixes air with the water, producing a slightly foamy flow of water. Aerators save on water usage because they limit flow while producing a stream that cleans as well as a stronger unaerated flow. So avoid the temptation to simply remove the aerator, unless you have severe flow problems.

An aerator can be cleaned quickly and with little difficulty. However, aerators are inexpensive, so if yours is scratched or dented, go ahead and replace it with a new one.

1 **UNSCREW.** Close the drain plug, or cover the drain with a cloth, to keep small parts from dropping down the drain. First, try unscrewing the aerator by hand. If that doesn't work, use a pair of slip-joint pliers. (Remember that when you unscrew, you must turn counterclockwise—which appears to be clockwise when you're looking from this point of view.) Wrap the pliers with a cloth to prevent scratching. If you have trouble grabbing firmly with the cloth, try moistening it first. Finish unscrewing by hand and pull out carefully, so the parts don't disassemble.

2 **DISASSEMBLE.** Aerators come in different configurations. For example, the one shown at right simply has a body and a small screen inside the metal housing, whereas the one shown below has a double screen for extra-foamy flow and a pair of rubber washers. Pry the pieces apart with your fingers and fingernails; if that doesn't work, use a utility knife.

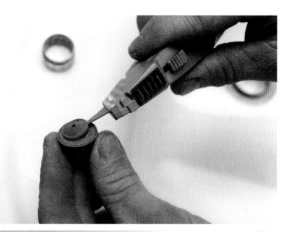

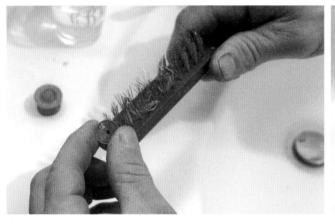

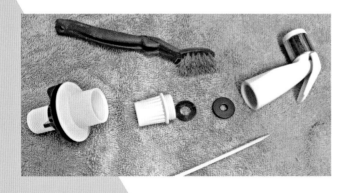

3 **CLEAN OUT DEBRIS.** Use a toothpick, needle, or a few wires of a wire brush, as shown, to pop out crumbs and debris. Examine the parts from all sides.

4 **SOAK IN VINEGAR.** If things are gunky or if crumbs are stuck, soak the parts in household vinegar for a half-hour or so. If you still can't clean the screen, buy and install a new aerator.

Cleaning a Kitchen Sprayer

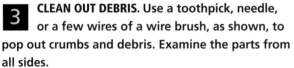

Kitchen faucets often have sprayers, either on the end of the spout or as separate units. There are many different models with different configurations. Simply unscrew the sprayer from the hose. Cleaning is a matter of carefully disassembling, looking for particles and buildup, and using a brush, sharp-pointed tool, and perhaps a bowl of vinegar.

Cleaning a showerhead

Showerheads have plenty of pin-sized openings that can get clogged up with even small amounts of debris, so they often need cleaning or replacing if you want to restore a full, strong shower flow.

There are many styles of showerhead—the types shown here are just some examples. As you disassemble, pay attention not only to the order in which the parts need to be reassembled but also to the orientation of each piece.

TIP If you have low water pressure in your home and your showerhead has a flow restrictor, first try cleaning it thoroughly. If water pressure is still low, you may choose to remove the restrictor.

1 **REMOVE THE HEAD.** If you can't unscrew the showerhead by hand, use a strap wrench to unscrew it, in order to avoid scratching the finish. If you don't have a strap wrench, try a cloth, as shown on p. 32.

2 **REMOVE AND CLEAN THE SCREEN.** There is usually a screen where the showerhead meets the shower arm. Carefully pry it out; the screen is easily damaged. Flush away any debris, then poke out any remaining particles.

3 **DISASSEMBLE.** Look carefully for ways to disassemble the head, if any. Some inexpensive showerheads cannot be disassembled; if general cleaning does not solve the problem, replace the showerhead. The model shown here has a flow restrictor that can be removed using longnose pliers.

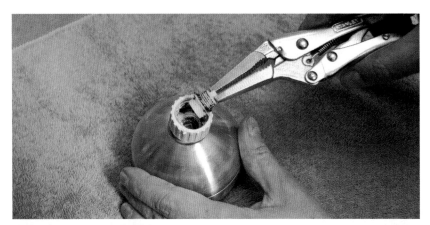

4 **SOAK IN VINEGAR.** Mineral deposits can form on front openings even when there is a screen in place. First try running water backward through the head, and scrub gently with a bristle brush. For more thorough cleaning (both to increase water flow and for good looks), soak the front of the head in vinegar overnight, then clean again.

Washing Machine Inlets

If a washing machine fills slowly, shut off the valves attached to the two hoses and unscrew the hoses from the inlets on the back of the machine. You should find a screen filter in each inlet. Remove and clean it as you would an aerator.

Zipping and Grabbing

Start with the easiest solutions: If the drain is not completely stopped, wait for the water to drain out and clean away hairs and gunky debris at the sink's or tub's drain strainer. If that doesn't solve the problem, remove the strainer, or remove a stopper if it is the type that can be removed without first removing the pop-up lever (see p. 42), and try pulling out the blockage. If the blockage is very near the top, you may be able to reach it with a pair of longnose pliers. Or try one of these tools:

ZIP-IT TOOL. This long flexible plastic zip tool has backward-facing barbs that slide past a blockage while going down but grab on the way up. To push it down, you may need to twist or use an up-and-down movement. Pull up while twisting slightly for more grabbing power. If you succeed in pulling out some stuff, do it a couple times more, to make sure you get all you can.

GRABBER. This flexible grabbing tool works well if there is a solid object in the trap, like a pen, a ring, or a child's action figure. Push it down until you feel an obstruction. Pull back just a bit, push the button to open up the grabbers, push forward, and let go of the button to grab. It may take a number of attempts to extract the treasure.

Using a Pressurized Drain Opener

Several types of drain openers work with air pressure. Tools that use aerosol cans or CO_2 cartridges may work, but sometimes they do not form a good seal around the drain and do not allow you to adjust the pressure. The type shown here allows you to work a simple air pump until you have achieved the desired air pressure, and then shoot the pressure into the hole. Start with a small amount of pressure and gradually increase the pressure until the clog is cleared.

Plunging

Back in the day it was called a "plumber's helper," and a plunger is still often the quickest and simplest way to eliminate a clog. Before you reach for a plunger, try some even simpler measures: Pour hot water down the drain. If there is a strainer, clean it of any hair or greasy debris. You may also want to try a zip tool or a flexible grabber (see the facing page). If that does not solve the problem, spend a few minutes with a plunger.

Plunging can sometimes create a mess, spraying water out of the sink or toilet. Have a towel or absorbent rag on hand.

1 **PARTIALLY DRAIN THE SINK. There should be some standing water in the sink so the plunger can seal tightly, but not too much, because water may slosh and splash. If water is draining slowly, wait for it to go down. If it is completely plugged, bail with a cup.**

2 **PLUG THE OVERFLOW. Bathroom sinks have an overflow hole in the front or back, which makes another pathway to the drain so water cannot over-flow the sink. Plug this up with a wet rag. You may be able to poke a wet rag into a large hole, as shown here, or you may need to have a helper hold a rag against smaller holes, as shown in the next step.**

3 **PLUNGE. Use a medium to small plunger that can easily seal all around the drain hole. Make sure the stopper (if any) is in the up position. Start plunging slowly, pushing down and pulling up.**

TIP If you have a stopped-up drain on a shower-only unit, there is no overflow hole to stop up; just plunge the drain.

4 **PUSH DOWN AND PULL UP. You should feel water being forced down and up as you work. You may push the obstruction forward and into the drainpipe in the wall, or you may pull the obstruction up and into the sink. If at first you don't succeed, try again with more vigorous motions. If plunging does not do the trick, your next move is probably to dis-mantle the trap (pp. 39–41).**

CUTE BUT EFFECTIVE. This plunger is small and inexpensive, but it generates a surprising amount of pushing and pulling power. Because it is small, you can operate it with one hand while you use your other hand to stop up the overflow hole. It might do the trick for you.

PLUNGE A DOUBLE SINK. The two bowls of a double sink have drains that are connected in some way, so plunging one may create a waterspout in the other. Have someone else use a plunger to deal with the second sink, either to hold back the water or to actively plunge the second bowl while you plunge the first.

Drain Cleaners

Liquid or crystal drain cleaners, also called drain openers, often contain toxic substances that may even be harmful if they touch your skin. And they usually do not dissolve a clog unless it is very near the surface. Biological cleaners are less of a risk, but in general are even less effective. If you do use a drain cleaner, follow instructions carefully, and store the product out reach of children. For the most part, however, mechanical measures—plungers, augers, and dismantling a trap—are not difficult and are more effective.

PLUNGE A TUB. To plunge a tub, first remove the drain strainer and stuff a small wet rag up under the overflow's cover plate. If that doesn't seal the overflow while you plunge, you may need to remove the overflow flange first (see p. 45).

Dismantling and Clearing Traps

Taking apart a trap may seem like serious plumbing, but it's actually a pretty simple matter of loosening nuts and pulling the pieces apart. However, some factors can complicate things:

- Rubber and (less often) plastic washers can disintegrate over time, so you may have to replace some. If possible, have washers on hand to make the job easier. Otherwise, you'll need to shop for replacements while the trap is apart.

- Traps are often located in small, hard-to-access cabinets. Make things as comfortable as you can, with thick towels and good lighting.

- Things could get messy. Place a bucket under the trap to collect water that pours out, as well as a large sponge or two.

- If the trap is chrome plated, there's a good chance that parts of it have eroded; disassembly may reveal or cause holes or tears. If that happens, install a new trap—preferably a plastic one, unless you need chrome for looks.

PLASTIC TRAP. If your trap is plastic, it may have nuts that you can easily unscrew and tighten by hand. If not, use slip-joint pliers. Usually you need to loosen only two nuts to remove the trap portion. Use longnose pliers or a grabbing tool to remove any debris, hair, or long-lost toys or jewelry. Flush the inside of the trap with a stiff flow of water, then reattach, making sure the washers are snugly in place. Test for leaks.

Removing and replacing a chrome trap

If the trap is chrome, things can be more complicated. Rubber washers are often dried out so they cannot seal, and the chrome parts often develop leaks. Because these traps are so often damaged, we include instructions for installing a new trap.

If water still does not flow freely, the blockage is farther down the line. The next step is to auger where the trap meets the drainpipe in the wall.

1 **DISASSEMBLE. Use a pair of slip-joint pliers to loosen at least the two nuts that hold the curved trap portion of the P trap. Remove the trap portion, allowing water to pour into a bucket below.**

2 **CLEAN OUT AND INSPECT. Clean out any blockages in the trap. If the washers look worn, replace them with washers of the same type and size. If you see a hole, a tear, or any sign of deterioration, replace the entire trap, including the arm and perhaps the tailpiece as well.**

3 **DRY RUN AND MARK FOR CUTTING. Use slip-joint pliers to loosen the tailpiece, then unscrew it by hand (above left). Also remove the trap arm, and replace it with a new arm. Attach a new trap piece to the arm, but do not tighten. Temporarily screw the new tailpiece in place. Mark the tailpiece for cutting to length (above right). The tailpiece should slide most of the way into the wider portion of the trap piece.**

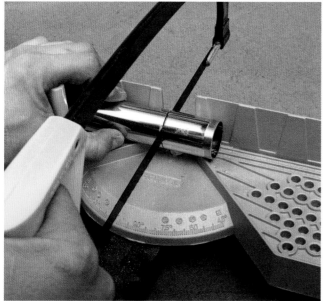

4 CUT PARTS. Cut metal parts with a hacksaw, pressing gently as you cut to keep from bending the metal out of round. Use a file or a sanding block to remove any burrs.

5 TAILPIECE. On a bathroom drain, the tailpiece screws up into the sink's drain body, as shown. Spread a bit of pipe thread compound (also called TFE paste) on the threads, or wrap with Teflon tape. Tighten by hand, then tighten another half turn or so with pliers; do not overtighten, or you may distort the tailpiece out of round. (On a kitchen sink the tailpieces attach with nuts and special flanged plastic washers.)

6 REASSEMBLE. Assemble the entire trap. Nuts need to tighten against washers, so in most cases you must slip on a nut, then the washer, and then slide the two down or over to tighten the nut. Make sure the washers are positioned to form watertight seals at the joints; take care that they do not fold over. Fit the pieces together and tighten the nuts with slip-joint pliers. Test for leaks.

Augering

A modest-sized plumbing auger, also called a snake or a plumbing wire, can be used to clear (or "rod") a trap, a bathtub, or a vertical drainpipe in a wall. Larger augers are used to clear main drain lines. Nowadays, many homeowners use augers that are attached to a power drill for fast augering. However, hand-cranking an auger has the advantage that you can better feel when you reach an obstruction.

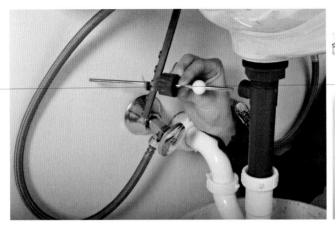

1 **REMOVE POP-UP LEVER. If water remains in the sink, place a bucket under the plumbing.** From underneath the sink, unscrew the nut that holds the pop-up lever (or rod) in place. Pull out the rod.

2 **REMOVE STOPPER. Pull the stopper out. If a good deal of blockage material comes out with it, you** may have solved the problem; replace the stopper, re-attach the pop-up lever, and test. If blockage remains, remove the lever and stopper and move on to augering.

3 **AUGER. Loosen the setscrew or push down on the metal tab at the front of a hand-crank or** drill-attached auger, pull out a foot or two of cable, and insert it down the drain. Keep inserting until it stops. Position the auger so less than a foot shows above the sink, and tighten the setscrew. Crank or drill the auger until it starts to move forward. Loosen the setscrew and keep working downward.

TIP Auger carefully; don't push the auger with force, and pull the auger out as soon as it feels like you have caught something. Occasionally, an auger's tip may get caught in a severe blockage so that it cannot be removed; you want to avoid that fate.

4 **PUSH THROUGH OR PULL OUT. Augering may push an** obstruction though, or it may grab onto an obstruction, or it may do both. Pull the cable out, and clean away any hair and other fun stuff, using a rag and pliers if needed. Test for flow; repeat if needed.

Augering a sink trap

If a trap is difficult to access, you may choose to auger it instead. Augering a kitchen sink trap is usually not possible, because the basket strainers' openings are not large enough for inserting the auger's tip. If a bathroom sink has a stopper that is not linked to a pop-up assembly, simply pull it out. If there is a pop-up assembly, you probably need to disconnect it in order to pull out the stopper.

Clearing the wall pipe

If water is still blocked up, move on to augering the pipe in the wall. Disassemble the trap, as shown on p. 40. You can auger with the trap arm still in place, but it's easier to work with the trap arm removed, so you can insert the cable directly into the trap adapter.

TRY PULLING OUT. Before using a snake, take a peek with a flashlight to see if you can spot the blockage. You may be able to grab and pull it out with longnose pliers or a grabbing tool.

DRILL/AUGER. Attach the auger's rod to a drill's chuck and tighten firmly. Work the cable forward in stages, loosening the setscrew, pushing forward, tightening the setscrew, and drilling. Start drilling slowly, then increase the speed in order to help the cable make turns in the pipe. Pull out the cable after you feel you've hit something.

AUGER AT WALL. Use a hand-crank or drill-operated auger as directed at left to push a blockage through or pull it out. Usually you need only push the cable a few feet to get the job done. However, if the blockage remains, try going farther. If the blockage remains after extensive augering, you may need to auger the main drain (pp. 48–49).

PUSH IT THROUGH. You can also use a pressurized drain opener (see p. 36) to push the blockage through. Or use a blow bag, as shown below: The blow bag may have a tip that seals against the trap adapter, or you may be able to insert and expand it inside the pipe. Attach the blow bag to a garden hose, and either press it firmly or insert it into the pipe. Turn on the water; after a few seconds, it will exert very strong pressure and should remove the blockage.

DOUBLE-BOWL UNBLOCKING. Under a double-bowl kitchen sink, blockages most often occur at the trap or traps; disassemble and check these first. As long as a garbage disposal is operating, there should be no blockage inside it. If the blockage is farther downstream, you may need to run an auger, as shown, into the wall.

Clearing a Tub Drain

A bathtub drain can be cleared in the same ways as a sink: First try cleaning away or pulling out obstructions near the surface. If that doesn't work, you can use a plunger (as shown on p. 38), a pressurized drain cleaner (p. 36), or a blow bag. Or pull out and clean the tub's drain assembly. If that doesn't work, use an auger.

CLEAR OUT A NEAR-SURFACE BLOCKAGE. First try removing the drain screen (left) or whatever type of assembly you have. The type shown at right has a plastic part that unscrews. Often, a stoppage can be resolved by pulling out gunk with a pair of longnose pliers or a grabbing tool.

TIP When you pull out the linkage, you may find a cylindrical plunger instead of a spring at the end (see p. 199). This plunger assembly can be cleaned and adjusted in much the same way as the one shown here.

1 PULL OUT THE DRAIN ASSEMBLY. Remove the mounting screw for the overflow's cover plate. Pull out the cover plate and gently work the attached linkage out of the overflow hole.

2 CLEAN THE ASSEMBLY. Pull the assembly all the way out. There is a spring at the end, where hair often gets stuck. Use longnose pliers to pull away any blockage material. Clean the entire assembly.

3 ADJUST THE LINKAGE. If the tub's stopper does not seal well, so that water drains slowly, use a screwdriver or pliers (depending on the type of assembly) to lengthen the threaded rod by ½ in. or so. You may need to readjust after testing the stopper.

4 AUGER THROUGH THE OVERFLOW. If cleaning the assembly does not clear the clog, try augering through the overflow. See p. 42 for instructions on augering.

5 GET AT THE TRAP. In some cases, the tub's trap may be accessible from a basement below or from behind an access panel in an adjoining room. It is sometimes easier to disassemble a trap and/or auger from those locations.

TIP Some older tubs have a rocker-arm drain assembly that attaches to the drain rather than to the overflow. To get at it, flip up the tub's trip lever, which will release the assembly. Then pry and pull the stopper (at the bottom of the tub, not at the overflow hole) up and out. Clean out hair and debris, and run hot water through the drain. Carefully thread the assembly back into the drain hole until the stopper seats.

Clearing a Toilet

Toilets have their own built-in traps, which of course cannot be disassembled. But the toilet's drainpipe (called a closet bend) is very large in diameter, so serious clogs rarely occur there. And the toilet's trap passageway is short, so clearing a toilet is often easily done, either by plunging, pressure-blasting, or augering (see the photos on the facing page).

Stop That Rising Water

If when you flush a toilet the water level keeps rising ominously, looking like it may overflow onto the floor, you maybe able to prevent a flood if you think and act fast: Remove the tank's lid and pull up on the float—which may be a sort of hollow piece that fits around the drain line, or, in the case of an old valve, an oblong ball attached to a rod. (See pp. 112–113 to learn about toilet valves.) This will stop the water from flowing into the bowl. If the toilet is draining slowly, you can wait a minute or two for water to subside, then release the float. If the toilet is completely stopped up, have a helper hold the float in the up position while you bail water out of the bowl.

Whether you are plunging, blasting, or augering, it is best to have a few inches of water in the bowl—enough to help seal around the opening, but not so much that you could splash water onto the floor. To get the right amount of water, either flush and wait (if the toilet is not completely clogged), or bail out water with a small bucket (if water does not drain at all).

If all else fails...

Sometimes a toilet is blocked or partially blocked with something that cannot be removed with a plunger or an auger or with pressure. There are two types of recalcitrant clogs: those that are very soft (like pickles), so that the auger goes right through them without being able to grab, and hard objects (like small children's toys) that are really stuck.

In either case, the solution is to remove the toilet, turn it upside down, and work from the bottom up (see the photos on p. 48). This may seem like a drastic measure, but unless there is some problem with the mounting flange, removing and replacing a toilet should take less than an hour; see p. 132–137 for instructions.

Have a thick towel on the floor to collect spilled water and to protect the toilet from damage. Shut off the stop valve supplying the toilet. Flush the toilet if it is sluggish rather than fully blocked. Bail out as much water as you

PLUNGE A TOILET. Use a plunger with a flange, which reaches inside the bowl's opening to make a tight seal. Seat the plunger firmly in the hole, and press down gently at first, to clear the plunger of air. Then work the plunger up and down; it should be sealed well enough that you can feel it sucking strongly on the upstroke. Push up and down several times, then pull the plunger out to check whether water flows down quickly. If not, plunge again in the same way, applying a good deal of muscle power—don't be shy; go at it with plenty of might and main. In most cases, this will push the clog through or pull it up into the bowl.

PRESSURE-BLASTING. A pressure-assisted drain opener works well for clogs that can be pushed forward into the wall's drainpipe—which is usually the case. Fit the opening with a rubber head that fits snugly inside. If your blaster allows you to choose the pressure, start with 150 lb.; if that does not clear things up, make succeeding attempts with the pressure increased by 50 lb. each time. Press firmly when you blast; if you create air bubbles in the bowl, you need to push harder.

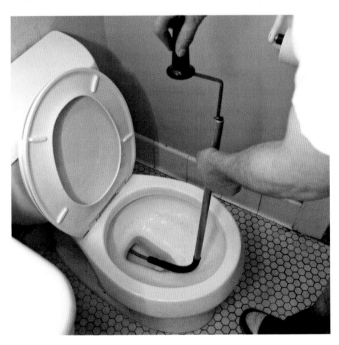

AUGERING. A special toilet auger is just the right size for the job, and it has a rubber sleeve that protects the porcelain from scratches and stains. It can sometimes push or pull smaller objects that are bypassed by plunging and blasting. Pull the cable all the way up through the sleeve, and insert it into the bowl's drain hole. Push the cable forward gently until it reaches an obstacle, then turn the crank as you continue to push forward. If you feel the cable's end grab onto something, pull back, cranking backward if necessary. Repeat until you can move the auger's cable all the way forward.

TIP Wear rubber gloves, long clothing, and protective eyewear when clearing a toilet, because splashing does happen.

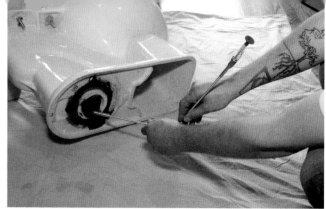

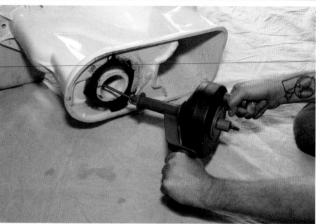

can, and use a large sponge to remove the rest of the visible water from the tank and the bowl. Remove the mounting nuts and pull the toilet up. Gently lay the toilet on its side, so the hole in the bottom of the bowl is easy to reach.

You may be able to see the obstruction from here, in which case you might be able to remove it with longnose pliers, perhaps together with a large screwdriver for prying. For objects a little farther away, try using a grabbing tool. If the object cannot be seen, an auger may be the best tool.

WORK FROM THE BOTTOM. If a clog cannot be removed by plunging, blasting, or augering, you'll need to remove the toilet, turn it upside down, and work through the hole in the bottom of the toilet.

Clearing Large Drains

If more than one sink, tub, or toilet is clogged or sluggish, and if the steps on the previous pages do not clear things up, it's probably time to auger (or rod) large drainpipes. Your house should have cleanouts in fairly convenient locations, where you can remove a cleanout plug and insert an auger. A modest-sized auger attached to a drill often works for pipes that are 2 in. to 3 in. in diameter; for larger pipes, especially the house's main drain, you

probably need to rent a large auger or hire a rodding company that specializes in clearing large drainpipes.

Cleanout plugs

In a newer home, removing a cleanout plug is usually a simple matter of unscrewing a plastic plug using a pipe wrench or a very large adjustable wrench. After augering, wrap the plug's threads with Teflon tape or spread pipe thread compound on them, then screw the plug back in. In an older home with cast-iron pipes, rust and perhaps decayed rubber may make the task more difficult.

Augering the main drain

The main drain line runs from your house to the utility's line, usually located under a nearby street (see the illustration on p. 11). Consult with a local plumber or a knowledgeable plumbing salesperson before doing this job yourself. In some cases, tree roots actually break into the main line and have to be cut through. When you rent a large auger that rests on the floor—which may be called a drum machine—be sure it includes at least one "cutter head," which bores through roots.

You may be able to access your main drain through a cleanout plug near the floor, or you may need to remove

Jetting and Vacuuming

If your sewer line is badly clogged, a standard auger may not be able to clear it out. In that case, consider hiring a company with a sewer truck that performs jetting and vacuuming. Both actions are pretty much what you might expect: Jetting, or jet cleaning, uses extremely high water pressure to flush out sludge and debris. If there is too much debris to flush out at one go, the company may need to jet, then vacuum the loosened debris, then start again.

REMOVING THE OLD PLUG. If a plug is really stuck, try spraying it with penetrating oil and waiting a few minutes. If the pipe and the plug are entirely made of metal, it can help to heat the plug up with a propane torch. Unscrew using a pipe wrench. If the plug has a rubber seal, unscrew a wingnut to loosen it.

AUGERING A CLEANOUT. You can try running a drill-driven auger into the cleanout, and sometimes this will enable you to push the obstruction through or pull it out. Work slowly and carefully: You don't want to get the auger's tip so firmly embedded in an obstruction that you cannot pull it back out. You may also use a pressurized drain opener (see p. 36).

a floor drain's cover and go through there. If you remove a low cleanout, do so slowly; if your situation is severe, sewage may back up, sometimes with a good deal of pressure. If that's the case, wait some hours or days until the pressure subsides, or call in the pros.

Plug in the auger. Many units have foot pedals so you can operate the motor hands-free. Feed cable into the opening until you hit an obstruction, then spin the auger, gently pushing the cable as it spins. Take it easy: once you feel the cutter grabbing, pull it back. Don't let the cutter keep cutting into the obstruction because it may become stuck.

Keep cutting, pulling back, and pressing forward again until the sewage breaks free—often with a happy whoosh sound. Pull out the cable and run water through the line with a garden hose.

If the going gets tough and the cutter does not work through the obstruction, call in the pros.

AUGERING A MAIN DRAIN. A main drain may be accessed through a cleanout near the floor, or through a drain hole in the floor, as shown here. Hire a rodding company or rent a large floor auger for the job.

CHAPTER THREE

REPAIRING & REPLACING FAUCETS

IF YOUR FAUCET DRIPS, or if it is clogged so that it lacks full flow of either hot or cold water, it can cost plenty to have a professional plumber come out and fix it. And many plumbers are reluctant to make faucet repairs, because old faucets can develop other problems, leading to call-backs. A pro will likely want to replace a faucet rather than repair it.

You may want to do the same. Many attractive faucets cost less than $80, and fairly high-end faucets are often less than $150. Most can be installed in an hour or two.

Still, it often makes sense to repair rather than replace, as long as you can get the right parts. Years ago, faucet repair was a matter of replacing a number of small parts, such as rubber washers and O-rings, or valve seats. Nowadays, most "repairs" are almost replacements: Take out a large part generally referred to as a "cartridge," which contains all the rubber and metal parts that create seals, and then pop in a new cartridge.

Though these repairs and replacements are small and fairly simple, the golden rule of plumbing applies: Before starting disassembly, *shut off the water, and test to be sure that the water is shut off.* This usually means shutting off the hot and cold stop valves under the sink. If your faucet does not have stop valves, you'll need to shut off water elsewhere (see pp. 6–8).

Choosing a New Faucet

The following pages give instructions for repairing various types of faucets—for a kitchen sink, a bathroom sink, and a tub/shower. However, you may want to consider replacing rather than repairing a faucet, especially if you have an unusual faucet with hard-to-find parts, or if you just don't like the looks of your existing faucet.

People are often pleasantly surprised what a difference a new faucet makes in the appearance and function of a room. It may be a small feature, but it is highly visible, and when it looks and works well, it is an upgrade that is well worth the cost.

Choosing finishes

In a small room like a bathroom, it usually looks best to harmonize metal surfaces, and faucet manufacturers tend to offer matching accessories. On the other hand, in the kitchen, mixing metals can add spice to the overall design. If you have a stainless sink and a brushed-nickel faucet, you may not need to stick with brushed nickel everywhere in the room. Adding a bit of contrast is a trend in kitchen design; for instance, it's common to incorporate a different color or style of cabinetry in one section of the kitchen. Similarly, metals can vary as long as there is overall balance. A rule of thumb is to have three or more items that match spaced throughout the room to establish a theme—perhaps door knobs, lighting fixtures, and a section of cabinet knobs. When mixing metals, a clear contrast works best, so that black matte or oil-rubbed bronze might work well with brushed nickel.

Unusual finishes like copper, gold, or oil-rubbed bronze add an elegant touch in the kitchen or bath, but tend to be expensive.

> **TIP** Be careful if you're combining different brands with the same finish, especially in the bathroom—a bronze finish from one company might look different from that of another.

FINDING THE RIGHT PARTS. Often, shopping is the most time-consuming part of a faucet repair. At a home center or hardware store you can find a wide assortment of parts for the most common faucet models. When shopping for parts, bring in the old faucet, or the make and model number (if you can find it on the body). Or take a photo of your faucet to show the salesperson.

Bathroom faucets

Whether you're upgrading both your sink and faucet or just the faucet, make sure your faucet will fit your sink's hole configuration. You can often replace a two-handle faucet with a single-handle model, but it will have a base plate that covers the other two holes.

A single-hole faucet is the usual choice for a bowl or vessel sink. A deck-mounted faucet like this needs to be tall enough to clear the rim of the bowl. Because water and grime tend to accumulate around a faucet, it's a good idea to allow at least ¼ in. or so behind the faucet so you can fit a finger or toothbrush in for cleaning.

Like widespread faucets, mini-widespread faucets have three individual components, 4 in. apart, on top of the sink, but under the sink they are a single unit.

> **TIP** When choosing a bathroom faucet finish, keep in mind that shinier, "polished" finishes will tend to show water spots and fingerprints. Matte or brushed finishes are more forgiving.

Four-inch centerset faucets are easiest to install. The handles and faucet are connected via an escutcheon (the flat bottom piece) and form a single unit on top of the sink. The "four inches" refers to the on-center distance between the two inlet holes.

On a widespread faucet, separate handles for hot and cold are spaced farther apart from the faucet for a more traditional look.

If you're installing a new wall-mounted faucet, you'll need to hook into water-supply lines that run in the wall above the sink's height (rather than below the sink). Make sure the faucet spout extends far enough out and is at a good height to work with your sink/counter arrangement.

Shower faucet heads

A shower faucet upgrade can really enhance your showering experience. Be sure to check out the range of possibilities before you choose.

Hand-held showerheads can be removed from the mounting and have a lot of handy uses, from washing hair (especially children's) to cleaning large items (perhaps the family dog). Look for a model that snaps back in place easily and securely. It's also possible to buy a two-in-one combo with both a removable and a fixed shower head, like the one shown here.

In this traditional arrangement, the showerhead, valve handle, and spout emerge from three different locations.

TIP Faucets with sharp corners are stylish and great for an overhead rain shower, but sharp corners may be hazardous for a showerhead placed at a lower level; also, the finish can wear around corners.

Water Conservation in the Shower

There are two ways to conserve water in the shower: Reduce either the flow rate or the length of time in the shower.

Water-saving showerheads work by restricting flow. To earn the EPA WaterSense® label they use no more than 2.0 GPM (gallons per minute), while at the same time meeting performance standards for water coverage and spray intensity. As for time in the shower, well, the average shower lasts just over 8 minutes.

For parched areas, a recirculating water system may be worth the extra expense; it recycles the bath water.

This showerhead slides up and down along a rail, making it possible to tailor the spray height for children. These heads are also nice for those who like to sit while showering, due to a disability or just a preference—for shaving legs, rinsing off feet, and so on. The showerhead may be fixed or removable.

Some shower faucets come with separate handles or buttons for controlling both water temperature and volume, which is a nice water-saving feature. For instance, when washing hair, you can turn off the water pressure while you soap up, and when you turn it back on to rinse, the temperature will be right where you want it.

A rain showerhead provides a spray of water directly overhead, like a blast of rain. These may be installed directly on the ceiling or may attach at the traditional spot for a showerhead, with an extension arm running up to the ceiling. Some real estate experts say they are good for home resale value.

Kitchen sink faucets

The kitchen sink faucet is heavily used, so a better-quality product is worth the extra money. Cheaper faucets are lightweight because they use plastic parts. A heavier faucet with copper, brass, or stainless-steel parts will tend to perform better and last longer. There are lots of choices for finishes, styles, and design. Until recent years, most kitchen faucets mounted onto the rim of the sink, but some new faucets can also be installed behind the sink—in the counter or in the wall. Here are mounting options:

Most undermounted sinks have deck-mounted faucets, which offer a neat, seamless appearance. Two-hole bridge faucets like this have an appealing antique quality, currently very popular. Leave a little space behind the faucet for cleaning, because grime will collect there on the deck.

If you're happy with your existing sink that has a sink-mounted faucet and just want to upgrade the faucet, select a faucet that works with the number of mounting holes in the sink. If a new faucet leaves you with an extra hole or two to fill, you can always add a new feature like a soap dispenser or buy a hole plug from the sink manufacturer.

A wall-mounted kitchen faucet can be charming, but be careful with this installation. If the faucet will be installed in an outside wall, check whether local codes will permit it; you may need insulation in a climate with freezing winters. Installation can be tricky, because the spacing and location of plumbing must be precise. In the event you encounter a wall stud where your faucet or handles need to go, you will need to relocate it.

Two-handle faucets have a traditional quality with enduring appeal. Some people complain that it's inconvenient to adjust two separate knobs when hands are full or dirty.

TIP If you have hard water, look for a faucet that has solid brass parts. Hard water will corrode other metals.

Pulldown versus Pullout

Most people want a kitchen faucet they can pull out or down to wash pans and other large items. Either way, check that the faucet stays securely in place when you put it back—cheaper faucets may use magnets to stay put, which may cause the faucet to wobble or dangle after a while.

Pulldown faucets (below left) have a higher arc and pull down vertically toward the bottom of the sink. Many people find the downward motion feels right, and prefer the more dramatic height. Some homes

with low water pressure may find the high arc slightly reduces it further.

Pullout faucets (below right) have a lower arc and you can more easily pull them sideways (e.g., toward the side or front of the sink), offering more flexibility. This lets you bring a garbage bin (or a fish tank) over to the side of the sink and pull the sprayer over to reach inside. However, because the faucet arc is lower, very high items may not fit under it (without pulling it out).

Repairing a Two-Handle Compression Faucet

A compression faucet, also called a stem faucet, is the oldest type of faucet. These faucets can last a long time, and many older homes still have them. The handle is attached to a part called a stem, which has a rubber washer at its bottom. When you twist the handle clockwise, the stem lowers, causing the washer to press tightly against a small round piece called a seat inside the faucet body, thereby shutting water off. If the rubber washer starts to fail, or if the seat develops pitting, the seal will be incomplete and the faucet will drip.

Most often, a stem faucet can be fixed by replacing the rubber washer. If the washer gets damaged after a short time, or if replacing the washer does not solve the problem, then try replacing the seat. If those measures do not help, either replace the stem(s) or the entire faucet. If water leaks out the handle, you may need to replace an O-ring or (in the case of a very old faucet) some packing material that winds around the stem near its top.

Before you begin disassembly, shut off the water by turning off the stop valves under the sink. Or see pp. 6–8 for other ways to shut off the water. Open the hot and cold valves to ensure that the water is shut off.

1 **REMOVE THE HANDLES.** If there are decorative caps on top of the handles, pry them off with a small screwdriver or a putty knife. Remove the screws that hold the handles. Pull the handles up and off. You may need to tap gently with a hammer from side to side and pry up to loosen the handles. If none of these methods works, use a handle puller, shown on p. 28.

2 **REMOVE THE RETAINING NUT.** Use a crescent wrench to loosen and remove the retaining nut. Grab the stem with a pair of pliers and pull it out.

TIP Rubber washers for stems come in many sizes; some are flat, whereas others are beveled. You may need to buy a small tub of rubber washers to get a washer that matches yours exactly.

3 **REPLACE A WASHER.** If the washer is pitted or deeply indented, replace it. Use a screwdriver to remove the screw holding it in place. Gently pry the washer out, taking care not to damage the stem. Replace with an exact duplicate.

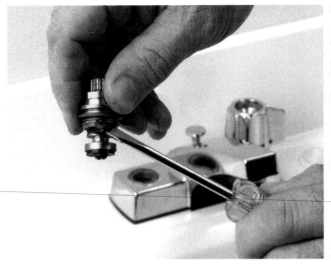

4 **REPLACE AN O-RING.** If water leaks out the handle or if an O-ring looks damaged, pry it off with a small slot screwdriver. Clean the groove and replace with a new ring of the same size. If you find crumbly or thread-like material around the stem, clean the area. Buy some "packing" string and wind it around the stem in the same place.

5 **REPLACE A SEAT.** If replacing a washer does not solve a drip from the spout, use a seat wrench to remove the seat, which is a small ring inside the faucet body. Get a duplicate seat and use the seat wrench to screw it tightly in place. Reassemble the faucet, restore water pressure, and test.

Repairing a Reverse-Compression Faucet

This type of faucet has been made by Chicago Faucets®, Crane®, and other companies for many decades and is still being made. It looks like a stem (compression) faucet but actually opens and closes in the opposite direction. The seat is attached to the stem body rather than the faucet body. The washer is beveled; be sure to get one of the same size and shape. When the faucet is closed, the seat moves up, sealing against the washer.

Because these faucets have been made for so long, replacement parts are available. If your local plumbing supply store does not have them, they can be ordered online. You can order repair kits, which include the washer, seat, and O-ring. Or just buy a new stem, often referred to as a cartridge.

Before you begin disassembly, shut off the water by turning off the stop valves under the sink. Or see pp. 6–8 for other ways to shut off the water. Open the hot and cold valves to ensure that the water is shut off.

1 **REMOVE A STEM.**
Remove the handle.
Use a crescent wrench to remove the hold-down nut (seen just above the wrench in the photo). Pull out the stem. You may be able to do this by hand; if not, use a pair of locking pliers. If the stem is encrusted with minerals, soak it in vinegar and brush it clean.

2 REMOVE THE WASHER AND RETAINER. Hold the stem firmly with pliers; use a cloth as shown to prevent damage to the stem. Use a crescent wrench to remove the bottom nut (above left). Now you can take off the rubber washer, which is encased in a metal retainer (above right).

4 REPLACE THE PARTS. Replace the parts that seal against each other: the O-ring, seat, and washer with retainer. Reinstall the metal washer and the hold-down nut. If the stem has other rubber O-rings, replace them as well.

3 REMOVE THE SEAT AND O-RING. Remove the seat with pliers. Also remove any other rubber parts; in this case, there is a rubber O-ring behind the seat.

5 REINSTALL THE STEM. Slip the repaired stem (or, as shown in this photo, an entirely new stem) into the faucet body. Tighten the hold-down nut and any washers, attach the handle, and restore water pressure. Test for leaks.

Repairing Other Two-Handle Faucets

A wide variety of two-handle faucets are on the market and installed in homes. Some are described as "disk" or "diaphragm" types, but all have cartridges (or stems) attached to the handles. If you can find the faucet's manufacturer and model number, it may be easy to find replacement parts at a home center or plumbing store. If not, you can very likely get them from online sources.

Individual cartridges are often similar to single-handle cartridges, as seen on p. 62. In some cases you may be able to make inexpensive repairs by replacing individual parts like washers, seats, and O-rings. A surer fix, which costs more but saves time, is to replace entire cartridges.

Before you begin disassembly, shut off the water by turning off the stop valves under the sink. Or see pp. 6–8 for other ways to shut off the water. Open the hot and cold valves to ensure that the water is shut off.

TIP Take the whole cartridge, rubber parts and all, to the store to find an exact replacement stem, or replacements for rubber parts.

FOUR STEMS. Cartridges (or stems) for two-handle faucets may be brass or plastic. Though brass cartridges are generally more durable, plastic units can be very long-lived and are inexpensive. Here, the stem on the left is a diaphragm type, and the one on the right is much like an old-fashioned compression stem. The two in the middle are disc-type valves.

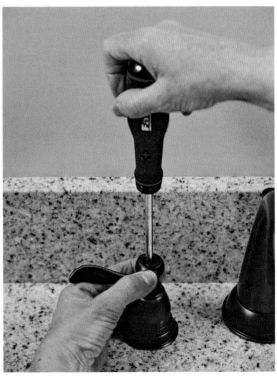

1 **REMOVE THE CAP AND HANDLE.** After ensuring that the water is shut off, pry off any decorative cap on top of the handles (above). Remove the screw that attaches the handle to the cartridge, and remove the handle. If the handle is stuck, you may need to tap it lightly from side to side, pry up on one side and then the other, or use a handle puller (p. 28).

TIP It's easy to forget which little parts go where, especially if your work is interrupted by a trip to the store. Jot down the order in which parts were disassembled or removed, or take phone photos of the parts prior to disassembly so you won't get confused.

2 REMOVE THE CARTRIDGE. Use a crescent wrench to remove the nut that holds the cartridge. Pull the cartridge out. If it is stuck, grab it with longnose pliers or locking pliers and wiggle it out.

3 REMOVE SMALL PARTS. Peer inside the faucet body and carefully remove any small parts. In this example, there is a spring and a rubber seal. In other cases, you may need to use a hex wrench or other tool to remove other parts.

4 REASSEMBLE. Buy a repair kit and replace the parts as instructed. This may mean replacing rubber and brass parts, or simply replacing an entire cartridge. Insert any small parts into the faucet body, insert the cartridge, tighten the hold-down nut, and reinstall the handle. Restore water pressure and test for leaks.

MAIN TYPES. From left to right, a ball with its cap, a cartridge, and a (ceramic) disk. All three types have small rubber and other parts that can be replaced (see p. 64 for a ball valve's seals and springs), but it is common to simply replace the entire innards with a sealed part that may be called a cartridge.

Repairing Single-Handle Faucets

Single-handle faucets are often divided into three types: cartridge, ball, and disk (also called ceramic disk). The distinction between the three types has become blurred over the years, and in newer models the major replacement part for all three types may be called a "cartridge."

To make repairs, shut off the water and follow the instructions on the next page for disassembling. Once you pull out the insides, you can determine which type of faucet you have, and you can look for exact replacement parts. If parts are difficult to find, consider installing a new faucet.

Disassembling a single-handle faucet

To get at a single-handle faucet valve, you usually need to remove the handle, then a retainer ring or clip of some sort.

Before you begin disassembly, shut off the water by turning off the stop valves under the sink. Or see pp. 6–8 for other ways to shut off the water. Open the hot and cold valves to ensure that the water is shut off.

SIDE MOUNT. Valves mounted on the side, like this one, are growing in popularity. Many models use disc valves, like this one. For repair purposes, the valves are the same; only the orientation changes.

1 REMOVE THE HANDLE. If there is a plastic decorative cap, pry it off with a small flat screwdriver or a putty knife, then remove the screw that holds it down. On the type of handle shown here, raise the handle and use a small Allen (hex) wrench to back off the setscrew (do not remove it) far enough so you can pull the handle off.

2 REMOVE THE RETAINER. Unscrew the retainer ring (also called a collar). If you cannot unscrew it by hand, wrap it with a cloth to protect it from scratches and use a pair of slip-joint pliers.

3 REMOVE THE VALVE. Now you can easily get at the disk, cartridge, or ball. In this example, there is a plastic cap with a rubber gasket fitted to it on top of a ball valve. In the case of a cartridge faucet, there may be a retaining clip that you must remove first (see p. 68, Step 2; if a cartridge is difficult to pull out, see the tips on pp. 68–69).

Repairing a Ball Faucet

If you have a ball faucet, a repair kit for your model will include springs and rubber seats, and perhaps a new ball as well.

TIP Pull the ball out gently and slowly, to ensure that the springs don't fly out.

1 **REMOVE THE SEATS AND SPRINGS.** Use a nail set, awl, or small screwdriver to take out the rubber seats and the springs that are under them. Also remove any other rubber parts that appear worn. If the ball itself is scratched or pitted, replace it as well.

2 **REPLACE THE PARTS.** Carefully slip a spring into the opening, then press a seat over it and press until it seals tight. Or slip the seat onto the spring first, then push them into the opening as a single piece. Insert the ball so that its slot is aligned with the pin in the faucet body.

3 **TIGHTEN THE CAP.** Keeping the ball aligned correctly, add the cap, making sure it aligns with the notch in the faucet body (above). Taking care to keep the ball and the cap correctly positioned, press down with the retainer, then screw it on by hand. Finish screwing using a pair of pliers as shown at right.

Repairing a Disk or Cartridge Faucet

A ceramic disk cartridge rarely wears out, but the rubber O-rings and gaskets do. Still, you may find that a repair kit includes the cartridge, just to make installation easier.

TIP If a ball-type faucet leaks at the base of the spout, remove the spout and replace the large O-ring that seals the spout at the bottom.

1 **CLEAN AND REPLACE RUBBER PARTS.** Remove the cartridge and pry out the rubber parts, which may be individual O-rings or a single gasket that goes around all the openings. Use a toothbrush or small brush and detergent to clean away scum and debris on the cartridge, then rinse clean. Apply plumber's grease (which will come with the repair kit), then press the new rubber parts into place.

2 **REASSEMBLE.** Slide the cartridge back into the faucet body and reinstall any retaining clip. Hand-tighten the retainer ring (or collar). Replace the handle and fasten with a setscrew or hold-down screw. Restore water pressure and test for leaks.

TIP To repair a long narrow cartridge faucet, see p. 68. (The procedure is similar for a tub/shower faucet and for a sink faucet.)

Repairing Kitchen Sprayers

Inexpensive and older kitchen faucets often have separate sprayers that rise out of a fourth hole in the sink. These are notorious for getting clogged, producing anemic flow, and having sticky triggers. "One-touch" faucets have sprayers that pull out and also act as the main spout. More often than not, these are more reliable. In many cases you can solve problems by disassembling and cleaning out debris that clogs the sprayer head or the valve that sends water to the sprayer. But if a sprayer is a continuing source of frustration, consider replacing it with a better model. These are readily available at home centers, plumbing supply stores, or hardware stores.

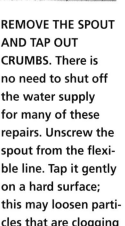

REMOVE THE SPOUT AND TAP OUT CRUMBS. There is no need to shut off the water supply for many of these repairs. Unscrew the spout from the flexible line. Tap it gently on a hard surface; this may loosen particles that are clogging the spout.

| TIP | Take special care to keep track of all the little sprayer parts, and be sure you remember the order in which they need to be reinstalled. It will help to put the parts in order on the countertop and then take a quick photo. |

REMOVE THE SPOUT COVER AND CLEAN PARTS. The spout cover may simply unscrew by hand or with the help of a pair of slip-joint pliers, or you may need to insert the prongs of longnose pliers into a pair of holes, as shown at top. Carefully remove all the parts inside; you may need to pry out the screen. If an O-ring or the screen is damaged, replace it.

A REPLACEMENT HOSE. This replacement hose comes with a variety of connections that allow you to replace many types of sprayers.

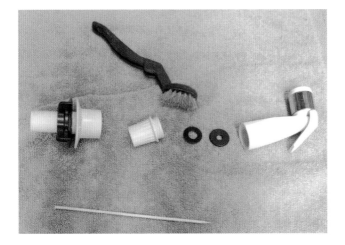

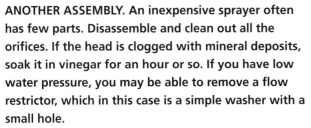

ANOTHER ASSEMBLY. An inexpensive sprayer often has few parts. Disassemble and clean out all the orifices. If the head is clogged with mineral deposits, soak it in vinegar for an hour or so. If you have low water pressure, you may be able to remove a flow restrictor, which in this case is a simple washer with a small hole.

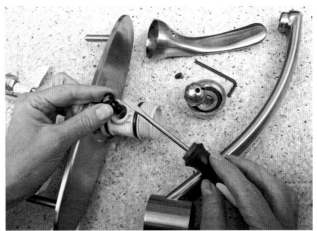

REMOVE THE DIVERTER. If after cleaning the sprayer's innards you still get a balky flow, the problem may be with the faucet's diverter. This is often located inside the faucet's body. Shut off hot and cold water to the faucet. Disassemble the faucet as described in the previous repair instructions for your type of faucet. Gently pry out the diverter. Clean away any debris, replace any damaged parts, and reassemble.

Repairing a Single-Handle Tub/Shower Faucet

Like sink faucets, tub/shower faucets may have cartridges, balls, or compression stems. The parts usually look and assemble much the same, except that they may be larger and are horizontal rather than vertical.

If, for instance, your faucet is a ball type, disassemble and remove the springs as you would for a sink ball faucet (see p. 64), taking extra care to ensure that the springs don't pop out and get lost.

In this section, we show a very common single-handle cartridge faucet, which gets repaired simply by replacing the cartridge. The main problem with this type is that

1 REMOVE THE HANDLE AND PLATE. Pry off the decorative cap, if there is one, and remove the screw holding the handle. Or use a hex wrench to loosen a setscrew. Pull out the handle. Unscrew the screws holding the plate (or escutcheon) and pull it off. If it is held in place with caulk or a dried gasket, use a putty knife to free it. Pull out the sleeve as well, to uncover the valve.

2 REMOVE THE RETAINER CLIP. Pull out the sleeve to fully expose the valve. In most cases, the cartridge is held in place with a retainer clip. Use a pair of longnose pliers or locking pliers to grab and pull it out.

3 LOOSEN THE CARTRIDGE. The repair kit includes a small plastic tool. Slip it over the cartridge's stem and use a pair of pliers to rotate back and forth. In most cases, this will break the seal and allow you to remove the cartridge without much trouble.

the cartridge may be difficult to remove. The pulling tool shown in Step 4 will often do the trick.

Before you begin disassembly, shut off the water. There may be stop valves behind an access panel in the adjoining room or closet. If not, you may need to shut off partial-house valves, or you may need to shut off water *to the whole house; see pp. 6–8. Open the valve to the middle position to be sure both hot and cold water are shut off.*

4 PULL OUT THE CARTRIDGE Try pulling the cartridge out using a pair of locking pliers (above left). If that doesn't work, try a cartridge-pulling tool made for your make and model (above right). Screw the tool into the cartridge's handle threads, taking care to keep the "wings" in the right position. Then use a wrench to turn the tool's bolt, which will slowly pull the cartridge out. Then pull it out the rest of the way by hand.

TIP Be sure that you pull the entire cartridge. Some cartridges have metal sleeves, and pulling with pliers may get just the inner portion, leaving the cartridge's sleeve still in the faucet body. In that case, you can use a tap tool, a bolt of the same size, and a heavy-duty socket wrench to pull out the sleeve. Unless you are familiar with this sort of technique, it is probably best to call in a pro.

5 CLEAN INSIDE. Look inside the faucet body with a flashlight and remove any debris. Use a bottle brush or a wadded-up rag to clean out the opening.

6 GREASE AND REINSTALL. You may choose to replace only rubber parts, but it's more common to replace the entire cartridge. Apply a bit of plumbing lubricant (which may be supplied with the repair kit) to the outside of the new cartridge. Insert the cartridge into the body, with the groove on the stem facing up. (If it faces down, hot and cold will be reversed.) Install the retainer clip, plate, sleeve, and handle.

Anti-Scald Faucets

Anti-scald faucets limit the temperature at which water can pass through your showerhead so you don't harm yourself with surprisingly hot water. These faucets come preset, usually to a maximum of 120°F. If you are not happy with the max temp, remove the faucet's handle and cover to expose the anti-scald mechanism, which may look like the one shown here. Turn the handle to the left and run water through the showerhead until it gets its hottest, then fill a glass and test with a candy thermometer. Use a screwdriver to turn the rotational limit stop to the left to increase the max temp or to the right to decrease it.

OTHER CARTRIDGES. Tub/shower faucet cartridges vary greatly depending on the manufacturer and model. Though each of these is called a "cartridge," the one on the left is a ceramic disk and the one on the right is a ball-type. All are designed to be easily replaced.

Repairing a Two- or Three-Handle Tub/Shower Faucet

Tub/shower faucets with two handles often have compression stems or other stems like those shown on pp. 57–59, though the stems will be larger. If there is a third handle, it controls a diverter that sends water up to the showerhead or down to the spout.

Before you begin disassembly, shut off the water. There may be stop valves behind an access panel in the adjoining room or closet. If not, you may need to shut off partial-house valves, or you may need to shut off water to the whole house; see pp. 6–8. Open valves to be sure both hot and cold water are shut off.

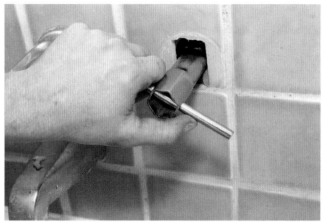

1 **REMOVE THE HANDLE, ESCUTCHEON, AND COLLAR.** Pry off the decorative plate, loosen the handle's setscrew, and pull the handle off. Loosen a setscrew (top) and remove the escutcheon, then unscrew and remove the collar (above).

TIP If water incompletely diverts up to the showerhead, you may need to repair or replace the diverter stem. Remove it as you would the other stems and replace the rubber parts, which usually include an O-ring and a rubber seat.

2 **LOOSEN THE STEM.** If the stem's nut protrudes out of the wall, you may be able to simply loosen it using an adjustable wrench. If it is inside the wall, use a stem wrench. Find a wrench that fits your stem, and try twisting by hand (top). If that doesn't work, use a pipe wrench for more torque (above).

3 REMOVE THE STEM AND INSPECT. Unscrew and remove the stem. Check the stem's washer and O-ring, and replace them if they are at all damaged. If the stem itself shows signs of wear, you may need to replace the stem.

4 REPLACE A WASHER. The most common repair is a washer replacement. Remove the screw holding the washer, pry out the washer, and replace with an exact duplicate. Also replace any other rubber parts, such as O-rings.

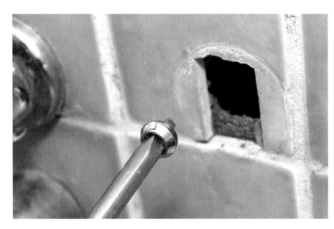

5 REPLACE A SEAT. If washers get damaged in less than a year, or if replacing a washer does not stop a leak, you may need to replace the seat. Insert a seat wrench (use whichever end of the wrench fits tightest) and unscrew and remove it. Replace with a new seat.

6 REINSTALL. Install the new or repaired stem and tighten firmly with a stem wrench or adjustable wrench. Temporarily place the handle on the stem, restore water pressure, and test. If there are no leaks, replace the collar, escutcheon, and handle.

Remodeling Kit

For many three-handle fixtures you can buy a remodeling kit that will make your faucet look and behave like new for less money and certainly less labor than installing a new faucet. This kit includes handles, escutcheons, valves, seats, washers, and extenders.

Installing Solid Supply Tubes

In most cases, the supply tubes—also called supply risers or risers—run from the stop valve to the faucet's inlets. Usually it's easiest to use flexible supply tubes, which come with nuts on each end that you simply tighten. Braided stainless-steel flexible supply tubes are easy to install and look good; plastic braided supply tubes are less attractive and less expensive.

If the supply tubes will be highly visible—as in the case of a wall-hung sink or, in some cases, a pedestal sink—you may choose to use old-fashioned solid supply tubes, which are usually made of chrome-coated copper. You'll probably also install a chrome rather than a plastic trap.

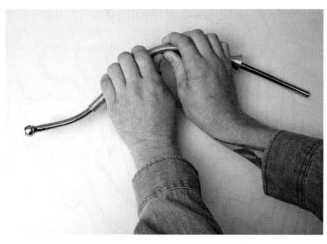

1 BEND THE TUBE. Slip a spring-type tube bender that fits as tightly as possible onto the tube, and use it to bend the tube into graceful curves. (If you try to bend without this tool, you will probably kink the tube.)

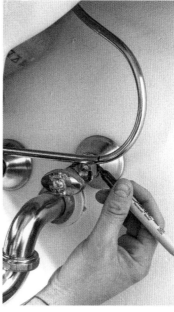

2 MARK FOR CUTTING. Test the fit; the tube must point straight into the inlets of the faucet and the stop valve. You'll probably need to rebend several times to achieve a good fit. Mark the tube for cutting.

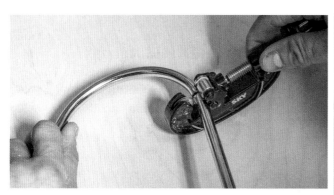

3 CUT THE TUBE. Use a tube cutter or, if you are careful not to press too hard, a hacksaw. You'll need to cut quite slowly: Tighten the cutter until it just barely cuts into the tube, rotate carefully so you don't go off track, then tighten just a little for each succeeding rotation.

4 ATTACH. The tube has a knob at the end that inserts into the faucet inlet. Screw on the nut, but don't tighten it. Slip a nut and ferrule onto the other end and poke it into the stop valve inlet. If it's not straight, you will not be able to tighten the nut. In that case, remove and rebend the tube. Tighten the nut at the valve, then tighten the nut at the faucet.

Replacing a Single-Handle Kitchen Faucet

These days, most single-handle kitchen faucets have pull-out spouts, so you can use them as sprayers as well. These faucets often have copper hot and cold inlets, to which you attach the supply tubes.

If you are working with the sink already installed, you'll need a basin wrench to get at the supply tubes' nuts.

Before you begin disassembly, shut off the water by turning off the stop valves under the sink. Or see pp. 6–8 for other ways to shut off the water. Open the hot and cold valves to ensure that the water is shut off.

The most difficult part of faucet installation is often reaching nuts and other connections from inside a cabinet below. Place plenty of large towels on the floor, have a good flashlight or two on hand, and have a helper nearby to hand you tools as you need them.

1 **DISCONNECT THE SUPPLY TUBES.** Use a basin wrench to disconnect the supply tubes from the existing faucet. Here we see them connected to two copper faucet inlets, but if you have a two-handle faucet they will be connected to a solid threaded pipe on each side of the faucet.

TIP Most kitchen sinks have three holes, but some have only one. The faucet shown here needs only one hole, but it has a baseplate that covers the other two holes. If you get a one-hole faucet, you can fill the other holes with a soap dispenser, a hot-water dispenser, or a filtered-water spout. Or you can simply buy hole plugs to fill the holes.

2 **DISCONNECT THE SPRAYER.** If you have a separate sprayer, you may be able to disconnect the old faucet's sprayer at the sprayer head and then thread the sprayer tube down through the sprayer hole. Or you may need to disconnect the sprayer below the spout. In the example shown here, a quick-connect fitting can be easily removed by hand. In other cases, you may need to use a basin wrench to disconnect.

TIP Measure to see that the existing supply tubes will reach your new faucet. The faucet may have inlets long enough to reach your stop valves. If not, you may be able to use the old tubes, or you may need to buy new tubes.

4 **INSTALL THE BASEPLATE.** This faucet has a baseplate that covers three holes. See that the baseplate's gasket is correctly aligned under it, set it in place, and have a helper hold it in place while you tighten the nuts from below.

TIP If you are installing a new sink, attach the faucet to the sink before installing the sink; it's much easier that way (see p. 152).

3 **REMOVE THE OLD FAUCET.** Loosen and remove the locknuts holding the faucet to the sink. You may need to start loosening with a basin wrench or pliers. Pull out the faucet. Clean any old putty or gunk from the top of the sink where the baseplate was.

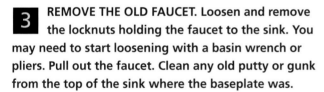

5 **INSERT THE FAUCET.** If there is a cover for the baseplate, snap it into place. Attach the supply tubes to the faucet's inlets; use pliers to hold the copper inlets still as you tighten the tubes so they do not kink. Thread the tubes and the faucet inlets down through the center hole.

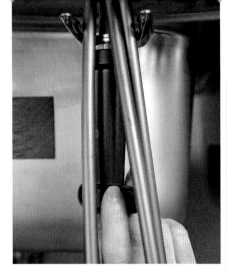

6 ATTACH THE FAUCET TO THE SINK. Faucets are fastened to the sink in various ways. In this case, you slip a U-bracket onto the mounting stud so it captures the three tubes, as shown. Use the wrench provided by the manufacturer (or a basin wrench) to tighten the center nut, which pushes the U-bracket up against the bottom of the sink.

7 ASSEMBLE THE SPRAYER/SPOUT. Attach the sprayer head to the threaded end of the hose. If supplied, put the little tapered hose guide on the other end, and feed it through the spout. Slide the spout/sprayer onto the faucet body.

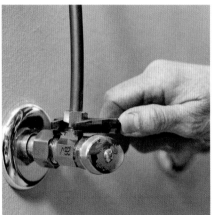

8 ATTACH THE SPRAYER HOSE. A doughnut-shaped weight hangs on the sprayer hose to help the spout/sprayer retract into the faucet. Slide the weight over the hose, and make sure there will be room for it to move freely inside the cabinet. Push the hose end onto the short tube coming out of the middle of the faucet. Connect it as shown, with a clip connector, or use pliers to tighten a nut.

9 CONNECT THE SUPPLY TUBES. Connect the faucet's inlets (or supply tubes that you fastened to the inlets) to the stop valves. Tighten by hand, then use a wrench to tighten one more turn.

10 FLUSH THE LINES AND CHECK FOR LEAKS. Restore water pressure and watch for leaks; you may need to tighten a bit more. Remove the sprayer head and pull the hose into the sink. Turn the faucet handle to the mixed position and flush the water lines for a minute or so to prevent debris from clogging the sprayer head. Reinstall the sprayer head and test again.

Installing a Bathroom Faucet

Most bathroom faucets come with a pop-up assembly, which raises and lowers the sink's stopper when you operate a push rod that comes up through the faucet body. The pop-up connects to the drain body, which is the tailpiece or topmost part of the drain trap.

Workspace under a bathroom sink is often very cramped. It may be worth the trouble to remove the sink from the wall (in the case of a wall-hung or pedestal sink) or lift it off the cabinet (in the case of a vanity sink) in order to remove the old faucet and install the new one. (In the steps on the following pages, we show installing with the sink removed.)

Most bathroom faucets cover three sink holes that are 4 in. apart. However, a bowl sink (see p. 86) or certain other types of sinks (see, for example, pp. 145–146) have only one hole, and one-hole faucets are available. These often do not have pop-up assemblies.

Make sure your supply tubes (see p. 79) are long enough to reach the stop valves below; you may be able to reuse the old tubes.

Before you begin disassembly, shut off the water by turning off the stop valves under the sink. Or see pp. 6–8 for other ways to shut off the water. Open the hot and cold valves to ensure that the water is shut off.

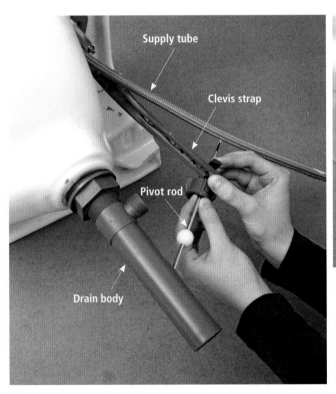

Supply tube

Clevis strap

Pivot rod

Drain body

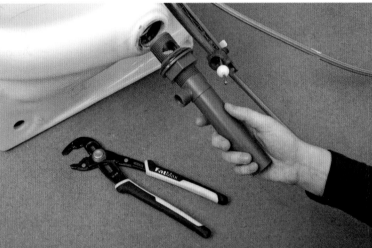

1 **REMOVE THE DRAIN BODY. To remove the old faucet, disconnect the supply tubes from the stop valves. Disconnect the trap piece (see p. 40). Unscrew the pivot rod's nut and remove the pivot rod (left). Use slip-joint pliers to loosen the drain body, then unscrew and remove it (above).**

Stop the Spin

When you work to unscrew the drain body, the drain flange that it attaches to (at the bottom of the sink bowl) may spin, and you will make no progress at unscrewing. In that case, have a helper hold the flange still using the handles of a pair of pliers or the jaws of longnose pliers.

2 PULL THE FAUCET OUT. From above, pull the faucet out. Clean away any putty residue or debris from the sink's deck. Disconnect the supply tubes if you will reuse them for the new faucet.

3 INSERT THE NEW FAUCET. Older faucets often called for a rope of plumber's putty under the faucet's baseplate, but most new faucets have a plastic gasket instead. Slip the faucet in place and have a helper hold it straight while you work from below.

Single- and Two-Handle Faucets

A single-handle faucet typically has inlets in the center; mounting nuts may attach to each side, as with this model, or there may be a single mounting nut in the center, as seen on p. 76. Sometimes the inlets are short and copper; in this case, they are long plastic supply tubes, so you probably won't need to add separate supply tubes. (These tubes usually have ⅜-in. nuts, so they won't fit if you have stop valves with ½-in. outlets.) A two-handle faucet usually has mounting nuts that screw onto plastic or brass inlets on each side.

If the sink is left in place, single-handle faucets are easier to install than two-handle models, because either they have supply tubes already or you can

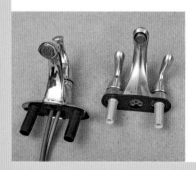

attach the supply tubes before mounting the faucet. With a two-handle model, you have to attach the supply tubes after the faucet is mounted.

4 MOUNT WITH NUTS. From below, screw on and tighten the mounting nuts. These may be plastic nuts on each of the inlets for a two-handle faucet, metal nuts with washers on each side for a one-handle faucet, or another arrangement. If you cannot reach the nuts with a crescent wrench, use a basin wrench. If you have a single-handle faucet, see p. 76 for an example of mounting hardware.

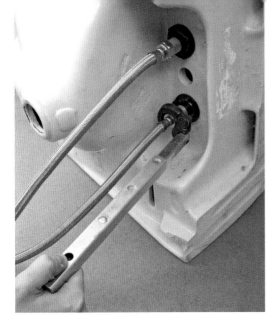

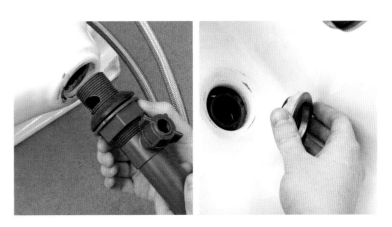

5 SUPPLY TUBES. If the supply tubes are not already connected to the faucet, connect them now, using a basin wrench if needed. Also connect them to the stop valves.

6 PREP THE DRAIN BODY AND FLANGE. Loosen the new drain body's nut and slide the rubber gasket down (above left) far enough so that the side hole will end up on the inside of the sink and the threads can reach up to meet the drain flange. From above, apply a rope of plumber's putty to the underside of the drain flange (above right).

7 SCREW ON THE DRAIN BODY. Poke the drain body up through the drain hole and hand-tighten it to the flange. Finish tightening with the drain body's hole for the pivot rod facing back toward the wall. From below, use slip-joint pliers to tighten the drain body. Putty will squeeze out of the drain flange; clean it away.

Tighten the Supply Tubes

If you have a single-handle faucet with copper inlets, tighten the supply tubes to them. Hold the inlets still with a small wrench as you tighten the supply tube's nuts, to keep them from twisting and kinking. If you have a two-handle faucet, you cannot attach the supply tubes yet, because you have to attach the mounting nuts first (see Step 4).

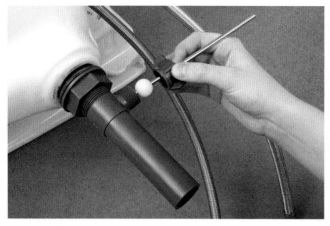

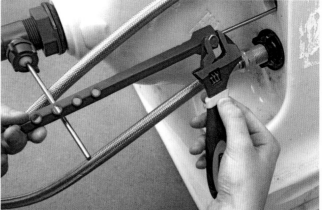

8 INSTALL THE PIVOT ROD. From above, insert the stopper into the drain hole. From below, insert the pivot rod into the drain body, so it slips into the hole in the stopper. Slide on the pivot rod's mounting nut and tighten; it should be tight enough to seal, but not so tight that it's difficult to move the rod up and down.

9 ATTACH THE CLEVIS STRAP. Slide the lift rod down through the hole in the faucet body, and attach the clevis strap to it. Tighten the nut to hold the strap to the rod.

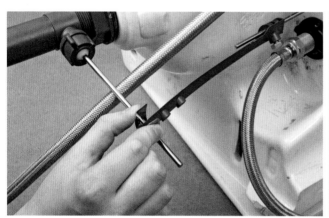

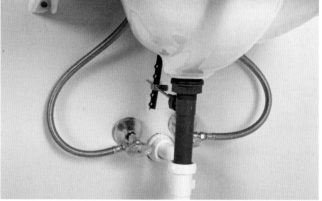

10 ATTACH THE PIVOT ROD TO THE STRAP. With the stopper closed all the way, slide the pivot rod through a hole in the clevis strap, using the clip to hold it in place. Test that you can easily open and close the stopper using the lift rod; you may need to loosen the clevis strap's nut and slide it up or down on the lift rod.

11 FINISH PLUMBING. Install the rest of the trap plumbing. You may need to cut a tailpiece or add an extension (see pp. 40–41). Restore water pressure and test for leaks: Fill the sink bowl with water, then open the stopper and watch closely. If there are any drips, tighten nuts or replace washers as needed.

Installing a Widespread Faucet

A widespread faucet has three separate parts—two handles and one spout—that connect together via flexible tubes, so they can be arranged in a variety of configurations, with no baseplate. There are a variety of types with different sorts of connections, but many of them use connections similar to those shown here.

Before you begin disassembly, shut off the water by turning off the stop valves under the sink. Or see pp. 6–8 for other ways to shut off the water. Open the hot and cold valves to ensure that the water is shut off.

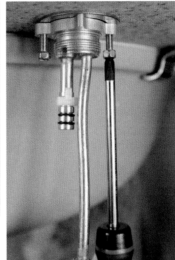

2 **FASTEN THE HANDLES. You** may need to apply a bead of silicone caulk under the escutcheons. While a helper holds the handles correctly positioned from above, work from below to tighten the nuts and screws.

1 INSERT THE HANDLES AND SPOUT. Slip the handles and spouts through their escutcheons and down through the sink's holes.

 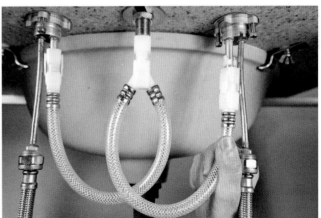

3 ATTACH THE SPOUT AND LIFT ROD. Slip the lift rod through the back of the spout. Slide the mounting washer in place, with its slot positioned so the rod can slide through. Screw on the mounting nut by hand, then tighten it with a crescent wrench. Don't overtighten, or you may crack the sink. Pull the lift rod out to make the next step easier to perform.

4 ATTACH THE SUPPLY TUBES TO THE HANDLES' INLETS. Use two wrenches or pliers and a wrench, to hold the inlets still while you tighten the supply tube's nuts. Connect the tubes that run from the handles to the spout. Slip the lift rod back down and connect it to a pop-up assembly. Restore water pressure and test for leaks.

CHAPTER FOUR

BATHROOM SINK AND TUB UPGRADES

THIS CHAPTER CONTINUES WITH PROJECTS that require running no new pipes in walls—only replacing or installing fixtures and traps. As long as you do not need to add a sink, toilet, or tub where there was none before, or need to move a fixture from one place to another, you can remake the look of your bathroom with only modest skills.

Some projects, like replacing a simple vanity sink or a tub spout, can be surprisingly quick and easy. A pedestal sink or a vanity with drawers may take some extra finagling to tuck the plumbing into tight spots. A bowl sink is usually simple plumbing-wise, but may take you a day or so of carpentry and finish work. A shower panel calls for carefully following manufacturer instructions. The most challenging project here is a claw-foot tub; if you do not already have plumbing in place (in the floor), you may want to hire a plumber for that.

Choosing a Bathroom Sink

Even if you don't want to spend a lot of money, you have plenty of design options for your bathroom sink. For bargain-basement prices, look for used sinks on Craigslist®, or check out discount remodeling stores. A home center will carry inexpensive to mid-priced options, whereas a design center will probably have pricier models.

You may want to choose a replacement toilet along with the sink, so they can coordinate in style. Replacing a toilet is not difficult (see pp. 132–137), so you might make a switch just for the sake of looks. While you're at it, consider also painting the walls and replacing your towel bars and medicine chest, to achieve a substantial bathroom makeover for a reasonable price. (Replacing a tub is a more involved project; see pp. 192–201.)

Bathroom sinks are often housed in some sort of cabinetry. There are four basic types: vanities, consoles, pedestals, and bowl or vessel sinks. All can be installed with relative ease, as long as your drain and supply lines are in place and are reasonably positioned. For a pedestal sink, the drain's trap adapter and the supply stop valves need to be pretty precisely positioned, so they fit behind the pedestal. For other types of sinks, you have more wiggle room.

TWO BOWLS. A double-bowl vanity allows two family members to wash up side by side, possibly reducing marital or sibling strife. This one has drawers in the middle. Before buying a model like this, make sure the plumbing will fit: There will be no problem if there are two drain lines with trap adapters that come out of the wall, but if there is only one trap adapter, you may need to snake a trap line behind the drawers.

VANITY CABINET. A vanity cabinet can be almost any style. Dark-stained veneered wood gives this cabinet a rich appearance.

| TIP | If your new sink will be wider than the old, check p. 242 to make sure it will not be uncomfortably close to a toilet, tub, or other element in the bathroom. |

ECLECTIC. Here's a jazzy arrangement: A rectangular white sink is undermounted to a shiny yellow counter-top, which is supported by chrome legs. The front bar could be used to hang towels.

CONSOLE. A console sink has minimal cabinetry below, often with open shelving. This model features a basket-like drawer just under the sink, which is shallow so it doesn't bump into the plumbing.

FLOATING. A "floating" or wall-hung vanity attaches firmly to the wall so no legs are needed. This makes it easy to clean the floor and gives a lofty, open feel to a bathroom.

PEDESTAL STYLE. Pedestal sinks are popular because of their classic lines. They are found in homes with both Victorian and modern style motifs. Here, the sink and toilet are clearly coordinated.

PEDESTAL PLUMBING. With a pedestal sink, the supply and drain plumbing is often at least partially visible, so gleaming chrome components are often used instead of more practical plastic parts.

VANITY WITH LEGS. Some bathroom sinks and cabinets blur standard distinctions. Here, a cabinet rests on metal legs, so it almost seems suspended. The sink is a metal bowl, but because it is set deeply into the countertop, it almost feels like a standard sink.

BOWL SINK WITH FANCIFUL SHAPE. Bowl sinks come in all shapes and materials. This one has a sort of boat shape and a flat bottom.

BOWL ON STONE. This simple bowl sink sits on a solid bluestone slab that has been well sealed. Note that bowl sinks require extra-tall faucets.

BOWL SINK WITH WALL FAUCET. This bowl sink is installed onto a wood countertop; the wood must be kept well sealed. A wall faucet works well for a bowl sink; see p. 53.

Preparing for a Bathroom Sink

You will probably need to remove an existing sink before installing a new one. Whether the old sink is wall-hung, pedestal style, or housed in a vanity, *first shut off the water and turn on the faucet to be sure the water is off*.

1 **CUT CAULK LINES.** Before you start prying or lifting, check to see if there is a line of caulk between the sink and the wall, or along the underside of the sink against a vanity cabinet or pedestal. If so, cut through the caulk with a utility knife. It may take several passes to cut all the way through.

2 **DISCONNECT THE PLUMBING.** Place a bucket and a thick towel under the plumbing to catch the water left in the lines. Use a crescent wrench or pliers to unscrew the supply tubes from the stop valves. Unscrew the nut that connects the trap's tailpiece (the straight piece attached to the sink) to the trap. You may need to loosen another nut or two as well. Pull the trap partially apart, so the sink is disconnected.

3 **LIFT THE SINK OFF.** Most wall-hung sinks or pedestal sinks rest on a bracket in the wall. Pull the sink straight up (you may need to wiggle it a bit at first) until it disengages with the bracket. If the sink is on a vanity, you can usually simply lift it up and out. Remove screws holding the cabinet to the wall, and remove the cabinet.

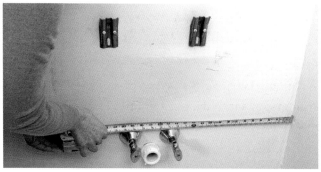

4 **TAKE MEASUREMENTS.** You may need to patch and paint the wall. Measure the distance between the plumbing and a nearby wall or fixture to make sure your new sink will fit. For a pedestal sink, the plumbing must be close together and centered on the sink, so it can fit in the pedestal. If you're installing a vanity, you have a good deal more wiggle room.

Installing a Vanity Sink

Adding a vanity is a common and usually straightforward project that can often be done in a couple of hours, as long as the wall plumbing is in good shape. (If it worked for the previous sink, it should be fine.)

Buy a sink along with the vanity cabinet; they often are sold as an ensemble. The type shown here, with a sink that is molded into the countertop, is the most common. For a custom look, you could buy a drop-in (self-rimming) sink and perhaps create your own countertop using tiles or other materials—which would greatly increase the difficulty of the project. The vanity shown here rests against the wall. Other types with legs may be installed an inch or two away from the wall.

> **TIP** Avoid shimming the bottom of the cabinet if possible, because this will create a debris-collecting crack. Usually you can shim the underside of the sink where it meets the cabinet instead. However, if the floor is way out of level, it may cause the vanity's doors to stay open. If that's your situation and you need to shim up the cabinet, consider covering the resulting gap with base shoe molding.

1 DRY-FIT THE CABINET. Set the cabinet where you want it, and measure on each side to be sure it is not too close to a toilet or tub (see p. 242). Check for level in both directions; you may need to apply shims to the wall.

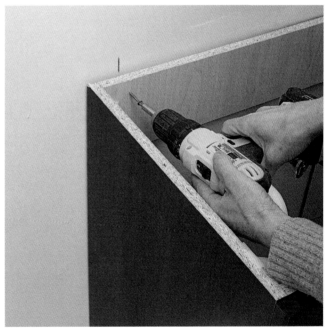

2 CUT A BASEBOARD. If baseboard is keeping the cabinet from meeting the wall, position the vanity and scribe a cutline (above left). Cut with an oscillating saw (above right) if you have one; otherwise, use a handsaw or reciprocating saw.

3 ATTACH THE CABINET. Use a stud finder to locate wall studs and mark their locations on the wall. Check that the vanity cabinet is at least close to level in both directions, shim if needed, and drive screws into studs.

4 PLUMB THE SINK. With the sink on a work surface, install the faucet onto the sink top, as shown on pp. 77–81. Attach the sink's tailpiece and the pop-up assembly if there is one. Screw flexible supply tubes to the faucet's inlets; make sure they are long enough to reach the stop valves in the wall.

5 PLUMB INSIDE THE CABINET. Carry the sink to the cabinet and set it on top. Lower it slowly to be sure you will not bend any plumbing inside the cabinet. Center the sink top on the cabinet and attach the trap. Attach the supply tubes to the stop valves. With a bucket under the trap, turn on the stop valves, turn on the faucet, and test for leaks.

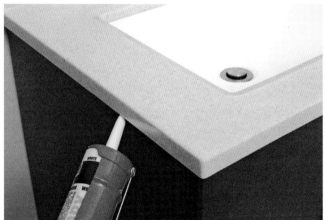

6 CAULK TO ATTACH. Apply a bead of caulk to the underside of the sink top to secure it to the vanity.

TIP For a no-doubt test of the plumbing, lower the stopper and fill the bowl most of the way. Then raise the stopper to let the water rush down. Stare at the trap and the cabinet floor with a flashlight to be sure the plumbing remains bone dry. If you see a leak, it can usually be fixed by simply tightening a nut.

7 FINISH. Add any knobs or other hardware. You may choose to run a bead of silicone caulk where the sink top meets the wall.

Installing a Pedestal Sink

Pedestal sinks are less forgiving than vanities: More of the wall will show, so be sure to patch and paint the wall carefully beforehand. Installation is a bit trickier as well, but not very difficult.

1 **CUT A HOLE FOR THE BRACE. Carefully read the manufacturer's instructions and measure to determine where you will install the sink's mounting brackets or where you will drive screws to attach the sink. Locate studs, and cut a hole in the wall that spans between two studs large enough to accommodate a 2×8 or 2×10 brace. Save the cutout piece to use as a patch.**

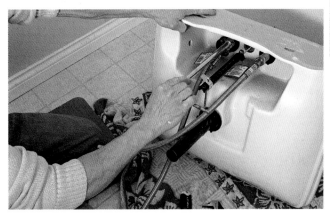

2 **ATTACH THE BRACE AND PATCH. Cut a 2×8 or 2×10 cleat to fit snugly between the studs, and attach it with three angle-driven screws on each side. Attach the cutout piece from Step 1 to the cleat. Apply fiberglass mesh tape around the perimeter, and trowel on joint compound to complete the patch. Allow to dry, sand, apply another coat, and repeat until you have a smooth patch. Prime and paint.**

3 **PLUMB THE SINK. Install the faucet and the drain tailpiece, and attach the pop-up assembly if there is one (see pp. 77–81). On many pedestal sinks you will need to use a basin wrench to attach the faucet. Screw on the supply tubes, making sure they are long enough to reach the stop valves in the wall.**

TIP At least some of the plumbing will be visible. If you have a narrow pedestal and your stop valves are widely spaced, you could open up the wall and install new pipes to move the stop valves closer together, using techniques shown in Chapter 7. Or proudly display your plumbing, perhaps replacing the stop valves with classier-looking valves and installing solid chrome supply tubes rather than flexible tubes (see p. 73).

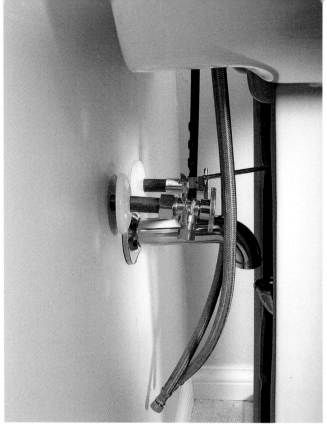

5 CUT OR ADD A TAILPIECE. If the trap is low, you will need to cut the tailpiece, as shown here. If the trap is too high, install a tailpiece extension, test the fit again, and cut the extension as needed.

4 TEST THE TRAP'S FIT. Slip the trap arm into the trap adapter in the wall, but leave it loose so you can position it as needed. Attach the trap to the sink's tailpiece. Set the sink on top of the pedestal and slide them into position so the sink is against or close to the wall. Check the fit. In the example shown, the tailpiece is a bit long, causing the trap to be lower than the trap arm.

6 MOUNT THE SINK. If the sink mounts via a bracket or two, follow the manufacturer's instructions for positioning the brackets and screw them to the hidden cleat. If the sink mounts using long screws, as shown here, slide the sink and pedestal into position and loosely attach the trap to the trap arm so you can slide the pieces as needed. Working from underneath, use a drill or a socket and ratchet to drive the mounting screws into the bracket.

7 FINISH PLUMBING. Tighten the trap's nuts and attach the supply tubes. Turn on the stop valves, turn on the faucet, and check for leaks. You may choose to apply a bead of caulk where the sink meets the wall, but it is more common to leave this seam uncaulked.

Installing a Vanity with Drawers

Most vanities provide below-sink storage space that is difficult to reach and partially blocked with plumbing. The type of vanity sink and cabinet shown here, sold at IKEA, features a shallow sink bowl and a drain trap that snakes cunningly just under the sink, then snugs against the wall. That allows room for large drawers, which provide storage that is ample and easy to access. This system does not have a pop-up assembly, which would get in the way of the drawers. Instead, it has a drain stopper with a spring that pops up and down when you press on it.

The sink and cabinet come as a two-part ensemble. The model shown here has a pair of legs to support the cabinet in the front. Other models are "floating," meaning that there are no legs and the cabinet is held in place with strong screw connections at the wall (see the photo below).

DRAWERS ARE BETTER. The sink's low profile and serpentine drain trap assembly make it possible to include capacious drawers, turning this vanity into a serious storage unit.

FLOATING VANITY. This style of vanity has no legs and the cabinet is held in place with strong screw connections at the wall.

1 ASSEMBLE THE CABINET. This type of cabinet typically requires assembly, which calls for no special skills but will take some time. Following the manufacturer's instructions, slip in wood dowels and metal connectors, attach braces, and assemble with fastening nuts (top). Drive screws to attach the drawer glides (above).

2 ATTACH THE VANITY TO THE WALL. Use a stud finder or rap on the wall and drill test holes to find the wall studs and mark their locations. Position the vanity against the wall. Check for level in both directions; you may need to adjust the height of one or both of the legs. Once you've achieved level, drive 2-in. or longer screws through the vanity's back brace into wall studs.

3 INSTALL THE OVERFLOW FITTING. The overflow assembly has a front and back part (above left). Hold the back part in place as you screw in the front part (above right). In this case, a special tool has been supplied for this purpose.

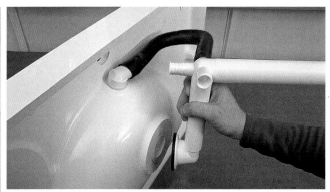

4 SLIP ON THE OVERFLOW HOSE. From the back of the sink, slip the rubber hose onto the overflow fitting. It can be swiveled as needed.

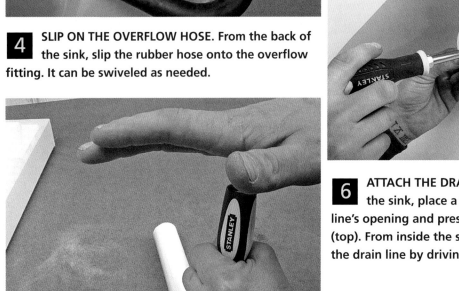

6 ATTACH THE DRAIN TO THE SINK. From under the sink, place a rubber gasket on the drain line's opening and press it against the sink's drain hole (top). From inside the sink, attach the drain flange to the drain line by driving a screw (above).

Pop-Up Stopper

Instead of a pop-up assembly with a lift rod, some vanity sinks have stoppers that work simply by fitting tightly. A better solution, shown here, is a unit that closes or opens when you press down and release.

5 PREPARE THE DRAIN LINE. The rubber overflow hose can be attached to either side of the drain line. Decide which side is more convenient, and use a large screwdriver to punch out the removable tab in that side. Use pliers to remove the tab.

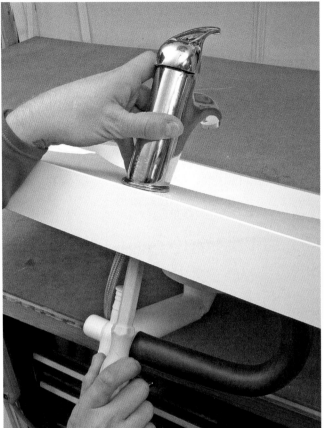

7 INSTALL THE FAUCET. See the instructions in Chapter 3 for installing your type of faucet. This sink has only one hole, and there will not be a pop-up assembly. Here, the manufacturer has supplied a plastic wrench for attaching the faucet. Make sure the faucet's inlets are long enough to reach your stop valves, or purchase supply tubes that are long enough and that have the same size fittings as your stop valves (either ¾ in. or ½ in.).

8 CUT DRAIN TRAP PIECES TO FIT. Set the sink in place and determine which trap pieces need to be cut. Mark with a felt-tipped pen, and cut with a miter saw or a hacksaw.

TIP As shown here, the instructions show installing where the wall's trap adapter (into which the trap is installed) is near the center of the cabinet. If your trap adapter is significantly off center, you will need to purchase trap arms and extensions so the drain trap can travel sideways as needed.

9 INSTALL THE TRAP AND SUPPLIES. Attach the supply tubes to the stop valves. Following the instructions on pp. 40–41, assemble and install the trap with all the washers facing the right direction. Restore water pressure and check for leaks.

Creating a Bowl Sink

A bowl sink, also called a vessel sink, is an updated version of the old "face bowls" people used to wash up in the days before running water and drainpipes. Newer versions retain the old-fashioned charm, but with modern plumbing. Most bowl sinks use a "vessel faucet," which has a raised spout and typically uses only one countertop hole.

There are companies that sell bowl sink sets, which include a cabinet and a countertop (or deck) that has two holes for the sink and the faucet, along with the sink and the faucet. These are simple to install. The faucet plumbing is standard, whereas the bowl's drain may have a drain line that hugs the bottom of the cabinet, like the one on p. 94.

The following pages show a popular project: converting a used table into a cabinet for a bowl sink. The table shown is fairly small—22 in. by 28 in.—but you may want a larger one. Bathroom sinks may be anywhere from 30 in. to 36 in. tall, depending on your preferences. Take into account the height of the bowl itself when selecting a cabinet; you may choose to cut the cabinet's legs.

If a sink will be lightly used by adults only, you may choose to simply cover the table top with solid coats of paint or clear finish. For better protection, install tiles or a solid piece of granite or marble. Here we use large (18 in. by 24 in.) travertine tiles, and end up with just a few grout lines. Natural stone like travertine, marble, or limestone can be porous and should be coated with a masonry sealer.

A BOWL SINK. A bowl sink adds a touch of old-fashioned charm, especially if you start with an antique table.

TIP It usually looks best to have the stone tiles or slab overhang the table by ½ in. or so on the two sides and in the front. If you want the sink to fit snugly against the wall, install tiles flush with the back of the table.

1 **LAY YOUR TILE or stone slab on top of the table or cabinet that you have chosen. Measure for cutting some tiles or the slab. Position the bowl where you want it to be, and place a tube or pipe (here we use a part of the drain trap assembly) to represent the faucet. Use a pencil or felt-tipped pen to trace outlines for both the faucet hole and the sink's drain hole.**

TIP You may choose to get masonry hole saws that are ⅛ in. larger than recommended, to make it easier to bore the holes in the table. Just be sure that the faucet and the drain flange will cover the resulting holes.

2 **CUT TILES OR SLAB.** Use a wet-cutting tile saw to cut tiles. You can rent a tile saw or purchase an inexpensive one. Or your home center or tile store may cut tiles or a stone slab for you, for a reasonable price.

3 **DRILL HOLES IN THE TILES.** Buy or rent masonry hole saws that are the required sizes for the two holes. Bore the holes, exerting medium pressure while a helper sprays the tile surface with water or glass cleaner to keep the hole saw from getting dull.

4 **DRILL HOLES IN THE TABLE.** Place the tiles or slab on top of the table, positioned for best effect. If you are using tiles, secure them with pieces of tape so they won't shift while you work. Switch to a wood-boring hole saw, and use the holes in the tiles or slab as guides to start the holes in the table. Remove the tiles, and finish drilling the holes.

5 **APPLY ADHESIVE.**
Set the tiles or slab in place and test to be sure the drain and faucet will fit in the holes, then remove them. You may apply tile mastic or thinset mortar with a notched trowel. Or, as shown here, apply squiggles of silicone caulk, which will hold very well.

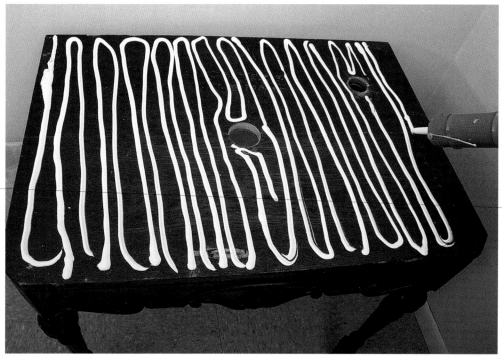

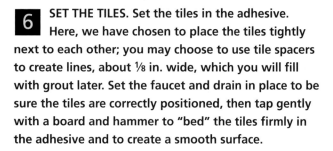

6 **SET THE TILES.** Set the tiles in the adhesive. Here, we have chosen to place the tiles tightly next to each other; you may choose to use tile spacers to create lines, about ⅛ in. wide, which you will fill with grout later. Set the faucet and drain in place to be sure the tiles are correctly positioned, then tap gently with a board and hammer to "bed" the tiles firmly in the adhesive and to create a smooth surface.

7 **FINISHING TOUCHES.** Sand corners and perhaps top edges as well to slightly ease any sharp corners. Apply stone or masonry sealer, paying special attention to the joints between the tiles (left). If you have grout lines, fill with grout using a grout float, then wipe several times with a damp sponge, working to create grout joints that are consistent in depth and appearance.

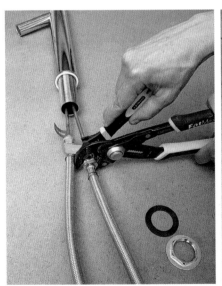

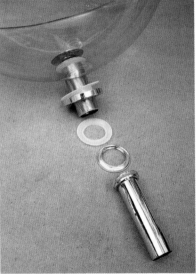

8 **ASSEMBLE THE SINK AND FAUCET PLUMBING.** A one-hole basin faucet usually has two copper inlets. Use two wrenches when attaching the supply tubes to the inlets so the copper lines don't bend (above left). Follow the manufacturer's instructions for assembling the sink drain; it's a simple matter of attaching pipes, washers, and nuts in the correct order (above right).

9 **MAKE PLUMBING CONNECTIONS.** Attach the drain trap, as shown on pp. 40–41; you may need to cut one or more parts. Attach the supply lines to the stop valves in the wall. Turn on the water and test for leaks.

Replacing Tub Spouts

Bathtub spouts may simply be screwed onto a threaded galvanized pipe sticking out of the wall, but don't just grab a pair of pliers or a wrench and start unscrewing the old one. It may be attached to an unthreaded copper pipe with a setscrew, and trying to unscrew it could damage the pipe.

LOOK FOR A SETSCREW AND REMOVE IT WITH A HEX WRENCH. Use a mirror to see if there is a setscrew on the bottom of the spout. If so, use a hex wrench to loosen the setscrew. Be sure to use find a wrench that fits tightly, or you could strip out the hex hole; it may be metric or SAE. Once the setscrew is loose, pull the spout out.

A Spout Retrofit Kit

Some spouts have threads at the back, whereas others have threads near the front. Others have no threads and attach with a setscrew. A retrofit kit will probably include the parts you need in order to extend the pipe out from the wall or attach with a setscrew, so you can attach the spout securely.

UNSCREW FROM A THREADED PIPE. If there is no setscrew, use pliers or a pipe wrench to remove the spout. If you will reuse the spout, wrap it with a cloth or use a strap wrench (p. 34) to prevent scratching. In some cases, you can insert a hammer handle or a dowel into the spout's opening and unscrew it that way. Or, if the spout is square at its end, you may be able to use a crescent wrench, as shown above right.

TIP If there is a leak inside the wall behind the spout, remove the spout, then remove the threaded pipe. Wrap with plumber's tape and tighten firmly.

Installing a Hand-Held Shower Spout

Some flex-line shower spouts attach to a special tub spout and require that you drill holes in the tile and attach a mounting bracket to the wall. A model that is easier to install, shown here, attaches to the shower arm. Remove the existing showerhead and replace it with the unit's large showerhead. Then screw the flex line for the hand-held showerhead to the large showerhead. Now you can operate the large and small heads at the same time, or use one or the other.

Installing a Shower Panel

A shower panel, sometimes called a shower tower, allows you to customize your shower experience. In addition to a standard showerhead that may be positioned to mimic an overhead waterfall, most models include several body jets with various massage settings located at various heights, plus a handheld spray wand. The body jets can be aimed at, for instance, the lower or upper back, creating the same therapeutic effects as the jets of a tub spa, but without the wait for the tub to fill.

The model shown here is a retrofit unit, so it can be installed in an existing shower with little difficulty: The only plumbing connection is to the showerhead's arm, and several screws with plastic anchors are all that's needed to attach the unit. With a retrofit unit, you control water temperature with the handle(s) you already have.

Other hard-piped models are hooked to the supply pipes, and so can be installed only while the plumbing wall is opened up. A piped unit may have its own standard hot and cold knob, or it may have a thermostatic control.

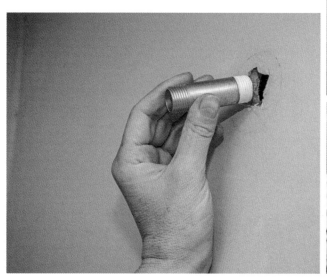

1 **SCREW ON THE EXTENDER PIPE. Use slip-joint pliers to unscrew and remove the shower arm. Wrap the threads of the unit's extender pipe with plumbing tape and screw it into the pipe in the wall. Check that the extender pipe protrudes the correct amount from the wall; if it doesn't, you may need a different sized pipe (a galvanized nipple will work fine).**

2 **MARK AND DRILL HOLES. Tape the unit's template onto the wall and check that it is plumb, or parallel with grout lines. Mark for the position of the screws. Drill holes at these positions. If the wall is tile or solid-surface, drill holes large enough for the plastic anchors (next step). If the wall is thin sheeting, drill holes slightly smaller than the screws you will drive.**

3 **MOUNT THE BRACKETS.** For a tile or solid-surface wall (as shown), tap in plastic anchors and drive screws to fasten the mounting brackets. If the wall is covered with plastic sheeting, just drive the screws to attach the brackets.

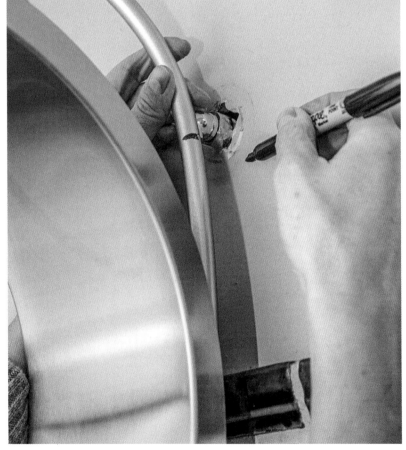

4 **MEASURE AND CUT THE FLEX LINE.** Temporarily screw on the elbow fitting at the extender pipe. Hold the tower in place, or measure with a tape measure to find the desired length of the flexible supply line. Cut the line with a knife, pipe cutter, or heavy-duty scissors.

TIP Because they have several water outlets that operate at the same time, a shower panel requires a minimum water pressure to ensure effective spray. Check the manufacturer's literature for the required pressure.

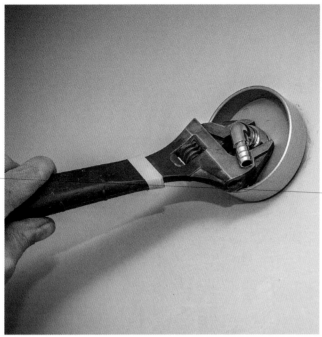

5 **CONNECT AND ADD TRIM.** Apply the trim piece to the wall (this one is self-stick). Firmly screw the elbow fitting to the extender pipe (above left). Connect the panel's flex tubing to the elbow with a clamp (above right). Slip on the showerhead cover to conceal the elbow joint (left).

6 **HOOK UP THE WAND.** Screw the wand's flex line to the holder/elbow fitting at the side of the unit.

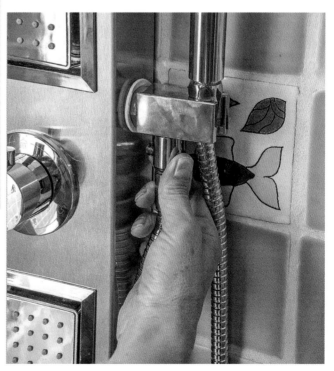

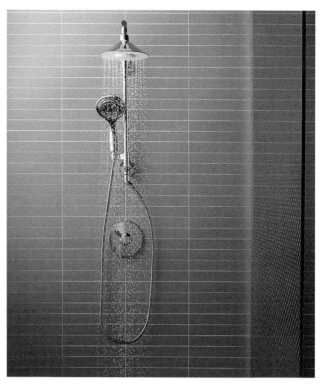

A SIMPLER MODEL. A unit like this blurs the distinction between hand-held showerhead and shower tower. The shower wand can be moved up and down on the pole to act like a body jet, or it can be removed to be hand held. This may be a good option if your water pressure is not sufficient for a genuine shower tower.

7 **HANG THE PANEL.** Raise the shower unit an inch or two above its final location, press it against the wall, and slide it down to secure it onto the mounting brackets. You may choose to apply a bead of silicone caulk to the outer edges of the shower tower to ensure a firm connection.

Installing a Claw-Foot Tub with Curtain Surround

Retro-look claw-foot tubs are mighty popular these days. They look great, as long as all the exposed plumbing (and there is a lot of that) is made of attractive materials—in this case, a gleaming chrome finish. If you are replacing an existing claw-foot tub, measure to see that the plumbing parts—the supply risers and the drain—will match. Otherwise, or if you are installing a claw-foot tub where there was none, you will need to move the plumbing under the floor.

> **TIP** If your tub is cast iron, have a helper or two on hand to move the tub around. When you turn it upside down, set one end on a thick book or block of wood, so you don't trap your fingers. An acrylic tub is much lighter and easier to maneuver.

1 INSTALL THE LEGS AND CHECK FOR LEVEL. Turn the tub upside down and install the legs. Tighten the bolts and turn the tub right side up where it will go. If it wobbles or is seriously out of level, loosen a bolt or two and insert rubber shims to slightly lengthen one or more of the legs.

2 ADD THE WASTE-AND-OVERFLOW. If the waste-and-overflow assembly is not already cut to fit, temporarily attach the two parts to the waste and the overflow holes and mark for cutting the pieces (top). Assemble the parts as you would for a standard tub (see p. 199) and tighten the nuts (above). At this point, the bottom of the assembly should be slightly above the floor; you will add the final part that goes into the floor later.

106 ■ BATHROOM SINK AND TUB UPGRADES

STANLEY

3 ASSEMBLE AND INSTALL THE FAUCET. A typical claw-foot's faucet mounts on the tub's deck and turns 90 degrees; it also has connections for both a shower and a hand-held shower wand, so it is somewhat complicated. Follow the manufacturer's directions carefully to assemble the basic faucet (be vigilant about keeping track of all the little parts). Mount it into the tub's holes.

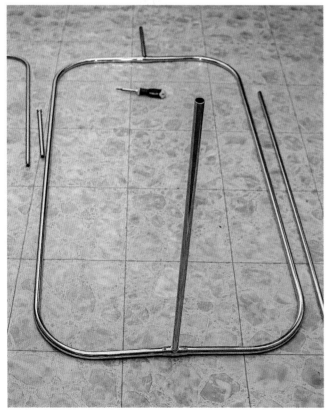

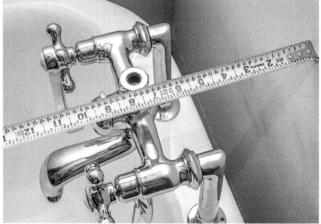

4 PREPARE THE CURTAIN ROD. Assemble the curtain rod, the horizontal rod that attaches to the wall, and the vertical rod that attaches to the ceiling. Measure up from the tub's floor to the ceiling and subtract the desired height of the curtain rod; 80 in. is standard. Cut the vertical rod to that length using a tube cutter (see p. 169). Then measure out from the back wall to the faucet's plumbing hole and subtract the length of the fitting; cut the horizontal rod to that length.

5 **ATTACH THE FITTINGS AND SHOWER ROD.**
Follow the manufacturer's instructions to assemble the fittings needed for the shower wand (above). These usually join with rubber washers, so no plumber's tape is needed. Measure from the top of the fitting to determine the height of the showerhead. Slip the showerhead's rod through the fitting in the curtain rod and tighten a setscrew to hold it in place (right).

Claw-Foot Plumbing

If plumbing does not already exist in the floor, cut an access hole and run a drain and supply lines positioned so the tub's plumbing can be inserted straight down into them. (See the chapters that follow for instructions on running new pipes.) Here, we show supplies of PEX tubing and drop-ear elbows; you can screw the supply tubes directly into the elbows. Install the supply risers and the trap arm so they rise out of the floor, then install the subflooring and the finished floor around the pipes.

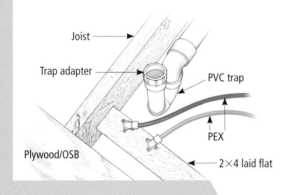

Joist
Trap adapter
PVC trap
PEX
Plywood/OSB
2×4 laid flat

6 **ATTACH THE CURTAIN ROD.** Have a helper check with a level and eyeball the curtain rod to be sure it is parallel with a side wall; then drive screws to attach the vertical rod to the ceiling. Also attach the horizontal rod to the end wall. Unless you are fortunate enough to hit a stud or a joist, you will need to drill pilot holes, move the flange to the side, tap in plastic anchors, and then drive screws into the anchors.

7 ATTACH THE SHOWER ROD AND WAND ASSEMBLY. Mark the bottom of the shower rod (below) and cut it so it can slip into the fitting. Slide the shower wand's holder up onto the rod, slip the rod into the fitting, and tighten the nut. Screw on a showerhead.

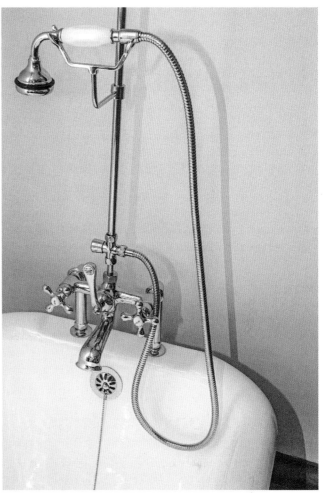

8 FINISHING TOUCHES. Turn on the water supply and test for leaks. Hang two shower curtains. Here we have just cloth curtains, which will work fine, but you may prefer plastic liners as well, perhaps with the cloth curtains hanging outside the tub.

TOILETS

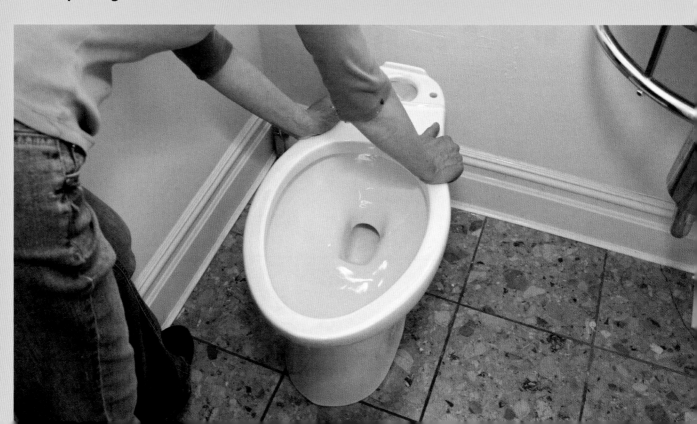

FEW HOUSEHOLD FIXTURES DO MORE TO make our lives comfortable than the humble toilet. Toilets are amazingly reliable and durable, typically providing many thousands of flushes before they need to be repaired or replaced. A toilet's bowl (the lower part that you sit on) and its tank (the upper part that fills with water and empties into the bowl when a flush occurs) are almost always made of vitreous china, which stays shiny and easy to clean virtually forever. But the toilet's innards—including some sort of valve, float, flapper or stopper, and tubes and a chain—do wear out and need to be adjusted, repaired, or replaced.

Manufacturers have been vying for years with each other to produce valves and other products that cost very little, are quick to install, and will last a long time. If you just want to keep your toilet in running condition, don't hesitate to make a repair. However, if you don't like your toilet's looks, or if you'd like one that uses less water or one that flushes with more power or that is more comfortable to sit on, go ahead and replace it. Removing an old toilet and installing a new one is easier than you may expect, and will make you a home-repair hero for less than a half day's labor.

Don't be afraid to touch the water in the tank; it is clean. Water in the bowl may of course contain contaminants, but after a few flushes it will be fairly clean and danger-free as well.

How a Toilet Works

Residential toilets come in a variety of shapes and sizes, but the basic configuration is the same for most of them. A toilet has two parts: The bowl rests on the floor, and the tank sits on top of the bowl. (Some high-end toilets are one-piece, but even there the arrangement is pretty much the same.)

Most of the time the tank is filled with water. When the handle or push button is operated, a flapper or stopper is raised above the flush valve seat at the bottom of the tank, which causes water to rush into the bowl via an opening called a siphon jet, which is precisely sized for maximum force. Water exits the bowl through another siphon jet at the bottom and passes through a trap, then through a pipe called a closet bend, and then to the house's stack. The trap acts like a sink's trap, staying full in order to seal out noxious gases.

When the tank is empty after a flush, a flapper or stopper seals the opening at the flush valve seat at the tank's bottom so water cannot flow into the bowl. The tank's valve has a mechanism that calls for water when the float cup or ball sinks below a certain level. When the tank fills with enough water, the cup or ball rises to turn off the valve and shut off the water.

Older and newer valves

Older toilets may have a float ball attached to a ballcock valve, as well as a stopper attached to a lift wire (see the drawing on the facing page). This arrangement can last for decades, but it has disadvantages: The lift wire can get bent so that it cannot slide smoothly. This leads to the common problem where you need to jiggle the handle in order to get the stopper to slide all the way down and fully stop the water. In addition, older (usually brass) valves have inner

HOW A TOILET WORKS

This is a very common toilet setup, with a float-cup valve and a flapper. Most better-quality toilet bowls feature rim openings so water cleans the sides of the bowl during a flush; some inexpensive models do not have them.

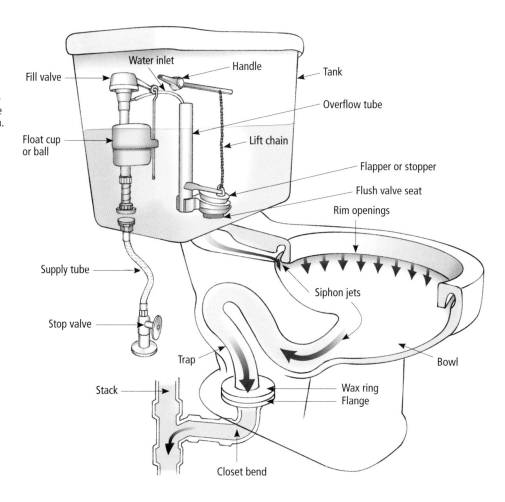

rubber parts that eventually need to be replaced. Newer toilets, or toilets that have been upgraded, often have a float cup that slides up and down the fill tube, or a diaphragm-type valve. These look like cheap plastic, but they actually are more reliable and durable.

Low-flow problems and solutions

In the 1990s, U.S. regulations required all toilets to be "low flow," meaning they would use only 1.6 gal. per flush, as opposed to the 3.5 gal. commonly used by older toilets. Early low-flow toilets had notoriously weak flushes. In response, some people opted for expensive pressure-assist toilets, which forced water into the bowl with a strong whoosh. But designers got to work, and today's low-flow toilets have plenty of power, so pressure-assist toilets are not needed for most of us. Some even use only 1.28 gal. In addition, dual-flush toilets can use only 1 gal. of water when only liquids are being flushed.

TOUCHLESSNESS. A toilet with a no-touch switch activates when it senses your hand above the tank for completely germ-free operation.

OLDER TOILET VALVE

Older toilets often have a float ball attached to a ballcock valve. A very old model also has a stopper with a lift wire, as shown here. Newer toilets, or those that have been partially upgraded, have a flapper with lift chain instead. (The toilet shown on the facing page shows this combination of parts.)

TIP Unless it is cracked, a toilet can almost always be repaired and even upgraded; the following 12 pages show how to do that. If you would prefer to replace your toilet, see pp. 132–137.

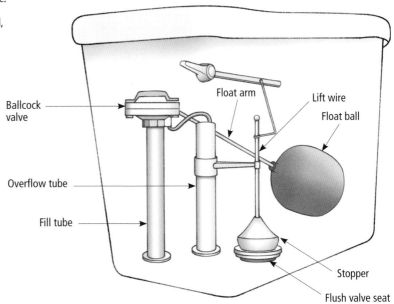

Ballcock valve

Float arm

Lift wire

Float ball

Overflow tube

Fill tube

Stopper

Flush valve seat

Troubleshooting a Toilet

In most cases it will take only a few minutes to diagnose a toilet problem. Most repairs take less than half an hour. Following the instructions in the pages that follow, you may spend most of your time going to the hardware store or home center for the parts you need. Here are the most common ailments and their cures:

- Toilet is clogged and overflows or will not flush with force: Clear the clog with a toilet auger, plunger, or pressure-assisted drain opener (pp. 46–48).

- Water leaks from the bowl onto the floor: Deal with this problem immediately, because it could damage your flooring and even your home's structure. Shut off the water, remove the toilet, and replace the wax ring (pp. 133–134).

- "Phantom flushes": If your toilet makes soft flushes on its own from time to time, water is leaking out of the tank and into the bowl. To verify that this is happening, pour a few drops of food coloring into the tank, wait a half hour or so, and see if the color has seeped into the bowl's water. To repair, clean the valve seat and adjust or replace the stopper or flapper, so water cannot leak out of the tank (pp. 122–124).

- Water constantly runs (often with a hissing sound): Most likely, the tank water is all the way up to the top of the overflow tube and running into it. Adjust the float cup, valve, or tank ball to bring the water level down at least ½ in. below the top of the overflow tube (p. 117). If that doesn't solve the problem, install a new float cup assembly or other type of valve (pp. 119–121).

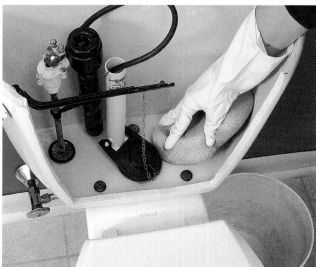

SHUT OFF WATER AND FLUSH. Turn off the water at the stop valve that supplies the toilet. If there is no stop valve, shut off a partial-house valve or even the house's main valve. (It is recommended that you install a stop valve at this time; see p. 20.) Then flush the toilet, which will mostly drain the tank. If you want the tank completely free of water, soak it up with a large sponge.

| **TIP** | If you will empty the bowl as well as the tank, flush the toilet, wait for it to refill, and flush again. This will ensure that the water in the bowl is at least fairly clean. |

- You sometimes need to jiggle the handle to stop the sound of running water: This happens if you have an old ballcock valve with a lift wire and stopper. You can try to bend the wire to get it to slide more smoothly, but a better solution is to replace it with a flapper and lift chain—and perhaps a new float cup valve while you're at it (pp. 119–121).

- A leak that comes from the tank: If the leak is at the water inlet, tighten the water-supply nut or replace the supply tube. If the leak is elsewhere, tighten the tank bolts (there may be two or three). On an old toilet, you may need to replace the rubber washers. If the tank is cracked, replace it (if you can find an exact replacement) or replace the entire toilet (pp. 132–137).

- Weak flushes: If the water level in the tank is lower than ½ in. below the top of the overflow tube, adjust the float cup or ball or the valve to bring the level up (pp. 117, 124). If the flapper or stopper sinks down onto the flush valve seat too soon, replace it. If the toilet has always produced inadequate flushes, it may be an early-model low-flush toilet; replace it with a newer model.

- Turning the handle does not produce a flush: See that the handle is connected to the flapper or stopper; if not, reattach. If there is no water in the tank, make sure the stop valve is turned on and squirting water; you may need to replace the stop valve or the supply tube.

Draining a tank and bowl

Though many of the repairs on the following pages can be done with water in the tank and the bowl, some require dry conditions, and you may feel more comfortable with at least the tank empty.

EMPTY THE BOWL. If you want to empty the bowl, first bail with a small plastic container. Then soak up as much of the water inside the trapway as you can, using a balled-up towel or large sponge.

Handles

Handles can come loose and simply require tightening. Or you may choose to replace yours. The handle is the only visible piece of metal on a toilet, and replacing one can provide a quick and inexpensive visual upgrade.

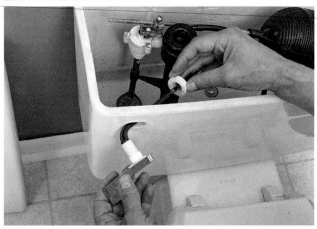

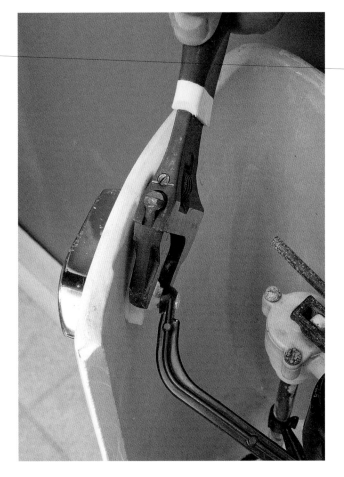

INSTALL A NEW HANDLE. You can buy handles to mount on the front or the side of a tank. Disconnect the lift chain (there is usually a clip) from the handle's arm (top), and remove the mounting nut (by turning it clockwise). Make sure the new handle has an arm facing the same direction as the old one. Slip the new handle's arm through the hole, slip on the nut (above), and tighten. Reattach the lift chain to the handle's arm.

TIGHTEN A HANDLE NUT. If a handle is wobbly, remove the lid and tighten the nut, which is typically a reverse thread—meaning you turn it counter-clockwise to tighten it. Tighten by hand, then use a wrench.

Replacing a Float Ball

If a float ball is cracked, water will seep in and it will no longer float well. You can buy a replacement ball: Just unscrew the old one and screw on the new one.

Adjusting water level

In most cases, your toilet will run best if the tank water fills up to about ½ in. or 1 in. below the top of the overflow tube. Adjusting the level is usually a simple matter.

OVERFLOWING WATER. If water fills to a level above the top of the overflow tube, it will continually run. If the level is too low, your flushes may not be powerful enough. Here, the water level is too high.

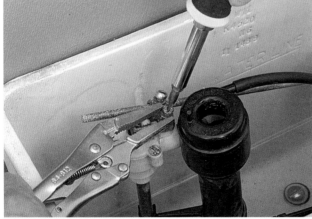

ADJUST A TANK BALL. If you have a tank ball, you can adjust it downward (to lower the water level) or upward (to raise the level) by simply bending a metal float arm (top). You can also adjust the angle of the arm by screwing or unscrewing the adjustment screw at the valve (above). (If the arm is plastic, this is the only way to make the adjustment.)

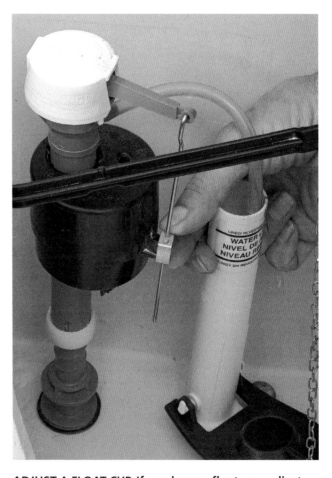

ADJUST A FLOAT CUP. If you have a float cup, adjust the cup's height, usually by squeezing a clip and sliding it up or down. (Here we show working dry, but don't be afraid to do this with water in the tank, because it is clean.)

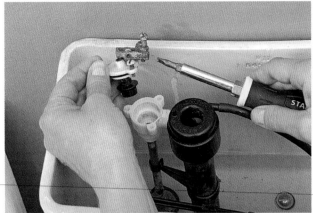

Repairing a Valve

Usually, if a valve leaks or gets clogged and sluggish, the best solution is to replace it, because valves are inexpensive. However, it may be worth your while to repair a valve like the one shown here, because it will save you the trouble of draining the tank. You may or may not need to replace the rubber parts. Your valve may not look like this one, but the steps are pretty much the same.

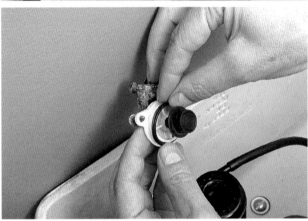

REMOVE AND INSPECT. Shut off water at the stop valve and flush the toilet. Remove the hold-down screws and pull out the valve's top. Check the rubber parts; if any are damaged, replace them or replace the valve.

CLEAN AND LUBRICATE. Use a lint-free, damp cloth to clean out any debris and mineral buildup. Apply some plumber's grease to the parts, and reassemble the valve.

Clearing Rim Openings

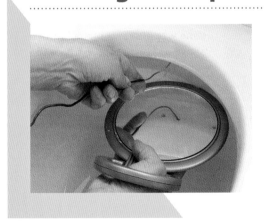

If you notice that water runs unevenly through rim openings around the top of the bowl, use a mirror to locate the clogged openings. Poke a wire up into the openings to clear them.

Installing a Fill Valve

Replacing a fill valve is one of the most common toilet repairs, because it takes less than an hour, costs less than $10, and can make your toilet run like new. Here we show one of the most common types of valves, called a float cup, but other types can be installed in much the same way.

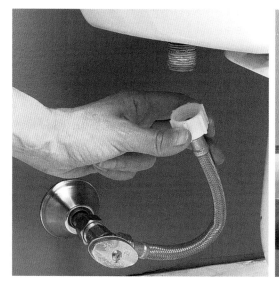

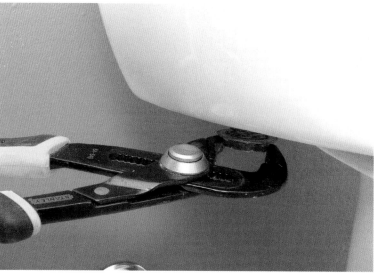

1 **SHUT OFF THE WATER AND REMOVE THE NUT. Shut off the water at the stop valve and flush the toilet to remove most of the water from the tank. Sponge away the rest of the water. Unscrew the supply tube (above left). Use a wrench or slip-joint pliers to remove the nut that holds the old fill tube in place; it is located under the tank (above right).**

Other Fill Valves

These fill valves install in much the same way as shown in the instructions above and on the following pages, with the "critical level" mark 1 in. below the top of the overflow tube. The white-topped vertical column valve (far left) has a float inside its body. It can be easily adjusted for height after installation. The yellow-and-black unit (left) operates much the same way as the one shown in the instructions.

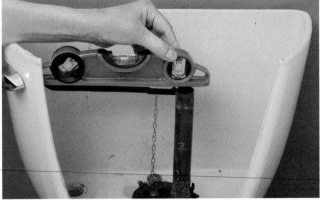

2 **REMOVE THE OLD VALVE.** Disconnect the water inlet (a thin rubber tube) from the overflow tube; it is usually attached via a clip that you just pull off. Lift the old fill valve assembly up and out. (Yours may look different from this, and may have only one tube rather than a tube plus a water inlet, but it probably removes in the same way.)

3 **CHECK THE OVERFLOW HEIGHT.** Use a small level to see that the top of the overflow tube is about 1 in. below the handle's hole.

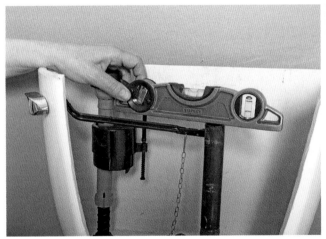

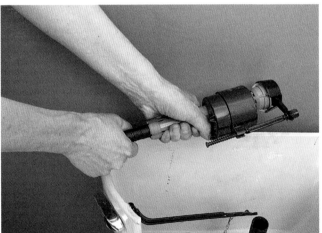

4 **ADJUST THE HEIGHT OF THE FLOAT.** Set the new fill valve in the hole, but do not attach it yet. Use a level to check that the critical level mark (usually "CL") on the float is 1 in. below the top of the overflow tube. This will ensure that water rises to ½ in. below the top of the overflow tube. If the float needs to be adjusted, twist the valve's shank to move it up or down (above right).

STANLEY

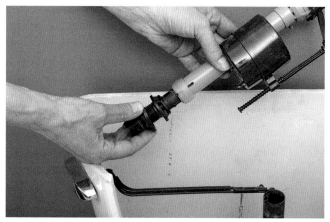

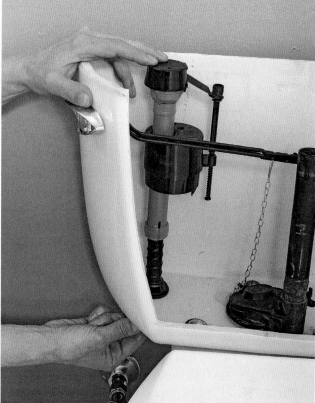

5 **MOUNT THE VALVE.** Once the cup height is secure, slip a rubber washer, positioned as shown (above), onto the valve's threads. Slip the valve into the hole in the tank and tighten the mounting nut under the tank (right).

6 **HOOK UP THE WATER SUPPLY.** Clip the water inlet so it will shoot into the overflow tube. Attach the supply tube under the tank: Hand-tightening may be tight enough, but you can give it another quarter turn with pliers to be sure. Turn on the water, and test to make sure the water rises to the right level and that the unit flushes smoothly.

Leak at the Bottom

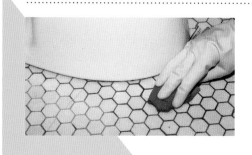

If water appears on the floor, flush the toilet and watch closely to see if water is coming from the tank, the seal between the tank and the bowl, or from the bottom of the bowl. If water is coming from the bottom of the bowl, remove the toilet and install a new wax ring, as shown on pp. 132–137.

Sealing at the Flapper and Valve Seat

If the seal where the flapper (or stopper) meets the flush valve seat at the bottom of the tank is not nice and tight, water will seep from the tank into the bowl, causing phantom flushes and a hissing or gurgling sound. You may need to replace the flapper, clean the valve seat, or replace the valve seat by replacing the whole overflow unit or installing a flush valve repair kit.

CLEAN THE SEAT. If the seat gets corroded or gunked up, even a good flapper will not seal. Clean it with a slightly abrasive pad, and feel for any ridges or holes. If you find any, replace the overflow unit, or install a flush valve repair kit.

INSTALL A NEW FLAPPER. If your flapper is cracked or deformed so it won't seal, replace it. There are many shapes and types, so take the old one to the store and get an exact replacement. Some snap onto two little posts at the side of the overflow tube, whereas others slide onto the tube itself. If you can't find an exact replacement, try a "universal" flapper like the ones shown above right, which are made to seal at various angles. You may need to try several before you find one that seals tightly. The one shown being installed at right has a yellow float that helps keep the chain from getting tangled.

Installing a New Overflow Tube

If replacing a flapper does not solve the problem of leaking water, consider installing a whole new overflow tube. You can buy a unit that includes the tube, flush valve seat, and flapper for a modest price. However, you must remove the tank, as shown on p. 125.

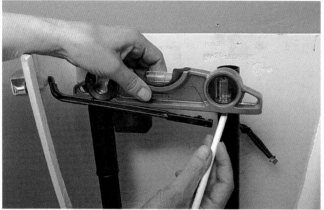

1 **MEASURE AND CUT THE TUBE. Shut off the water and drain and remove the tank. Remove the old overflow tube by removing the spud nut and spud washer (see p. 125, Step 2) and pulling the tube out. Attach the new overflow tube with the spud nut and washer, and set the tank on top of the bowl. Measure for cutting the tube, so its top will be about 1 in. below the critical level of the fill valve (top). Remove the tube and cut with a miter box or hacksaw.**

2 **REINSTALL THE TUBE. Remove the tank and reinstall the overflow tube with the spud nut and washer. Install the tank and tighten the tank bolts. Clip the water inlet to the top of the overflow tube and attach the chain to the flapper so it can rest completely on the seat, but with as little slack as possible to avoid tangling.**

Install a flush valve repair kit

If you can't get a flapper to seal tightly against the seat, installing a flush valve repair kit may be the easiest solution, because you don't have to remove the tank. The kit has a new seat that seals against the old seat with a thick sticky washer, and a flapper that seals against the seat.

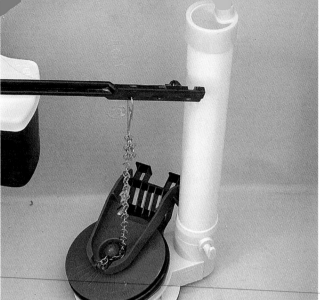

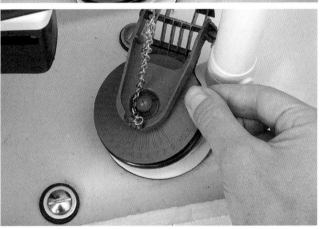

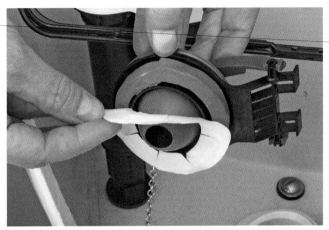

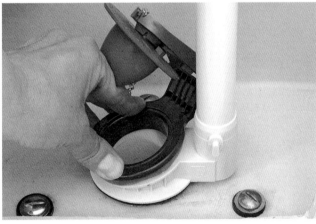

1 **PRESS IN PLACE.** Scrape away any debris or raised ridges from the toilet's seat. Remove the paper backing from the kit (top), and press the kit onto the old seat (above).

2 **ATTACH AND ADJUST.** Attach the chain to the handle's arm (top). The flapper shown above can be adjusted to use more or less water.

Sealing a Leak from the Tank

If water leaks at the bottom of the tank at the two or three tank bolts, you may only need to tighten the tank bolts. If the rubber washers look damaged, replace them. If the tank is cracked, replace it or the whole toilet.

Replacing a Seal between Tank and Bowl

If there is a leak where the tank meets the bowl, the rubber spud washer may need replacing. Buy a washer that is an exact replacement, made by the same manufacturer.

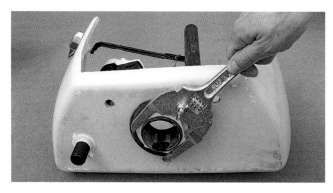

2 **REMOVE THE SPUD NUT.** Using a spud wrench, unscrew and remove the large spud nut.

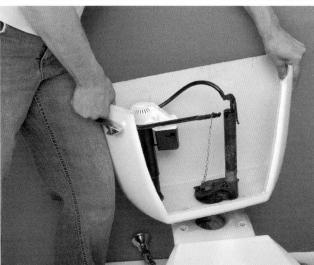

1 **REMOVE THE TANK.** Shut off the water at the stop valve, flush the toilet, and sponge out any remaining water. Remove the supply tube at the bottom of the tank. Unscrew the (two or three) tank bolts (top). Lift the tank up and out.

3 **REPLACE THE WASHER.** Pull the old spud washer out and clean away any debris. Push on a new washer, which may look like any of the three shown here. Replace the nut, set the tank in place, and replace the tank washers.

Dual-Flush Valve

A dual-flush toilet saves water by offering two flush levels: a small flush of about 1 gal. for liquid only and a more forceful flush of 1.2 gal. to 1.6 gal. for solids. You can replace your existing toilet with one that has a dual-flush feature, or you can save money and effort by retrofitting your current toilet with a dual-flush valve. These valves are now widely available at hardware stores and home centers.

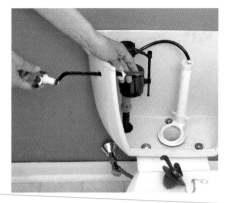

TIP The unit shown here is installed at the overflow tube only. Some kits also include a replacement for your fill valve.

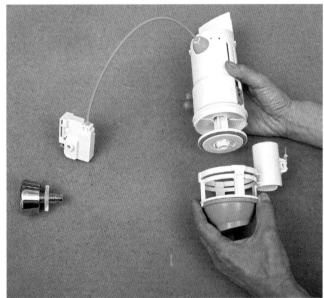

1 **REMOVE THE HANDLE AND FLAPPER. Shut off** the water, flush, and sponge out the remaining water from the tank. Remove the existing handle and flapper.

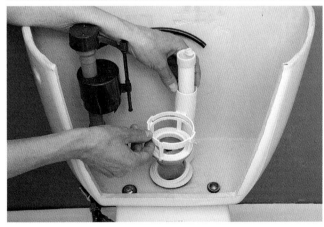

2 **DISASSEMBLE AND BEGIN INSTALLATION.** Disassemble the new valve and slide its lower part down over the overflow tube; it has a rubber flange that fits into the flush valve seat at the bottom of the overflow tube.

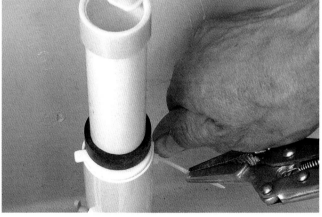

3 **TIGHTEN THE VALVE.** To hold the lower part of the valve in place, slip a plastic cam lock down onto it (top). Then slide down a rubber washer and tighten the zip tie (above).

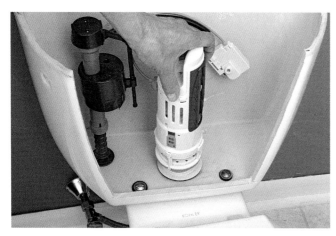

4 **ATTACH THE REST OF THE VALVE.** Reassemble the new valve: Place its main body on top, press down, and rotate until it clicks into place.

5 **INSTALL THE NEW BUTTON.** Attach the new handle (or in our case, control button) into the handle's hole, and tighten a plastic nut (counterclockwise) to secure it. Thread the control wire around so it doesn't interfere with the fill valve's water inlet, and slip the control unit onto the handle, pressing until it clicks into place.

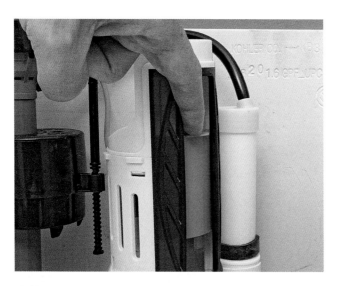

6 **ADJUST FLUSH FORCES.** Clip the water inlet into the top of the fill valve. Test the flushes. If you want flushes to be stronger, or to use less water, you can make the adjustments for both types of flushes by simple moving an adjustment bar up or down.

TWO BUTTONS. The new control has two buttons, one for a weak flush and one for a more powerful flush.

TIP If the existing flush valve seat is not compatible with the dual-flush valve, you will need to replace it with one that is compatible; see p. 122.

Choosing a Toilet

Some toilet choices are easy: white versus color, elongated bowl versus the traditional round shape, standard height versus the higher ADA (Americans with Disability Act) height. But then it gets a little more complicated. How do you find a toilet that flushes well, that's easy to clean, and that uses as little water as necessary?

NEAT LOOK. A one-piece skirted toilet costs more but has clean lines that cover the stop valve and supply tube. It is not much more difficult to install than a standard toilet.

CLASSY PLUMBING. A brass stop valve, solid supply tubes, and flange will cost more but can really class up a bathroom. A dual-flush mechanism on top conserves water.

CONSIDER COLOR. Most people choose gleaming white toilets, which are cheaper, but a colored toilet can add interest to the room. This toilet has a concealed trap-way, making it easier to clean.

CORNER TOILET. A corner toilet can solve bathroom layout problems and takes up minimal space.

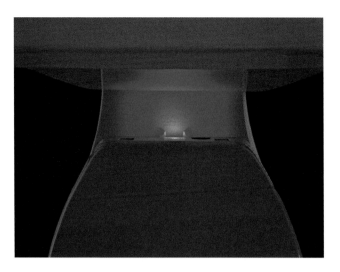

NIGHT LIGHT. A toilet with a night light barely disturbs your slumber while guiding you to the right spot.

TIP Standard toilets are 14 in. to 15 in. tall; ADA toilets measure 16 in. to 19 in., to make it easier for elderly or disabled people to sit down and stand up. For persons who are shorter in height, the tallest models may feel too tall; you may want to test ahead of time.

SLEEK TOILET. A toilet with a narrow tank snugs up close to the wall to provide a few extra inches of space in front.

Making sure it will fit

Before you head to the store, take some measurements to find the toilet's rough-in dimension: the distance from the wall behind the toilet to the center of the toilet's floor drain pipe. Your existing toilet's bolt caps align with the center of the drain pipe, so just measure from the wall surface (not from the base molding) to the center point of one of the bolts. The standard size is 12 in., but in an older home you may encounter a 10-in. or 14-in. rough-in, which will limit your selection.

Also consider space around the toilet. If you're adding a new powder room or bathroom with a toilet, experts recommend that you allow 15 in. to a wall or other fixture on each side of the toilet—and preferably 18 in. for improved comfort. In front of the toilet, allow a minimum of 24 in. to the nearest obstruction. See p. 242 for recommended clearances.

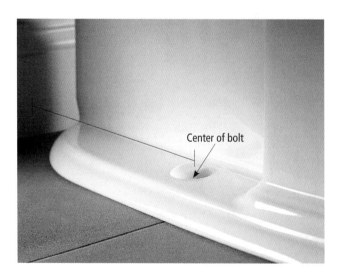

Center of bolt

MEASURE FOR TOILET SIZE. To find the size of your existing toilet, measure from the wall to the center of one of the bolts.

Flush performance

Toilet technology has come a long way in recent decades, producing great flushing power with little water. But how do you find a toilet with a proven track record? Check the toilet's MaP score, which stands for Maximum Performance Testing Program. The MaP score is a respected, standardized measurement of grams of solids removed with a single flush; scores range from 250 to 1,000. Highly rated models are not necessarily the most expensive, and water-conserving models are often among the top rated. To find a database with MaP scores for hundreds of brands of toilets, do an Internet search for "toilet MaP scores."

DUAL-FLUSH BUTTONS. A dual-flush lever on top of a toilet usually looks like this, with two buttons within a circle. The smaller one on the right uses less water.

NO-TOUCH SWITCH. Some toilets offer a motion-sensor flush mechanism, which reduces bacteria.

If Space Is Tight

Most people find an elongated bowl, commonly called "EB" on product boxes, more comfortable; the bowl length is about 2 in. longer than the standard-size round bowl, extending up to 31 in. out from the wall versus 28 in. for a round bowl. Round bowls are usually cheaper. If you're willing to spend more, some manufacturers offer a compact elongated bowl like the one shown, which provides longer bowl length with reduced tank depth to make the overall distance from the wall the same as a standard bowl; this is often accomplished by fusing the tank and bowl into one piece—a design aptly called a one-piece toilet.

Gravity-fed versus pressure-assist

Most homes have gravity-fed toilets: the traditional design with a snaking waterway at the back that siphons waste and water out of the bowl. Newer models have a re-engineered waterway for better performance. The highest-rated products have both better flushing performance and a quieter flush with less water turbulence.

Commercial toilets tend to be pressure assisted; they have a loud and very vigorous flush that may even spray water around a bit. If you're replacing a toilet with a weak flush, this may be tempting, but many people find them too much of a good thing, and in a home with older pipes the pressure can be a strain on the plumbing.

Trapway size

Most gravity-fed toilets have a 2-in.-wide trapway, which works well for light- to average-use toilets. But if your toilet will be in the heavy-use category, you might want a trapway that is 2⅜ in. wide, a small upgrade that can handle 70 percent more mass.

Water conservation

According to the EPA, toilets are by far the heaviest source of water use in the home, accounting for 30 percent of overall consumption. Look for a toilet with a WaterSense label, meaning it has passed EPA standards for high efficiency and uses no more than 1.6 GPF or gal. per flush. As of 2014, toilets sold in California can't use more than 1.28 gal. per flush. There are some toilets on the market today that operate on 1.1 gal. Dual-flush toilets have two flush options, one for liquid waste, which uses less water, and one for solids.

Cleaning considerations

To make cleaning easier, look for a toilet with waterways that are fully glazed. The gold standard here is double-glazing with anti-microbial elements in the glaze; waste flows smoothly away, leaving behind less stain and odor.

"Top-flushing toilets" are often advertised as better at keeping the toilet bowl clean. They may have a wider opening, as wide as 4 in., where water from the tank enters the bowl, and the bowl is cleaned both as water enters the bowl and in the traditional way, when water swirls on its way out.

A sleeker exterior design is also easier to clean. Most toilets have a visible trapway behind the bowl that snakes a bit to maximize the flush suction. Concealed toilets cover this over with a smooth surface that hides the waviness. Skirted toilets have a clean line from front to back, making them easiest to clean because the exterior surface has few crevices. Skirted toilets are often one piece, meaning tank and bowl are fused together.

"Dual Force" Flushing

Some manufacturers offer upscale toilets with flush valves that provide extra power without pressure assistance. Like the Kohler® "Dual Force" toilet shown here, they use precision engineering to create an extra-strong siphon when flushed. They also send the water into the bowl in a swirling motion rather than straight down, in order to wash the bowl more efficiently. In addition to greater power, these toilets typically use less than a gallon per flush. A toilet like this could cost three times as much as a standard toilet but may save enough water to be worth it in the long run.

Replacing a Toilet

Buy a toilet that is the same rough-in size (the distance from the wall to the bowl's bolts) as the old one—usually 12 in. Unless you buy a one-piece toilet, the new one will probably come in two boxes and you'll need to assemble the pieces—a job that takes only a short time.

The following pages show a very common installation approach, but you have other options:

- If lifting an entire toilet is daunting, you can remove the old toilet's tank first.
- The same is true of the new toilet: We show installing the bowl only, then adding the tank. But

some plumbers prefer to install the tank onto the bowl, and then install the whole toilet.

- A wax ring makes a time-tested seal at the floor, and it's really inexpensive. However, many old-school plumbers prefer to make the seal with massive amounts of plumber's putty. Newer rubber seals are also available.

> **TIP** Replacing a toilet is a job that can get wet and messy, so have some thick rags or towels on hand.

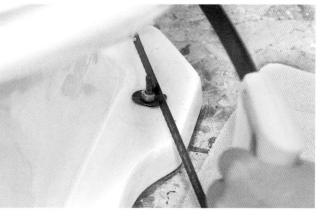

1 **DISCONNECT THE WATER.** Shut off the water to the old toilet at the stop valve. (If there is no stop valve, see pp. 6–8 for other shutoff options.) Flush the toilet and remove as much water as possible from the tank and the bowl. Disconnect the supply tube. Here we show disconnecting at the stop valve, but it may be easier for you to disconnect at the bottom of the tank.

2 **REMOVE THE NUTS.** Pry off the two decorative caps and unscrew the nuts on the flange bolts. If the nuts are rusted so this is difficult (which is often the case), squirt with penetrating oil, wait, and try again. If that doesn't work, cut down through the nut alongside the bolt (above); then the nut will come off very easily.

3 **REMOVE THE OLD TOILET.** If there is caulk around the base of the bowl, cut through it with a utility knife or a putty knife. Pick the toilet straight up and over the top of the bolts. At this point you can carry it while waddling with one foot on each side of the bowl. Or set the toilet on a rug or towel and slide it on the floor.

4 **SCRAPE AND REMOVE THE BOLTS.** Use a scraper or putty knife to remove the old wax ring or other type of sealant. The flange does not need to be clean, but make sure that the new wax ring can make a solid seal. Remove the old flange bolts by sliding them and then pulling out. If they are stuck, you may need to wedge a putty knife under the flange (above).

5 **ADD THE FLANGE BOLTS.** Most toilets include new flange bolts. Slip their heads into the wide portion of the hole, then slide them into position. Measure to see that they are each the same distance from the wall.

TIP If you need to leave the toilet flange open for any length of time, cover it with a wadded-up rag or towel to keep out noxious sewer gases.

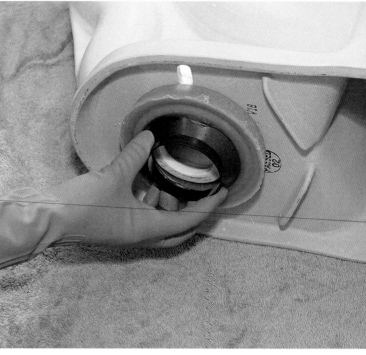

6 **POSITION THE WAX RING.** Press the wax ring in place. Some plumbers prefer to place it on the flange, and others like to put it on the bottom of the toilet.

If the Floor Is Raised

A toilet flange usually rests on top of the floor or is installed with its top level with the floor. New bathroom flooring can raise the floor level so the flange is too low to make a tight seal. Plumbers argue with each other over the best way to solve this problem, but the solution is usually not difficult.

Measure the distance from the top of the flange to the floor level (below left). If it is only ½ in. or so,

install an extra-thick wax ring. Or install a flanged wax ring on the bottom, as shown below middle, and add a ring with no flange on top of it. If the distance is greater than ½ in., purchase a flange extender, which can be simply bolted onto the existing flange. You can also buy a rubber extender like the one shown below right, which also takes the place of a wax ring. It can be adjusted to suit several heights.

MEASURE FLOOR HEIGHT

DOUBLED WAX RING

RUBBER EXTENDER

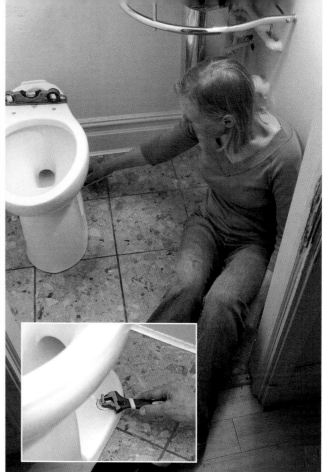

7 **POSITION THE BOWL.** Carefully lower the toilet bowl into place, taking care that the bolts slip through the mounting holes. If you get this wrong, so that one or both of the bolts falls over, lift the bowl out and try again. Press the bowl down most of the way; you will bring it all the way down when you tighten the bolts (next step).

8 **TIGHTEN THE FLANGE BOLTS.** Gently adjust the bowl's position so it looks parallel to the wall or to grout lines in the floor. Place a small level on top of the bowl, and start tightening the nuts, alternating between them until the bowl is snug and fairly level. Do not over-tighten; stop when the bowl feels firmly in place.

9 **PREP THE TANK.** On the bottom of the tank, install the supply tube and the spud washer (see p. 125). Tighten the mounting nuts.

TIP A common installation problem occurs when the flange bolts move or fall over while you lower the new toilet into place. Use the provided plastic washers to ensure that the flange bolts will stay standing upright during installation.

11 TURN ON THE WATER AND TEST. Connect the supply tube to the stop valve. Turn on the water and test: Allow the water to fill the tank, then flush and watch carefully for any leaks. You may need to further tighten the bolts holding the tank to the bowl. If there is a leak on the floor coming from the bottom of the bowl, shut off the water, remove the toilet, and take steps to make a full, tight wax-ring seal.

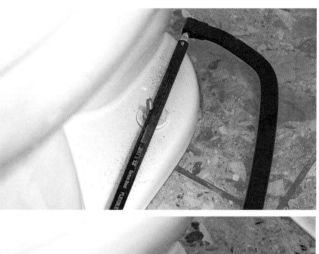

10 INSTALL THE TANK. Slip the tank into place, threading the mounting bolts through the holes in the bowl. Tighten the nuts under the bowl by hand, then use a wrench, tightening them alternately and checking that the tank ends up level.

12 ADD THE BOLT CAPS. Use a hacksaw to cut the flange bolts about ½ in. above the nuts. Slip on the plastic washers, then snap on the decorative caps.

13 **ADD THE SEAT.** A toilet seat installs quickly. Place the seat in position, insert the plastic bolts, partially tighten the plastic nuts from below, and use a screwdriver to finish tightening.

Shim an Uneven Floor

If the floor is uneven or significantly out of level, use plastic toilet shims to make your bowl firm and straight. Insert the shims as far as they need to go, then cut with a utility knife.

14 **FINISH.** In some areas, codes require that you apply a bead of caulk around the bowl at the floor. However, plumbers recommend that you do not make this caulk a complete seal, because if a leak does occur, the caulk would trap the water, causing damage to your flooring unbeknownst to you. Leave a gap or two, so any leaks can seep out onto the floor.

KITCHEN UPGRADES

THE KITCHEN IMPROVEMENTS SHOWN IN THIS chapter can be achieved in less than half a day and do not require running new supply or drain pipes. Some of these projects involve replacing existing fixtures, such as a garbage disposal, sink, or dishwasher. Others are additions that are simply accomplished, such as adding a filter, icemaker, or hot-water dispenser.

The process gets a good deal more difficult when you need to move a sink or dishwasher to a different location or add a major fixture where there was none. In that case, you will need to consult the chapters that follow for help with installing new supply and drain pipes.

In most locales, the projects in this chapter do not need to be approved by a building department, because no new pipes (only traps, and perhaps flexible supply tubes) are involved.

Installing a Garbage Disposal

If you already have a garbage disposal, replacing it should take less than an hour, as long as the new one is the same size and has its outlet in the same position. (If you upgrade to a larger disposal you will probably need to cut a trap pipe or two to make it fit.) If you will put in a new disposal where there was none before, see pp. 150–151 for instructions on assembling a new trap along with the disposal.

You will also need an electrical receptacle that is controlled by a wall switch, which you will plug the disposal into. If you don't have one, hire an electrician to install one, or consult a book such as *Wiring Complete* (The Taunton Press, 2013).

A ⅓-horsepower disposal does well for light duty; a ½-horsepower unit suits most household needs. If you often want to grind things like lemon rinds, it's a good idea to install one that pulls ¾ or even 1 horsepower.

KNOCK OUT THE DRAIN HOLE FOR THE DISHWASHER. If you plan to run the dishwasher drain line through the disposal (which may or may not be up to code in your area), open the drain hole by tapping the knock-out slug with a hammer and screwdriver. Be sure to remove the slug from the inside of the disposal.

ATTACH THE ELBOW. Some trap setups call for an elbow coming out of the disposal. (For a setup that does not use this elbow, see p. 150.) The elbow is usually provided along with the disposal. To install one, slip a rubber washer into the opening, set the elbow in place, and slide the mounting washer into place. Drive two bolts to attach the mounting washer, as shown.

TIP   If you are replacing a disposal with one of the same size, you can probably reuse the mounting bracket (the part that fits in the sink's hole), which will spare you the most difficult part of the job.

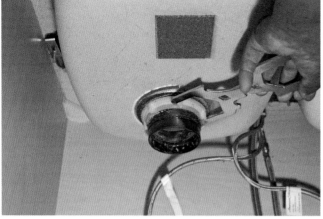

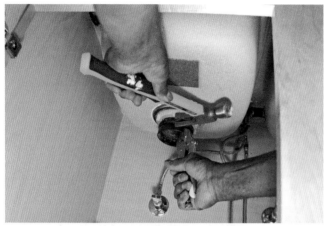

2 **DISASSEMBLE THE MOUNTING RING.** To disassemble the mounting bracket, loosen the three screws (top) and use a small slot screwdriver or two to pry off the ring (above).

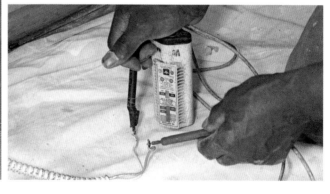

1 **REMOVE THE OLD BASKET STRAINER.** To remove the old basket-strainer mounting bracket, work from below and use a spud wrench to unscrew the mounting nut (top). Or tap with the claws of a hammer or with a hammer and screwdriver (above middle). Once the nut is off, pull the strainer out from above (above).

3 **PROVIDE POWER.** There should be a switched source of power. Test that it turns on with a switch. Before proceeding with the next steps, shut off power and test to verify that power is off.

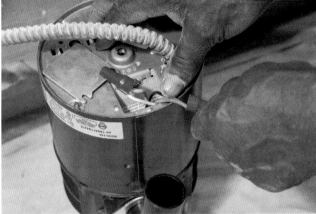

TIP The cable shown here is metallic sheathed, but yours may be plastic sheathed. The type of cable clamp shown here works for both types of cable.

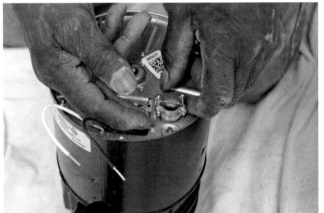

4 **INSTALL THE CLAMP CONNECTOR.** Loosen the screw that holds the electrical access cover and remove the cover. Pull the black and white wires out (top). Remove the nut from a clamp connector (inset). Insert the connector's threads into the hole in the disposal, and thread the nut back on from inside the disposal. It's usually easiest to hold the nut still while you turn the connector (above). Tighten the connector with pliers, but leave the clamping screws loose.

5 **MAKE THE ELECTRICAL CONNECTIONS.** Strip ¾ in. to 1 in. of insulation from all the wires. Poke the cable into the disposal's hole and pull its wires through the access opening. Tighten a ⅜-in. cable clamp to hold the cable securely (top). Use wire nuts to make firm electrical connections: black wire to black wire (or colored wire, in this case orange) and white wire to white wire. There should be no visible bare wire; wrap the connections with electrician's tape to be sure. If there is a third wire, green or bare, connect it to the green grounding screw. Push the wires back into the disposal, and replace the cover (above).

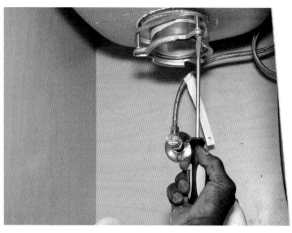

8 **TIGHTEN THE THREE SCREWS.** Tighten the three screws, alternating so they all end up about the same length. That will ensure that the disposal hangs straight down. Have your helper check that the flange is centered on the sink's hole. If not, loosen the screws, center it, and retighten.

TIP Unscrew the three mounting screws nearly all the way; that will make it easier to mount the bracket.

6 **PRESS THE FLANGE WITH PUTTY.** Roll out a rope of plumber's putty with your hands, place it on the underside of the bracket's flange, and press it all around to seal tight. Press the flange into the sink's hole. Have a helper hold the flange in place as you perform the next step.

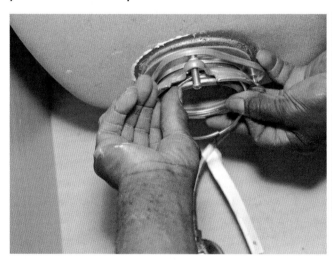

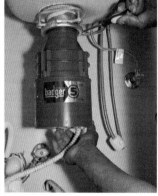

7 **ASSEMBLE THE BRACKET.** Working from below, slip on the cardboard washer, then the triangular washer, then the bracket with the screws. Now comes the first tricky part: Hold the ring in position, then use a screwdriver or two to slip the ring onto the groove in the bracket's body. This may take several attempts, but be patient and you'll get it.

9 **MOUNT THE DISPOSAL.** And now, the second tricky part: Holding the disposal straight vertically, push it up onto the mounting bracket. When you feel it slide up a bit, turn the locking ring by hand to get it started. Then use a screwdriver to finish turning the locking nut. If you don't succeed the first time, get yourself into a comfortable position and try again, taking care to keep the disposal plumb. Assemble the trap (see pp. 150–151) and perhaps the dishwasher hose, and test.

Choosing a Kitchen Sink

In the last couple of decades kitchen sink options have exploded, with various sizes, shapes, and bowl configurations. Here we'll talk about the main considerations.

Materials

Though some high-end sinks are made of exotic materials like natural stone, copper, brass, or even soapstone, for most of us there are four basic materials to choose among.

- Enameled (or porcelain) cast-iron sinks are solid and heavy, easy to clean, and very resistant to chipping. They are available in a range of colors and will last for decades unless abused by a very heavy object, which can produce a chip that will show the dark metal color underneath. They are quiet when water is running. However, they can be pricey, and many models can be installed only as self-rimming (see p. 145).

- Fireclay sinks are made of clay that has been heated to a very high temperature, 2,200°F, with the result that the sink is very hard and durable and has a nice shine. It resists most scratches and chips and is very easy to clean. This is a popular material for farmhouse or apron sinks.

- Stainless-steel sinks come in a wide range of prices, largely dependent on the thickness and quality of the metal. A good-quality sink will have a thickness of 16 or 18 gauge (the lower the number, the thicker the metal); a sink labeled in the "304" series has a good amount of chromium, for strength and durability. Be sure your sink also has a sprayed-on sound-deadening coating on the bottom; if it only has a couple of little foam pads, it may get noisy.

- Granite composite sinks are made of about 80 percent granite particles and 20 percent acrylic resin (polymers). These sinks have good resistance to scratching and chipping. Available in an array of matte colors, darker shades, especially black or slate, are most popular. In durability tests they beat quartz composite for strength and scratch resistance. These sinks are lightweight and easy to install. They are somewhat porous, so they may stain, but this is not a problem with darker colors.

ENAMELED CAST IRON. This retro-style enameled cast-iron sink has easy-to-clean curves and a low divider that makes it easier to wash items like cookie sheets. With heavy cast-iron sinks, the quality shines through, making the sink a satisfying focal point in any heavy-use kitchen.

FIRECLAY. Because they are made from clay, fireclay sinks come in a nice variety of colors. Some people claim they are less likely to chip than enameled cast-iron sinks, and even if they do, the color underneath is the same.

| TIP | Acrylic kitchen sinks are much more resistant to staining and scratching than they used to be, but they still are more easily damaged than the other options listed here. They also cannot handle high heat. The high-gloss finish is attractive, and they are an affordable choice for light use, but are probably not a good choice for a heavy-use kitchen. |

STAINLESS STEEL. Many people prefer stainless sinks, which are nearly indestructible. Even if they scratch, the blemish can be buffed out. The only downside is that hard water can leave spots, making cleanup more of a headache.

GRANITE. Granite composite sinks are popular in areas with hard water because they do not show water spots. The matte finish and darker color options are easy to keep clean and add spice to the overall design of the kitchen.

Self-rimming, undermounted, and apron

A self-rimming sink has a lip (or rim) that rests on top of the countertop. This makes it possible for a do-it-yourselfer to install, because the hole does not need to be precisely cut. However, some people do not like this option, because it's easy for crumbs and moisture to collect around the rim.

An undermounted sink is attached below the countertop, which must be made of a solid material like granite, quartz, or solid-surface. The hole for a sink like this will have exposed edges, so it should be professionally cut and polished; this is not a homeowner project. The advantages of an undermounted sink are its sleek look and the fact that you can easily wipe crumbs and moisture from the countertop into the sink.

An apron sink, also called a farmhouse sink, is usually made of enameled cast iron or heavily fired stoneware and consists of a single large bowl. The countertop is cut out in front to display its vertical apron, which may be plain or decorated. These sinks may be undermounted or self-rimming on three sides.

SELF-RIMMING. A stainless-steel self-rimming sink was the norm in the majority of kitchens for several decades. The combination of easy installation and sturdy materials continues to make this a popular choice.

UNDERMOUNTED. This charming beverage sink is undermounted. Its round shape and flat bottom make it easy to wash produce or clean glassware.

FARMHOUSE. A beautiful cast-iron farmhouse sink, here undermounted, has a satisfying sense of style and quality that makes it the perfect focal point in a hard-working kitchen. Often these sinks are available in either porcelain enameled cast iron or in fireclay.

Bowls and holes

A large, single basin is a popular choice in recent years. It offers a lot of versatility. Some of the reasons for choosing a two-basin sink can be handled with accessories (e.g., using a sink for both prep work and cleaning). Most sink manufacturers offer an appealing array of accessories.

Self-rimming sinks typically have one to four holes to accommodate the faucet and perhaps other amenities, such as a drinking-water spigot or an instant-hot-water faucet. Bridge faucets generally use two holes. Choose your faucet—which may need either one or three holes— and other products when you choose your sink. An undermounted sink usually has no holes, which means you will need to bore holes in the countertop. They are often coupled with one-hole faucets, for a modern appearance.

TWO-BASIN. This two-basin sink has two sizes of bowl. The smaller one is often used for washing vegetables, and the larger one is big enough to handle the kitchen's biggest stockpot.

SINGLE-BOWL. This spacious single-bowl sink comes with accessories that slide onto a system of ledges built into the basin, letting you position them where you need them.

PLUMBING HOLES IN COUNTERTOP. When you have an undermounted sink, plumbing holes are drilled in the countertop.

Installing a Kitchen Sink

If you are replacing an existing sink, remove it: Unplug the garbage disposal, disconnect the dishwasher hose, and unscrew one or more nuts on the trap. If it is stainless steel, remove the clips (see Step 11); if it is cast iron, cut through the bead of caulk around the rim. Then lift it out carefully, watching for any connections you missed. If you plan on keeping the countertop, choose a sink that fits into the existing hole.

If you are installing a new countertop (as shown in this sequence), position the sink above a "sink base" cabinet, which allows room for the sink. Measure to be sure the sink will fit, preferably with several inches to spare. There should be a drain line and supply stop valves nearby in the wall.

A RIM WITH NO GAPS. A carefully installed sink's rim will rest firmly and evenly on top of the countertop, with no gaps.

1 **MARK FOR THE OPENING. Measure carefully and position the sink, upside down, where it will go.** Usually, the front lip is 1½ in. to 3 in. from the front edge and centered over the base cabinet below. Apply a few pieces of tape to keep the sink from moving and scribe a pencil line around the lip (top). *This is not the cutline!* Next, mark the actual cutline, which is ⅜ in. to 1 in. inside the outer line (above). The easiest way to do this is to use the sink as shown; you will need to shift its position to scribe the other two lines.

2 **FOUR STARTER HOLES. Erase or at least blur the outside line to be sure you don't follow it. At** each corner of the inside line, bore a starter hole, about ½ in. or ¾ in. wide.

TIP To make absolutely sure a laminate countertop will not chip, some remodelers turn the countertop upside down and cut with a circular saw. Of course, this complicates things.

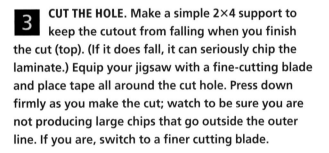

3 **CUT THE HOLE.** Make a simple 2×4 support to keep the cutout from falling when you finish the cut (top). (If it does fall, it can seriously chip the laminate.) Equip your jigsaw with a fine-cutting blade and place tape all around the cut hole. Press down firmly as you make the cut; watch to be sure you are not producing large chips that go outside the outer line. If you are, switch to a finer cutting blade.

4 **INSERT THE BASKET STRAINER.** In our example, one of the holes has a simple basket strainer, whereas the other has a mounting bracket for the garbage disposal. To install a basket strainer, roll out a rope of plumber's putty and wrap it around the bottom of the strainer's flange. With the sink right side up, press the strainer into place; some putty should squeeze out. Do the same for the mounting bracket in the other hole (see p. 143).

Cutting a Solid Countertop

The steps on pp. 147–148 show how to cut a laminate countertop. If you have granite, quartz, or solid-surface, you can cut it using a grinder equipped with a $30 diamond blade (see the bottom left photo on p. 152). Cut slowly and stop periodically to check that you are not overheating the blade. If the blade gets very hot, gently spritz it with water or glass cleaner, taking care that the water does not splash up onto the grinder itself.

TIP As shown in these steps, it will save trouble if you install as many parts as possible—the strainers, the disposal, the faucet, and the trap—with the sink upside down and resting on the counter or a pair of sawhorses. Use a drop cloth to protect the counter from scratches.

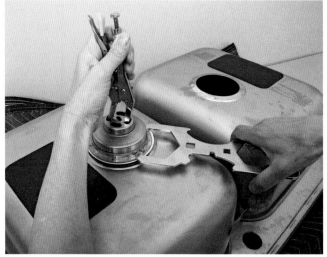

5 **TIGHTEN THE STRAINER NUT.** Turn the sink upside down. Gently (so as not to move the flange while you work) slip on the rubber washer, then the cardboard washer. Screw on the mounting nut. Hold the strainer in place with a pair of locking longnose pliers and tighten the nut with a spud wrench. Check the other side to see that the flange is centered in the hole.

6 **MOUNT THE DISPOSAL BRACKET.** At the hole for the garbage disposal (as shown on p. 143), slip on the cardboard gasket, the backup ring, the ring with the three screws, and the mounting ring. (This will be easier than doing it upside down inside a cabinet, but it is still a bit tricky to get the ring on.) Again, check the inside of the bowl to see that the flange is centered on the hole before the final tightening.

7 **INSTALL THE FAUCET.** Installing the faucet should be simple with the sink upside down (see pp. 74–76 for installation methods).

If There Is No Disposal

If you have no garbage disposal, here is a very simple trap configuration for a double-bowl sink, where both bowls share a single trap. However, codes in some areas require that each bowl have its own trap.

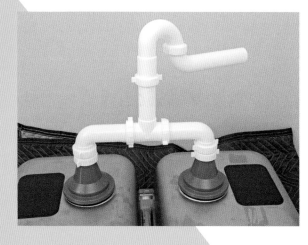

Boring a Mounting Hole

If you need to cut a hole for a faucet or appliance in your stainless-steel sink, it is usually not difficult. In most cases, a bi-metal hole saw, as shown, will do the trick. (If your sink is very thick and hard, you may need a titanium step drill bit.) The hole size is usually 1⅜ in. Determine the center of the hole, and tap with a hammer and nail set to create an indentation so the pilot bit will not wander. Then drill the hole, squirting oil on the bit regularly. Take your time; it may take 5 or 10 minutes to make the hole. If the bit heats up and starts to smoke, stop and let it cool for 15 minutes or so. The finished hole will be slightly rough around the edges but will accept plumbing fixtures well.

1. PUNCH AN INDENTATION.

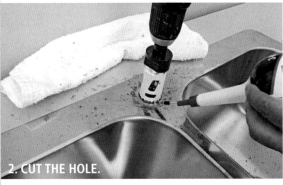
2. CUT THE HOLE.

3. THE FINISHED HOLE.

8 **START ASSEMBLING THE TRAP.** Install the garbage disposal (pp. 140–143). In this setup, the trap's tailpiece goes down from the basket strainer and has a T fitting for fastening to the disposal. Cut the tailpiece so the T is directly opposite the disposal's outlet, and install the T. Measure another tailpiece for cutting (top), and cut with a hacksaw or a miter saw. At the disposal's outlet, insert the rubber washer and attach with the diamond-shaped large washer and two nuts (above).

9 **COMPLETE THE TRAP.** Measure the height of the trap adapter in the wall and assemble a trap that will reach into it. Here, the disposal and the other bowl share a single trap; some codes may require separate traps for each.

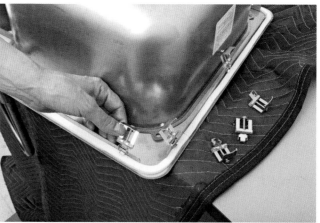

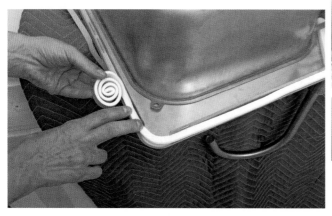

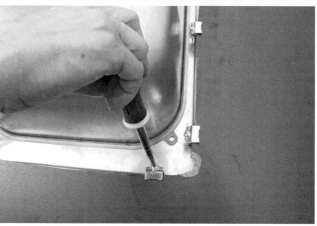

10 **SEAL THE RIM.** Seal the underside of the rim so water cannot seep underneath. This can be done with silicone caulk, but some sinks come with foam strips, which are less messy and make a surer seal. Pull off the paper backing as you press the strip into place.

11 **STAINLESS-STEEL CLIPS.** The sink should come with mounting clips. Slip them into the flange around the bowl and slide them so they are evenly spaced (top). Turn the clips so they do not get in the way, and carefully set the sink in place. From underneath, turn the clips and tighten them with a screwdriver (above) to firmly fasten the sink to the countertop.

Setting a Cast-Iron Sink

Cast-iron sinks are heavy, so they need no mounting clips. Just set the sink in place, make sure there are no gaps, and apply a bead of silicone or "tile and kitchen" caulk around the rim.

Installing an Apron Sink

Also called a farmhouse sink, an apron sink has one large bowl and a front apron that forms a decorative vertical front. This front does not cost you storage space; on a standard sink there is very little space in front, which is usually left blank. This section shows installing a self-rimming apron sink, which is a do-it-yourself-friendly project because it rests on top of the countertop on three sides. An undermount model should be installed, along with the countertop, by professionals.

Plumbing a farmhouse sink is not much different from a standard sink. However, the cabinet opening must be prepared with care. We show it installed with a garbage disposal, which most people will prefer unless local codes prohibit you from having one.

It's important that the countertop be level at all points, so the sink can rest firmly. This sink will be installed at the end of a countertop, so there is a panel on one side. The top of the panel is level with the top of the countertop.

1 PREP THE OPENING. An apron sink rests in a cabinet opening rather than a hole in the countertop. The sink's front may be flush with the faces of the abutting cabinets, or it may protrude an inch or two toward the person standing at the sink. Be certain you understand just how deep the opening needs to be. Because it will house a self-rimming sink, the cuts do not need to be perfect—they just need to be covered by the sink's rim.

2 CUTTING A STONE TOP. It is possible to cut a granite or quartz countertop for a self-rimming sink. Use a grinder equipped with a $30 diamond blade and cut slowly (see the sidebar on p. 148).

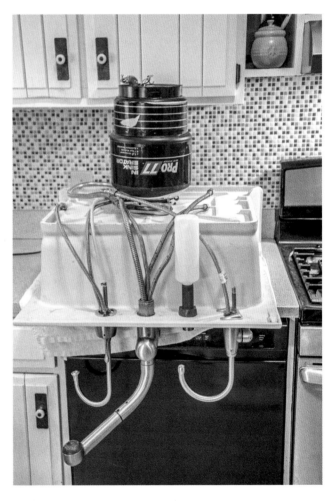

3 INSTALL PLUMBING BEFORE SETTING THE SINK. Install the faucet and garbage disposal as you would for a standard sink (pp. 74–76 and pp. 140–143). We've filled all four of this sink's holes with a faucet, hot-water dispenser, soap dispenser, and filtered drinking water faucet; those projects can be found on the following pages.

4 SET THE SINK. Working with a helper, set the sink in place and check underneath to be sure all your plumbing will line up. Then remove it, run a bead of clear or color-matched silicone caulk around the perimeter of the countertop, and set the sink on the caulk. Check that it is aligned correctly, with its back parallel to the wall, and wait at least a couple of hours for the caulk to harden before hooking up the plumbing underneath.

5 FINISH UP. Hook up the drain and supply lines under the sink. Open the supply lines and run the water through the faucet and any appliances, watching carefully for any leaks below. If drips do appear, you usually need only tighten connections. You may choose to apply a bead of silicone caulk around the rim, for a more finished look.

TIP A farmhouse sink is pretty heavy, so enlist some help in carefully lowering it into place.

Getting Ready for Added Water Fixtures

In order to install most of the water fixtures shown on the following pages—a water filter with its own spout, a hot-water dispenser, and a refrigerator's icemaker—you will need to hook up a new water supply. There's usually no need to run new pipes. Here are some easier methods.

Be sure to attach your supply fitting to the correct pipe: cold water for a filter or icemaker and hot water for a hot-water dispenser.

VALVE-MOUNTED T. This is probably the easiest method. If you have a nearby stop valve already installed, you can simply shut off the valve, remove the supply tube, and screw on a brass T fitting. Be sure to get one to match your stop valve's compression thread size—either ⅜ in. or ½ in. Now you can hook up the original supply tube, plus a tube for your new fixture. The great advantage of this fitting is that you don't have to shut off the water to the house in order to install it. With this setup, turning off the valve will turn off both fixtures at once, which is usually not a problem.

DOUBLE OUTLET STOP VALVE. A stop valve with two outlets is a good choice if it's not difficult to shut off water to the pipes. With the water shut off, remove the existing single-outlet valve and replace it with one of these. (Here we show a compression fitting, which does not need to be soldered on. To install one that is soldered, see pp. 170–173.) Again, this valve works for two supply tubes of the same size, either ⅜ in. or ½ in.

EXTEND A SUPPLY TUBE. If your supply tube does not reach the water supply, you can buy extensions for either ⅜-in. or ½-in. compression fittings.

Saddle T Valve

Though many plumbers are suspicious of saddle T valves, and they are not as strong flowing or as reliable as re-piping, they usually work for decades. And they are easy to install. There is no need to shut off the water to the pipe, though some people do so just to be safe.

Find a nearby location on a pipe, and clean away any corrosion or gunk from where the valve will go. Turn the valve off (if it is not already off). Check that the packing nut is tightly screwed on. Partially assemble the valve with one screw. Place the rubber gasket on the pipe, and position the valve so its needle will pierce through the gasket. Use a screwdriver to tighten the two bolts evenly.

Place a nut and ferrule onto the tubing (which is plastic here; you may use copper instead), slide the ferrule into the valve's opening, and tighten the nut. Turn the valve's handle until it bottoms out; it has now pierced the pipe, and is in the "off" position. Hold a small container under the tubing's end and turn the handle counterclockwise to open the valve. Let water run for a minute or so to flush any sediment, then turn the valve off and connect to the fixture at the other end.

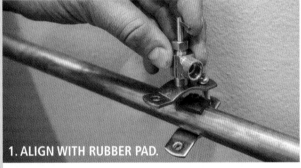

1. ALIGN WITH RUBBER PAD.

2. SCREW TO CLAMP.

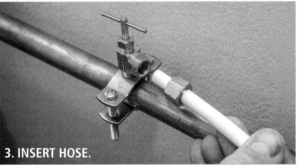

3. INSERT HOSE.

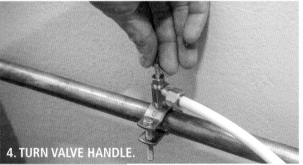

4. TURN VALVE HANDLE.

A push-on fitting

The push-on fitting with valve shown here may come in an icemaker hookup kit, or it may be purchased separately. It will require that you shut off water and drain the pipe, but you will not need to solder any joints. Here it is shown installed onto copper pipe, but you can also get versions made for PEX or CPVC as well.

TIP Saddle Ts work best on copper or CPVC pipe. If you want to install one on galvanized steel pipe, you will have to shut off the water and drill a hole first. However, because steel pipe often gets clogged with sediment, water flow may be restricted. If you have PEX tubing, a saddle T may not work well. Instead, shut off the water and install a T fitting, then a standard stop valve.

1 **CUT OUT A SECTION OF PIPE.** Cut out a section of pipe to accommodate the fitting. Use a tube cutter for copper, a PEX cutter, or a fine-cutting saw for CPVC.

2 **CONNECT TO THE PIPE.** Mark the pipe ends to indicate how deeply they should be inserted into the push-on fitting. Push the pipe into one end, then push on one end with the disconnect clip (removal tool) to help finish the connection.

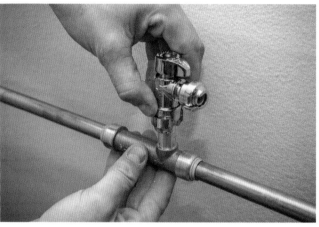

3 **ATTACH THE VALVE** To attach the valve, pull up on the sliding clip and push down onto the fitting. Make sure the bottom of the valve goes all the way down to the depth-indicator line.

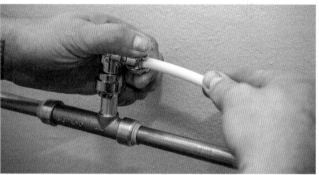

4 **INSERT THE TUBING.** You will not need a nut or ferrule to attach the ¼-in. supply tubing (which may be plastic or copper) into the valve. Just pull back on the sleeve and poke the tubing in until you feel it bottom out. Hook up the other end of the tubing to the icemaker or filter, restore water pressure, and check for leaks.

Installing an Under-Sink Water Filter

An under-sink water filter can be attached to the cold-water supply of the main faucet, but in that case it would filter all the cold water you use for cleaning as well as drinking, and you would need to change the filter often. Here, we show installing a filter with its own dedicated drinking-water faucet.

The faucet will require a hole in the sink's deck. The sink shown here came with four holes, so one was available. Some porcelain or fireclay sinks (like the one shown here) have knockouts, which you tap with a hammer and cold chisel to produce a hole. If you have a stainless-steel sink, see the sidebar on p. 150 for cutting a new hole.

The water path is easy to follow: It runs from the cold-water pipe to the filter, and then to the faucet.

2 **ATTACH THE BRACKET WITH FILTER.** Screw the filter canister onto the mounting bracket. Mound the bracket at a place convenient for running the supply tubes. The filter may shake a tiny bit, so make sure it does not touch any pipes.

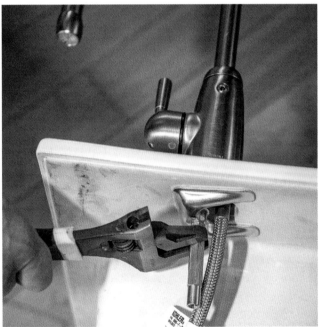

1 **MOUNT THE FAUCET.** Mount the faucet onto the sink with the hardware provided. Position the rubber gasket on the bottom of the faucet's body so it seals against the top of the sink. To be sure of the seal, set the faucet in a bed of clear silicone caulk. Here, there is a U-shaped washer and a long nut. If you cannot reach the nut with a wrench, use a basin wrench instead.

3 **CONNECT TO THE FILTER.** Connect the supply tube that comes from the filter to the port labeled OUT. (There may be arrows or other indications showing the direction of water flow.) Connect the other supply tube to the IN port. These supply tubes have plastic threads; wrap them with three windings of plumbing (Teflon) tape before screwing them in.

4 **CONNECT TO THE WATER SUPPLY. Attach the other end of the tube leading to the IN port to the cold-water supply.**

Under-Sink Water Filters

The steps on these pages show installing a simple single-stage filtration and absorption system, which will filter out most particles. It has a single small filter that takes up little space and needs to be replaced only twice a year or so. Two- and three-stage filters have, unsurprisingly, two or three canisters. Some filter systems add a tank as well. Here are some of the options:

• *Activated carbon* (sometimes called charcoal) filters are inexpensive. They will remove most particles and much of the chlorine, but cannot remove heavy metals like lead and copper and won't improve acidic water from wells. Over time, as particles collect, water pressure through the faucet will lessen as particles collect and clog.

• *KDF* (kinetic degradation fluxion) filters cost more, but do a better job of removing (actually, converting) chlorine and will effectively filter out heavy metals. They also kill microorganisms that are often missed by an activated carbon filter.

• An *ion exchange* filter is typically a canister (it may be one of the stages of a two- or three-stage filter system) containing tiny resin beads that "deionize" water, to remove nearly all inorganic particles. When used along with an activated carbon or KDF filter, pretty much all inorganic matter, parasites (including giardia), and chlorine will be removed.

• If you have serious water problems, the most common solution is a *reverse-osmosis* filter, shown at left. These typically have two or three canisters plus a tank, and so take up a good deal of under-sink space. In addition to the filtering power of KDF filters, a reverse-osmosis filter removes radioactive contamination, which is a problem in many areas, and turns hard water into soft, drinkable water.

Installing a Hot-Water Dispenser

A hot-water dispenser, sometimes called an instant-hot faucet, typically spouts 190°F to 200°F water in a matter of a second or two. This is hot enough to make tea, to cook thin asparagus, and to sterilize countertops. The tank plugs into an always-hot GFCI receptacle.

Three flexible supply tubes come from the faucet. Two go to the tank and one goes to the hot-water supply.

In our installation, we have complicated things a bit by running water through a filter on its way to the faucet. That way, your water will be purified as well as hot.

After installing the unit, don't plug it in yet. Turn on the water and check for leaks. Then open the faucet; it will hiss for a while, but keep it open until water starts to come out. (Plugging the tank in before this purging process can damage it.) Plug the tank into the receptacle, and adjust the knob to control the heat.

HOT-WATER DISPENSER WITH FILTER

Water runs from the hot-water pipe through a filter and into the faucet. Two lines then route water through the tank and back to the faucet.

TIP If water sputters out of the faucet even when it has not been opened, the tank is turned too hot. Turn down the temperature a bit.

THE POWER SUPPLY

Provide for standard 120-volt electrical power. There are a number of ways to do this; one common method (as shown) is to "split" the receptacle, so one plug is always hot (for the hot-water dispenser) and the other plug is controlled by a switch (for a garbage disposal). Power enters the receptacle box and attaches to the always-hot plug. The receptacle's hot tab is removed. A switch loop runs from the switched plug to a wall switch. If you are not confident of your wiring skills or have any concerns, hire an electrician.

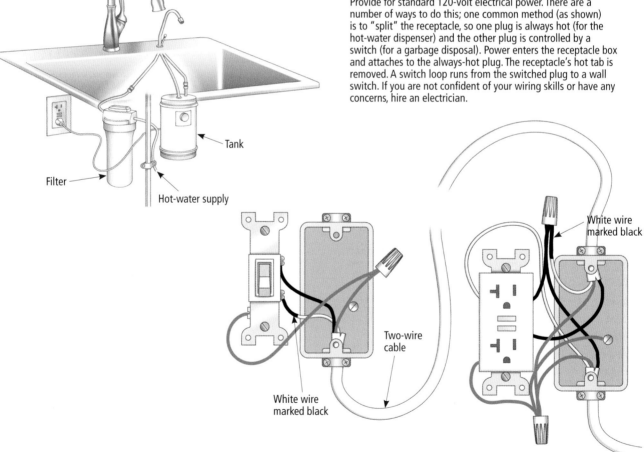

Tank

Filter

Hot-water supply

White wire marked black

Two-wire cable

White wire marked black

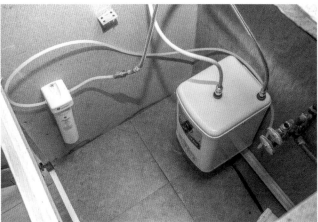

1 **MOUNT THE TANK.** Attach the tank's mounting bracket in a convenient location, so all the flexible supply tubes will be able to reach the faucet. Slip the tank onto the bracket now, or attach the tubes first and then mount the tank.

4 **RUN THROUGH A FILTER.** If you choose to install a filter as well, route the water supply line from the pipe to the filter, and then back up to the faucet.

2 **MOUNT THE FAUCET AND CONNECT A LINE.** Mount the faucet using the hardware provided. Be sure that the rubber gasket under the faucet's body seals well against the top of the sink. Three flexible supply tubes come out of the faucet; make any needed connections. For this model, a rubber hose connects via a squeeze clip.

3 **MAKE CONNECTIONS.** Connect the two lines that run into the tank. One hose and one line run to the tank and another runs to the water supply.

Soap Dispenser

Today's soap dispensers come with attractive spouts and are very easy to fill. This model has a brushed-nickel spout that coordinates with the sink's faucets. Mount it by screwing on a plastic nut. To fill, just lift the spout up and out and pour in the liquid soap.

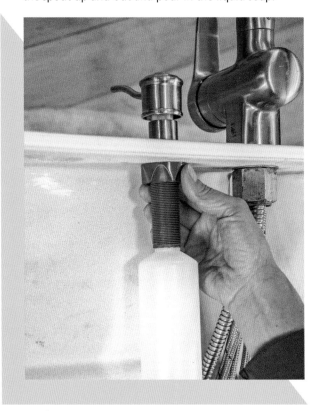

Connecting an Icemaker

Many new refrigerators come with icemakers, which need a cold-water supply. Running and connecting the water line is a DIY-friendly project, as long as a cold-water pipe is not too far away. Often the refrigerator is on the first floor and the exposed pipe is in the basement or a crawlspace, so you will need to run a line through the floor, as shown here. Or you may need to route the line through cabinets or a wall.

2 **FISH THE TUBING UP.** Firmly attach the tubing to the end of the drill bit. Wrap the tape tightly, so it doesn't scrape off. Pull the drill bit up to bring the tubing through the hole.

1 **DRILL A HOLE.** Using a very long ½-in. bit, drill a hole down through the floor and through the ceiling below. You should feel the bit drill through about 1 in. of flooring, then there should be an air space until you reach the drywall in the ceiling below (if there is any). If you encounter solid material deeper than 1½ in., you've hit a joist or other obstruction; try drilling in another location.

3 **CONNECT TO THE REFRIGERATOR.** Connect the tubing to the icemaker port on the refrigerator. If the refrigerator has a flexible line already installed, as shown, just connect to that line.

TIP An icemaker hookup kit may include a flexible ¼-in. tube as well as a saddle T valve, or the push-on fitting shown on p. 155.

STANLEY

Installing a Dishwasher

Replacing an existing dishwasher is usually a straightforward job: The opening between cabinets should be the right size, and the electrical and plumbing lines can usually be reused. If you are installing a dishwasher where there was none before, your main task will be to prepare the opening.

TIP When running a dishwasher drain hose, be sure to loop it up as high as possible at one point, near the underside of the countertop. This will prevent water from siphoning backward. If your hose is not long enough, you can buy an extension.

1 **PREP THE OPENING.** Make sure the opening is wide enough for the model you are installing. You'll need (from left to right) a drain line, a cold-water-supply tube, and an electrical line.

2 **HOOK THE DRAIN.** If your dishwasher has a permanently attached drain line, place the dishwasher near the opening and thread the line through holes in the back of cabinets and connect it to a garbage disposal or dishwasher tailpiece under the sink. If its drain line can be disconnected, you may choose to work in the opposite direction.

Taking Out the Old Dishwasher

If you have an existing dishwasher, shut off the water supply (usually at a stop valve under the sink). Also shut off electrical power at the service panel and test to verify that power is off. See the steps on p. 162 for disconnecting the water and wiring lines. Remove the screws holding the dishwasher to the cabinetry. Have small pails on hand to catch water as you disconnect the water-supply line. You may choose to disconnect the drain line from behind the dishwasher or from where it is hooked up to the plumbing under the sink. Then slide the dishwasher out, using towels to keep from scratching the floor.

Make sure the opening is 30 in. wide (unless you are installing an economy model that's only 24 in. wide). If it doesn't already exist, snake a drain line through holes or behind cabinets from the opening to below the sink, where it attaches to a garbage disposal or a special dishwasher tailpiece on the trap. Also supply cold water with a flexible supply tube made for dishwashers; it connects to a stop valve under the sink. You'll have to supply electrical power in the form of a flexible "whip." If you are adding a new electrical line, make sure you will not overload a circuit; otherwise, connect it to a new circuit in the service panel. (Hire a pro for this.)

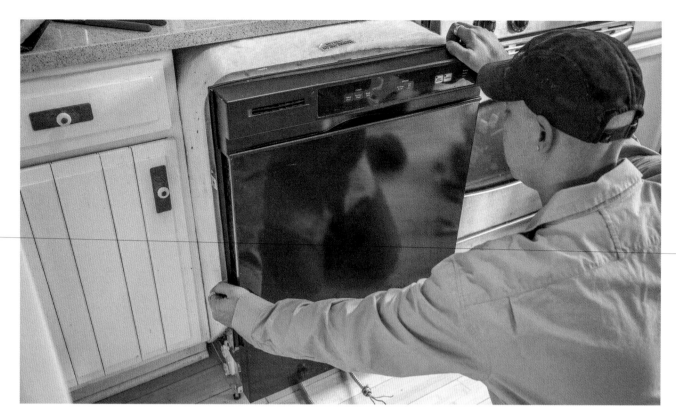

3 **SLIDE THE DISHWASHER IN.** Taking care not to kink the drain hose, and seeing that the electrical and water-supply lines are not pushed out of the way, slide the dishwasher most of the way into the opening.

4 **CONNECT THE WATER.** Connect the water supply to the dishwasher's inlet. This is usually a simple matter of tightening a hose-like fitting. If the existing water line is flexible copper, take care not to kink it as you work, and use a nut and ferrule to make the connection.

5 **ELECTRICAL CONNECTION.** Remove the cover from the dishwasher's electrical box. Slip the wires and the threaded electrical connector through the opening, and screw on a nut to tighten the cable to the box. (The cable shown is metal clad; yours may be plastic sheathed.) Use wire nuts to firmly connect the black or colored house wire to the dishwasher's black lead, the white wire to the white lead, and the ground wire to a grounding screw. Replace the cover.

6 **FINAL TOUCHES** Turn the adjustable legs to get the dishwasher aligned with the sides and the underside of the countertop. Drive screws at the sides or top to fasten the dishwasher to the cabinets and perhaps the countertop. Turn on the power and the water, and let the dishwasher run an entire cycle; make sure there are no leaks. Then install the metal base pieces.

CHAPTER SEVEN

WORKING WITH PIPE

THIS CHAPTER MARKS A MAJOR DIVIDING point in the book. Up until now, the projects have all been achievable without having to install "rough plumbing": running new supply and drain pipes. Most of the projects that will occur after this chapter do include "roughing in" some pipes. So now's the time to learn how to cut, prepare, and connect pipes and fittings made of copper, plastic, PEX, steel, and maybe even cast iron.

This book will deal only lightly with major projects such as complete kitchen or bath remodels. Instead, most of the new-pipe projects involve making simple pipe runs and a few connections. Still, you're in the big leagues now, and you need to make pipe connections that are every bit as watertight, strong, and durable as those made by the pros.

Hard pipes are most often hidden inside walls, so the connections and the pipes must be secure and capable of lasting a century or more. Fortunately, modern materials and fastening methods can achieve such durability without a great deal of special knowledge or skill. However, you do need to do things right the first time, and we'll show you how.

Tools for Cutting and Joining Pipes

The following pages arrange tools by the materials that they are used for. Though there is some overlap (for instance, a pair of slip-joint pliers comes in handy for almost everything), you can assemble tools as you need them for specific jobs. Almost all tools for actually working with pipes are fairly inexpensive. However, if you need to cut pathways in walls and framing for those pipes, then tools can get more pricey.

The tools shown here supplement the tool set on pp. 26–29; you'll need many of those as well when running pipes.

Tools for copper pipe

Soldering (or "sweating") copper pipe is still commonly done, though PEX is replacing copper in many areas.

Sweating copper calls for a distinct set of tools and materials. You'll need a *propane torch;* get one with a push-button igniter, for much greater ease of use. To clean pipe ends and insides of fittings, use a *copper cleaning wire brush* or a roll of *plumber's cloth,* which is actually a sort of sandpaper or abrasive mesh. A *large tube cutter* cuts copper pipe with ease, whereas you sometimes need a *small tube cutter* when working in tight spots. After cutting, you should ream out the inside of the pipe using the reaming tool on the cutter; you can also use a wrench or other metal tool that fits snugly inside the pipe. A *flame shield* keeps nearby surfaces from catching fire as you solder. To make the connections, you'll need *soldering flux,* a *flux brush,* and a roll of *solder.*

TOOLS FOR COPPER PIPE

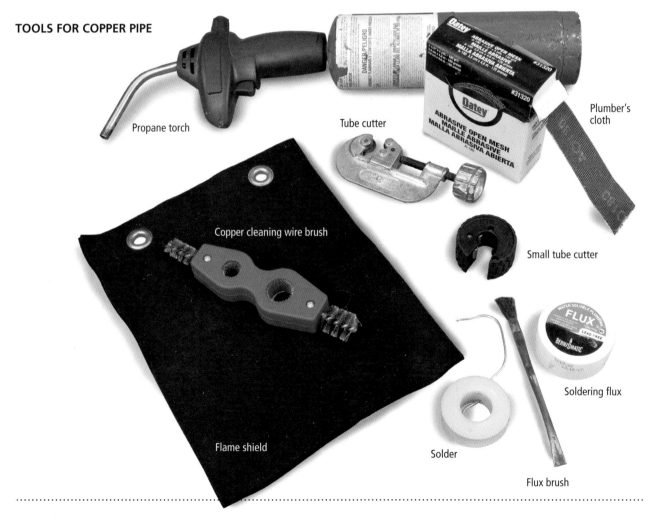

Propane torch

Tube cutter

Plumber's cloth

Copper cleaning wire brush

Small tube cutter

Soldering flux

Flame shield

Solder

Flux brush

Tools for threaded pipe

Threaded galvanized supply pipes are rarely installed nowadays, but threaded black pipe is still commonly used for gas piping. Not just one but two *pipe wrenches* are needed when making most connections. In addition, a pair of *slip-joint pliers* can come in handy for holding a fitting still or for starting a connection.

Tools for plastic pipe

Plastic (usually PVC) pipe is most often used for drainpipe, but CPVC supply pipes are still installed in some areas. A *plastic tube cutter* makes short and neat work of cutting small plastic pipe. A pair of *ratcheting cutters* provides more cutting power for less effort. To cut larger pipe, use saw blades that are as fine as possible to produce fewer burrs. A good-quality *hand miter saw* like the one shown below right holds the pipe in place and makes a fine cut. If you have only a few cuts to make, you can use a hacksaw. (A power miter saw, or chopsaw, cuts very quickly, but most blades will make a rough cut. If you have lots of cutting to do, equip yours with a plywood-cutting blade or another one that makes a clean cut.)

Use a *felt-tipped pen* to make reference marks to keep fittings facing in the right direction. To join plastic pipe, you usually need both *primer* and *cement*. Make sure the primer and cement you use are made for your type of plastic; PVC is the most common. After cutting, it's important to deburr the cut, or joining may be difficult. Scrape with a knife or the sides of a wrench or pliers.

Slip-joint pliers

Pipe wrenches

TOOLS FOR THREADED PIPE

TOOLS FOR PLASTIC PIPE

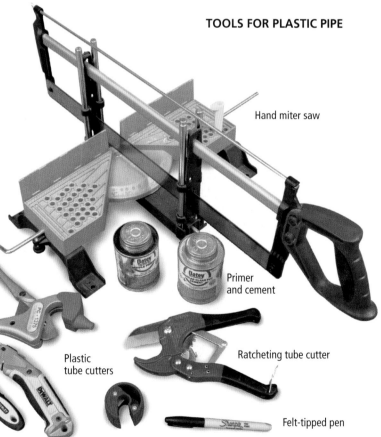

Hand miter saw

Primer and cement

Plastic tube cutters

Ratcheting tube cutter

Knife and wrench

Felt-tipped pen

Tools for PEX

PEX tubing is rapidly gaining in popularity. It can be cut easily using a tube cutter designed for plastic pipe, or get a special *PEX tube cutter*. There is also a *small PEX cutter* that you squeeze and rotate to make the cut. The tubing itself is quite inexpensive, but the tools can set you back a bit. Choose a connecting method (see pp. 174–176) and then buy the tools that apply to that method. Basically, you can choose to clamp or crimp. A *ratchet clamping tool* is used along with *PEX clamps* of various sizes. A *crimping tool,* unsurprisingly, is used in conjunction with *crimp rings*.

Tools for cutting pathways

If you need to run pipes through wall framing, you'll need a right-angle drill. The *cordless right-angle drill* shown here is surprisingly powerful and will enable you to make 15 or so holes before recharging the battery. (If you have major remodeling to do, consider renting a ½-in. right-angle drill.) Be sure to use high-quality *hole saws* that are ¼ in. or ½ in. larger than the outside diameter of the pipe you are running. Sometimes you will need to cut notches in framing. A *reciprocating saw* with adjustable angle for the blade allows you to cut easily in the tightest spots.

TOOLS FOR PEX

TOOLS FOR CUTTING FRAMING

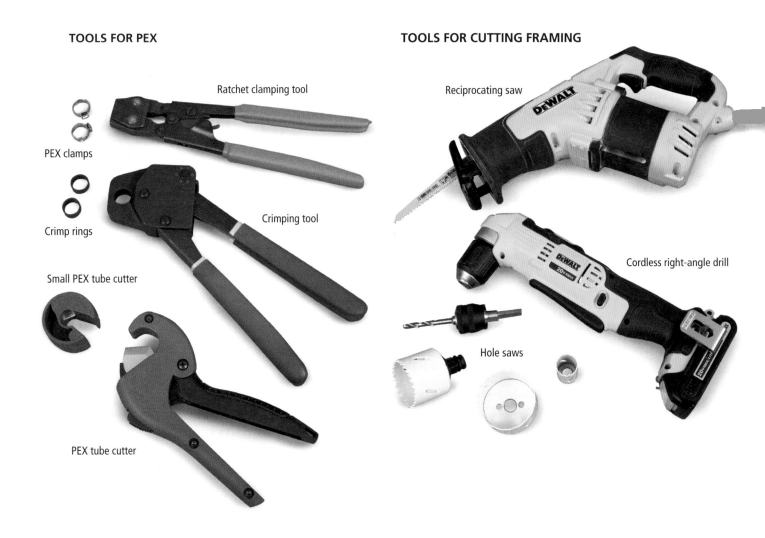

Ratchet clamping tool

PEX clamps

Crimp rings

Small PEX tube cutter

Crimping tool

PEX tube cutter

Reciprocating saw

Cordless right-angle drill

Hole saws

Cutting and Sweating Copper Pipe

In most areas, copper pipe is extremely long lasting. (In some areas with acidic water, copper can fail after some decades; check with your building department.) But it is expensive, which is why PEX is often used for large jobs.

However, if you will be running a modest amount of pipe for a remodel, it makes sense to continue with copper if that is what exists in your house.

> **TIP** Type M copper pipe is the thinnest and least expensive and is usually preferred for residential use. Types K and L are thicker, more expensive, and typically used only for commercial applications.

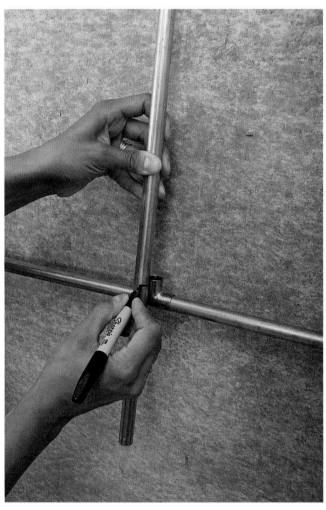

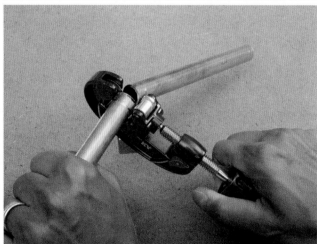

1 **MEASURE AND MARK.** Before cutting into supply pipes, be sure to shut off the water and test to verify that water is off. Measure to cut copper pipe so it enters a fitting about ¾ in. for a solid joint. Mark with a felt-tipped pen.

2 **CUT WITH A TUBE CUTTER.** Unscrew the handle to open a tube cutter until you can slip it over the pipe, then tighten—but not too firmly—until the cutting wheel snugs against the cutline. Rotate the cutter a full turn, then tighten the cutter and rotate again (either in the same direction or in the opposite direction). Repeat until the cut is complete.

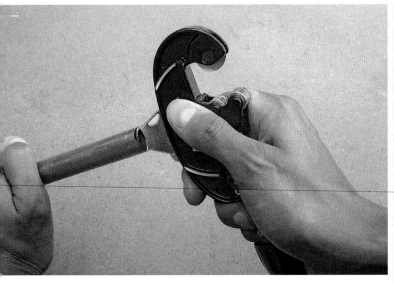

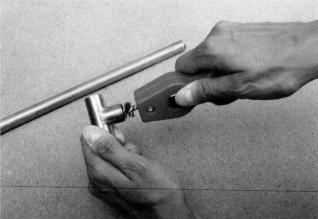

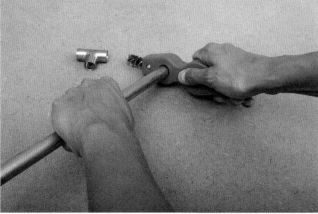

3 **REAM.** Use the reaming cutter on the tool to remove the inside indentation, which would slightly inhibit water flow. If you do not have a reamer, you can insert and twist a pair of lineman's pliers or another metal tool.

Cutting in a Tight Spot

If you need to cut a pipe that is near a wall or other obstruction, use a tight-spot tube cutter. Instead of turning the handle to tighten the cutting wheel, just squeeze the tool as you rotate. Be sure to make complete rotations, so the entire circumference is cut through.

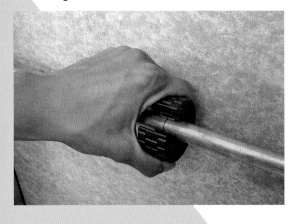

4 **CLEAN THE ENDS AND FITTINGS.** For a reliable joint, the two parts to be joined must be cleaned (or "polished") until they are bright and shiny. Use a wire brush tool to clean the inside of the fitting and the outside of the pipe. Do not touch the cleaned portions, or the oil on your fingers can ruin the joint.

TIP Work with multiple joints, rather than one joint at a time. Otherwise, you could melt a completed joint while soldering a nearby joint. In our example, three pipe ends and three fitting innards are cleaned, coated with flux, and soldered at the same time.

STANLEY

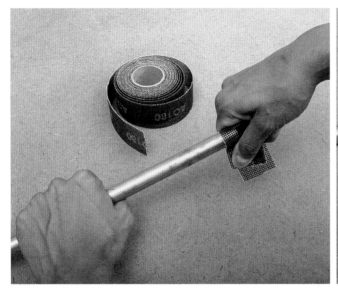

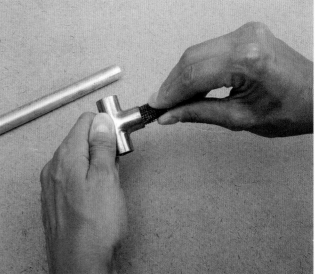

OR USE PLUMBER'S CLOTH. Many plumbers prefer to clean with plumber's cloth, which is a roll of sandpaper or abrasive mesh. Clean the outside of the pipe's end, and roll some cloth tightly in order to clean the inside of a fitting.

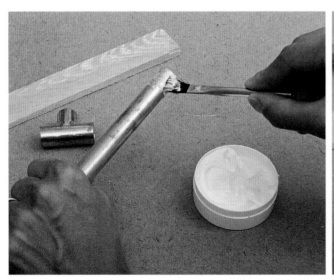

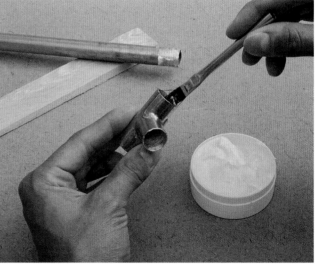

5 **APPLY FLUX.** Use a flux brush to apply a fairly generous amount of plumber's flux to the outside of the pipe ends and the insides of the fitting. Take care to keep the flux brush and the fluxed pipe ends from getting any debris on them.

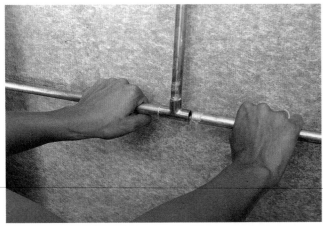

6 **PUSH THE PARTS TOGETHER.** Make sure that the pipes slip into the fitting by about ¾ in. See that the pipes are all facing in the correct direction for your installation. If there are globs of flux, very gently wipe them away.

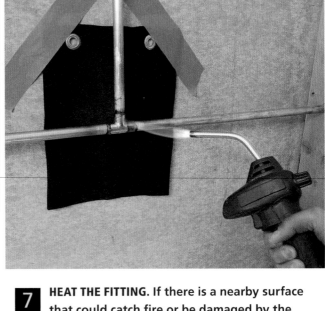

7 **HEAT THE FITTING.** If there is a nearby surface that could catch fire or be damaged by the flame, place a heat shield behind the fitting and pipes. (There should be some space between the shield and the pipes; if they are touching, the joint cannot be fully sealed.) Unwind a roll of solder and bend it at the end (see the next step) so you will be ready to apply it. Open the gas valve on a torch and start the fire. Apply the tip of the blue flame to the fitting—not to the pipes—and move it around to more or less evenly heat all parts of the fitting.

TIP Copper pipes and fittings must be dry during soldering. A slight amount of water will evaporate with the heat, but you cannot solder with a steady drip. Here's an old plumber's trick: If a pipe drips, stick a wad of white bread in it and solder the joint. The white bread will dissipate and not cause a clog.

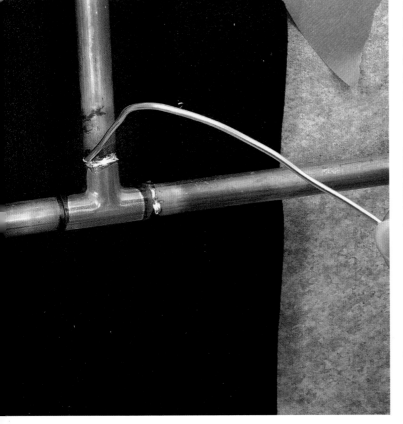

8 **SOLDER.** Once the fitting is heated, remove the flame. Touch the top of the solder to a joint between fitting and pipe. If it does not melt right away, take it away, heat the fitting some more, and try again. When you see the solder suck into the joint, move it to the back side quickly to make sure the entire circumference is soldered. Then quickly do the same for the other joints.

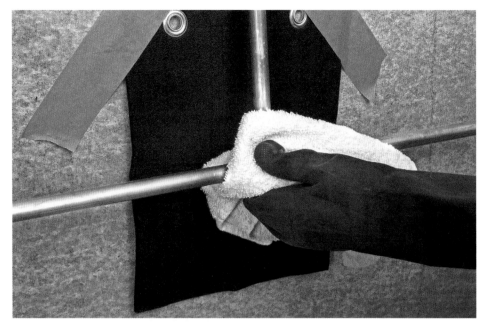

9 **WIPE**. Wipe the joint with a dry rag, taking care not to touch the pipe with your fingers. Test by turning on the water. If there is a leak, disassemble, and try again (see the sidebar below).

Disassembling a Joint

If a joint leaks or you need to disassemble it for remodeling, first heat the pipes with a torch, then pull the pipes apart with pliers and locking pliers. Before attempting to reassemble, be sure to clean the ends until all the solder is gone and they shine with a copper color. Use a new fitting to make the joint.

1. HEAT JOINED PIPES.

2. PULL APART WITH PLIERS.

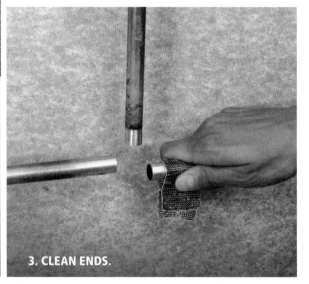

3. CLEAN ENDS.

Working with PEX tubing

PEX tubing is rapidly gaining in popularity throughout the country, though in some areas it is still prohibited. (Check with your local inspector for specific requirements where you live.) It comes in 100-ft. coils, and is generally available in ½-in., ¾-in., and 1-in. sizes. PEX is cheap, easy to install, and extremely durable. However, it can be easily punctured with a nail, so it must be protected at framing (see p. 241). PEX can be bent around corners, but an L fitting is often used where a sharp turn is needed.

There are several possible ways to join PEX. Professional plumbers often use expansion connections, but they require an expensive tool. If you will be running a whole lot of PEX, you may want to invest in the tool, but we will not show that in this book. Instead, we show less-expensive crimp and clamp methods. If you have only a few connections to make, or need to connect PEX to other pipe materials, push-on (SharkBite®) fittings are very easy to use and require no special tools, although each fitting is pretty expensive.

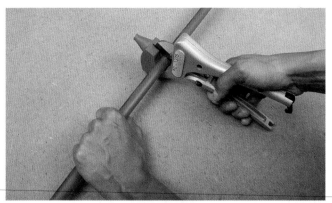

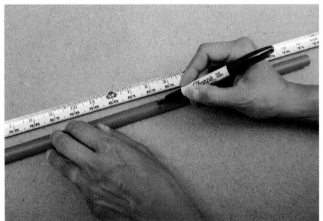

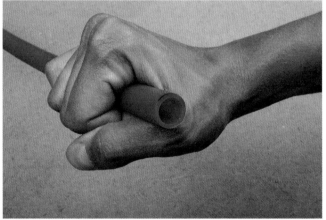

1 **MEASURE. Measuring for PEX lengths is not an exact science, because the tubing bends so easily. Cut pieces an inch or so longer than needed to be sure you will have some slack.**

TIP In Step 3 we show a plastic fitting, and in the next photo we show a metal fitting. Though many plumbers feel more secure using metal, plastic fittings have proved themselves quite reliable.

2 **CUT. You could cut PEX with a saw, but that would create burrs that need to be scraped away. Instead, use a plastic pipe cutter or a tube cutter made for PEX. It's important that the cut end be clean and straight; if the cut is at an angle, the connection may not be watertight. The tool shown at top makes it easier to ensure a straight cut.**

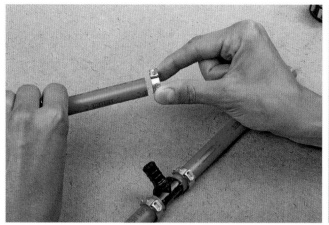

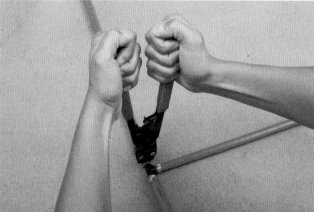

3 **ASSEMBLE WITH FITTING AND CLAMPS.** Slip clamps (or a crimp ring, see p. 176) over the ends of the pipes, slide them down a few inches, and push the tubing ends onto a barbed fitting. Then slide the clamps or crimp rings back, so their entire width is over the fitting's barbs.

If Clamping Is Difficult

If you find it difficult to clamp with two hands, it often helps to place the tool so that one arm is against a wall or other surface, and then just push onto the other arm.

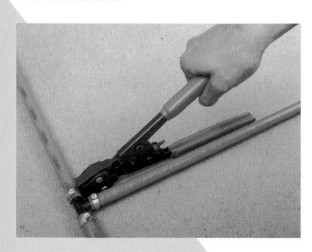

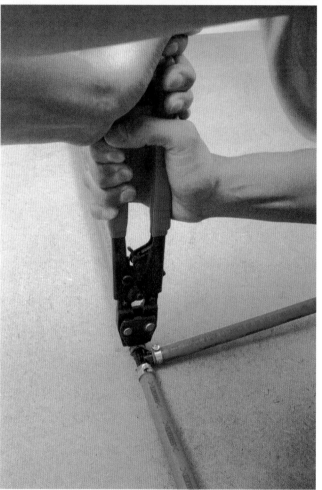

4 **CLAMP.** If you are using clamps, you need only one tool for any size pipe. Slip the tip of the tool over the wings of the clamp, and hold each handle with a hand to start clamping. Finish by squeezing the handles tightly together.

Making Crimp Connections

To crimp rather than clamp, slip on crimp rings when you assemble with a fitting. If you have only a few connections to make, the tool shown below top right will work, though perhaps with difficulty. The more-expensive tool shown below bottom left is easier to use. Place the tool's jaws over the ring and squeeze hard to exert even pressure all around the ring. Use a gauge (below bottom right) to test that the crimping is complete. If the ring does not slide into the "GO" slot, cut the pipe, slip on a new ring, and try again.

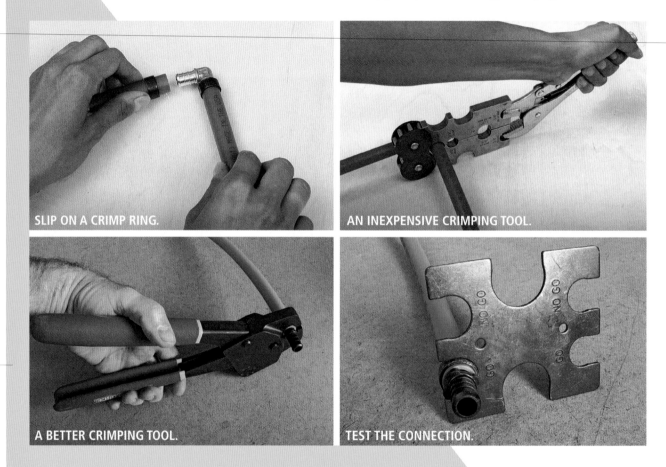

SLIP ON A CRIMP RING.

AN INEXPENSIVE CRIMPING TOOL.

A BETTER CRIMPING TOOL.

TEST THE CONNECTION.

Working with Threaded Pipe

Galvanized steel (sometimes called galvanized iron) pipe is no longer commonly installed for supply systems, though it is still often used for a short stubout pipe. Black threaded pipe is still often used for gas supplies, and it installs in the same way as galvanized.

Short lengths of threaded pipes are called "nipples." You can buy precut and prethreaded nipples in lengths of ½-in. increasing sizes up to 12 in. or so. If you need

a longer length of pipe cut, measure carefully and have it cut and threaded at a hardware store, home center, or plumbing supply store.

Here we show a procedure that involves most of the techniques used for threaded pipes: cutting into an existing pipe and installing a T fitting with a union. (Once installed, you can thread a new pipe into the T fitting, for new service.)

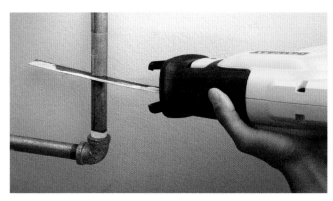

1 **CUT THE PIPE.** To tap into an existing line, first shut off the water and test to verify that water is off. You can cut a threaded pipe with a hacksaw, but it's easier to use a reciprocating saw with a metal-cutting blade.

TIP Unlike copper, CPVC, or PEX, you cannot simply cut a threaded pipe and then slip on a fitting; all connections must be made with threads. That may mean you'll have to remove a fairly lengthy pipe in order to make a connection.

2 **REMOVE PIPE SECTIONS.** Open or close the jaws of a pipe wrench so that you can slide it partway over the pipe, as shown. You can turn a pipe wrench only in one direction: Here it is positioned to turn counterclockwise to remove a pipe. As you turn the wrench, the jaws will tighten and grab the pipe.

3 **WRAP OR PASTE PIPE THREADS.** Before screwing a pipe into a fitting, wrap its end with pipe tape. As shown at top, wrap it while turning the pipe clockwise (as you face it, from the rear), so that it will not come unwrapped when you turn it clockwise in the fitting. Apply about three wrappings. Or you may prefer to apply pipe joint compound (also called pipe dope), which is a thick paste that you apply to the threads (above). Apply it only to the outside of the pipe end; do not apply it to the inside of the fitting.

TIP In most cases, you will need to use two pipe wrenches, one to turn a pipe and the other to hold adjacent pipes still as you work. This is shown in Step 4. Other photos on these pages do not show the other wrench for clarity sake, but you will likely need it in Steps 2, 5, and 7 as well.

4 **TIGHTEN PIPES AND FITTINGS.** Screw a pipe and/ or fitting by hand, and then use a pipe wrench. As shown here, use a second wrench to hold the pipe still as you work. Turn a pipe as far as you can, exerting a good deal of pressure. Turn a fitting very tight as well, but you may have to stop before exerting full pressure, in order to have it facing in the correct direction.

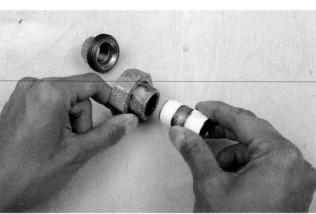

Three Types of Tape

Use standard white pipe (or Teflon) tape for water pipes and colored tape for gas pipe. Newer gray tape is stronger and thicker and requires only two windings. Pipe joint compound works for either water or gas pipe.

5 **ATTACH HALF OF THE UNION.** A union is a somewhat complicated gizmo that allows you to insert pipe thread in both directions, which you often must do. Here, a very short nipple is about to be threaded onto the end of the union that has a sliding nut (top). Thread the union half with the nipple into the fitting and tighten with a wrench (above).

6 **MEASURE FOR THE PIPE.** Temporarily assemble the other part of the union, and measure for the pipe that will go into it. Its threads should penetrate the fittings at each end by ¾ in. Have the pipe cut and threaded to fit.

7 **FINISH THE UNION AND PIPE ASSEMBLY.** Thread and tighten the other portion of the union onto the pipe end (top). Thread this end onto the union's nut, first by hand, then using two pipe wrenches (though only one is shown here).

Push-on Fittings

Also known by the brand name SharkBite, push-on fittings quickly and easily join almost any type of supply pipe, and no joining tools are needed. The connections are reliably watertight. The only downside is that they are pretty pricey—many individual fittings cost more than $10.

Do-it-yourselfers with only a few joints to make often find it money well spent. And many professional plumbers use them from time to time, when working in tight places where the other option would be to cut framing or open up a wall.

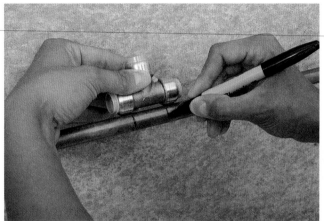

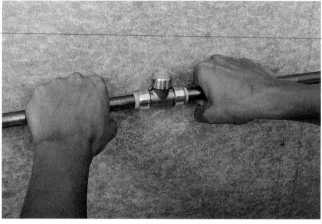

2 **PUSH TOGETHER. To make the connection, just push the pipe into the fitting. You should feel it go in an inch. Tug on the pipes to be sure the connection is strong.**

1 **CUT TO FIT. Mark and cut pipes so they can be inserted about 1 in. into the fitting. Make the cuts straight and remove any flares or protrusions that could cut the rubber gasket on the inside of the fitting.**

TIP Push-on fittings work only if the pipe to be joined is neatly cut, with no raised edges, debris, or burrs. Use plumber's cloth or a wire brush tool to smooth edges of copper, PEX, or CPVC pipe before connecting a push-on fitting.

Transition Fittings

You can buy transition fittings that allow you to tie into almost any type of supply pipe. Here, a copper-to-PEX transition fitting has been soldered onto a copper pipe.

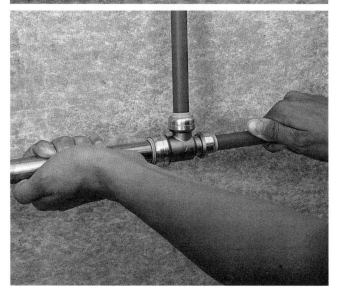

Sweating a Valve

If you need to attach a shutoff valve onto copper pipe, be sure to disassemble it if there are any rubber parts inside. Clean and apply flux to the pipe ends and the insides of the valve, as you would for a copper fitting (pp. 170–171). Assemble the pipes onto the valve, apply a torch flame to the valve (not the pipes), and solder the joints.

VALVE DISASSEMBLED.

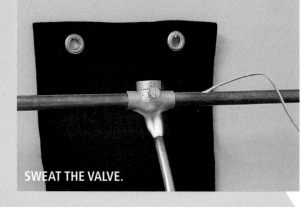

SWEAT THE VALVE.

CONNECT DIFFERENT PIPES. You can buy push-on fittings that attach to almost any type and size of fitting. At top, a ½-in. copper line has been tapped into for a new ½-in. PEX line. Above, a ¾-in. copper pipe is supplying two ½-in. PEX tubes.

CPVC Supply Pipe

PVC pipe is occasionally used for supply lines, but CPVC is much more reliable. CPVC pipes and fittings are slightly different in size from PVC, so you can't mix the two. Cutting and joining this plastic pipe is so simple it almost seems like child's play, but you do need to treat it seriously: Make the cuts straight and clean; remove any burrs or flares; take care that the pipes are facing in the right direction, because you won't be able to adjust the fitting later; apply primer and cement evenly; push all the way in when cementing; and hold each joint for 10 seconds before moving on.

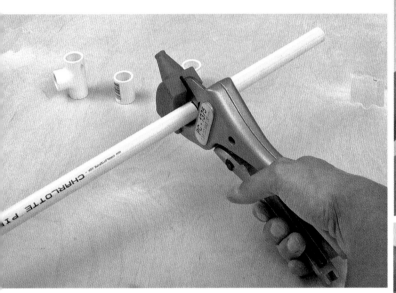

1 **MEASURE AND CUT.** Measure for pipes that will fit into the fittings by ¾ in. to 1 in. Cut with a plastic pipe cutter. (You can cut with a hacksaw or miter saw, but then you will need to carefully remove any burrs.) If a single squeeze does not cut the pipe completely, rotate the cutter and squeeze again. Dry-fit the pieces to be sure they will face in the right direction; make reference marks on a pipe and fitting if you need to (see p. 185).

TIP Keep pipe ends and fittings clean and debris-free as you work. If your workspace is dusty or grimy, be sure to place the pipes so their ends are hanging over and not touching surfaces.

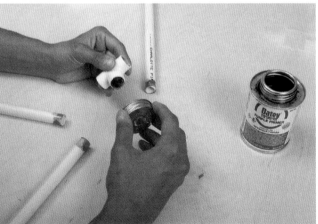

2 **APPLY PRIMER.** Do not skip this step; it is essential for making a watertight joint. The pipes are small, so you don't need a lot of primer. Dab the applicator against the edge of the can (top) to keep it from being too wet. Apply primer to the pipe ends and the insides of the fitting (above).

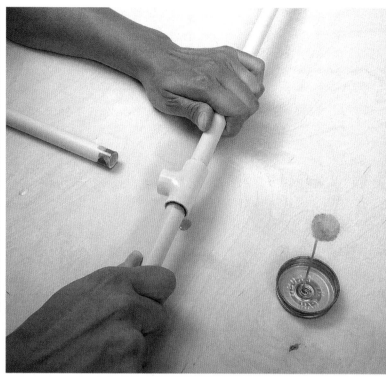

3 **APPLY CEMENT.** Apply an ample amount of CPVC cement to the inside of one of the fitting's inlets, and to the outside of the pipe end.

4 **PUSH TOGETHER.** Within a few seconds of applying the cement, push the pipe into the fitting and give it a slight twist. You should feel it go all the way in. Some excess cement should ooze out. Hold the pipe and fitting together for a count of ten, then let go.

CPVC Fittings

A number of CPVC adapter fittings have threads on one end—either male or female—so you can attach threaded pipe to them. Drop-ear elbows are designed to attach to a framing member in the wall so you can screw in a pipe that extends out of the wall, for a stop valve or a tub spout, for instance. Ball and globe valves are usually cemented to CPVC on each side.

PVC Drainpipe

Nowadays PVC is virtually the only type of drainpipe used in residential plumbing. (Black ABS is used in some areas, and it is cut and joined in the same way as PVC, but using ABS primer or cleaner and cement.) As with CPVC, PVC pipe is very easy to assemble, but you must have good habits in order to make tight joints and pipes facing in the right direction.

TIP Dry runs are essential to producing good drain lines. Assemble a dry run consisting of three or more pipes and a fitting or two, and put it in place to make sure everything fits well. Mark as needed, then disassemble and place the parts carefully, so you will be sure to reassemble them correctly. Now you can prime and cement.

1 **CUT PVC.** The best tool for cutting PVC is a power miter saw equipped with a fine-cutting blade. You can also use a hand miter saw, a reciprocating saw, or a handsaw, but you will need to take special care to make straight 90-degree cuts.

2 **DEBURR.** The saw will produce small burrs on the inside and outside of the pipe. These need to be removed so the pipe can fit easily into the fitting, and so liquid can flow without obstruction. You can scrape the burrs with a knife, or use plumber's cloth (or other sanding screen).

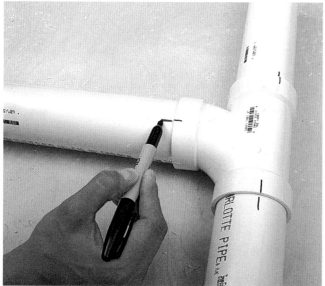

3 **MAKE A DRY RUN.** Assemble a number of cut pipes and fittings in a dry run. Make reference marks on the pipes and fittings to ensure that the pipes will face in the right direction.

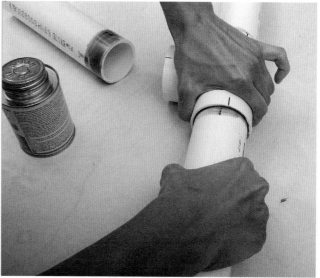

4 **APPLY PRIMER.** Apply primer to the pipe ends and to the insides of the fittings. The primer should completely cover the area where the fitting will be; in fact, it should show a bit after installation, so an inspector knows that you've primed. Take steps to ensure that the pieces will not get dusty or dirty.

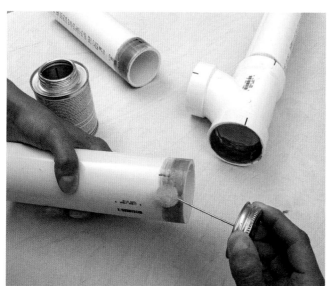

5 **APPLY CEMENT.** Apply an ample amount of PVC cement to the inside of one of the fitting openings, then to the primed outside of the pipe.

6 **PUSH, TWIST, AND HOLD.** Push the pipe into the fitting; some cement should squeeze out all around the joint. Give the pipe a short twist (perhaps to align the layout marks). Hold the pipe and fitting still for a count of ten.

BATHTUB AND SHOWER REPLACEMENTS

AFTER DECADES OF USE, A BATHTUB
may become dingy or outdated looking,
or its enamel finish may chip or deteriorate.
You could hire a tub refinisher, but likely
you'll be happier with a new tub. Installing
a bathtub is a pretty major job, but you
may find it less daunting than expected,
especially if the new tub and its plumbing
fit nicely where the old one was.

You can leave the old tub/shower faucet in place, as well as the wall
tiles, or you may want to go ahead and redo everything. Equipped with
pipe-joining skills learned in the previous chapter, you can install a new
faucet with spout and showerhead. Once that is done, you may want to
retile the surfaces or install a solid-surface surround.

Choosing a Bathtub or Shower

A bathtub or shower unit is the largest and most visible part of a bathroom, and one that may be used thousands of times a year, so it's worth time and money to get just what you want. Although alcove bathtubs are still the most common, today there are other options to choose among.

Types of tub installation

The type of tub you choose will determine the method of installation. Replacing an existing tub with the same type is the most common choice. But if, for instance, you have a traditional alcove tub and want something more stylish like a claw-foot tub or more comforting like a spa tub, an upgrade is doable as long as your space will accommodate the plumbing—and possibly electrical with a spa—modifications needed.

An alcove, or recessed, tub is the traditional or standard bathtub. Tightly enclosed on three sides by walls that are usually tiled (the alcove), it is an efficient use of space. When you buy an alcove tub, you'll need to specify the length from wall to wall and the drain location—either right hand or left hand, as you stand facing the tub. Most alcove tubs have a flange on three sides, which slips under the tiles or the shower enclosure. Some models permit you to build your own custom apron or skirt, which may be a tiled or wood-paneled surface to match cabinetry.

A deck-mounted, or drop-in, tub sits within a box specially built for it and covered with tiles or paneling. The frame may be on a platform or sunken below floor level. Often used for a spa tub, the structure usually has a ledge flush with the top of the tub along two or more sides; a wide ledge is handy for bathers but can make it a little more difficult to get in and out of the tub. One side should have a removable panel to access plumbing.

FOR THE DISABLED. It's easy to transform a traditional alcove into an ADA-friendly bath; simply add grab bars in custom locations to make getting in and out feel safer.

UNDERMOUNTED TUB. This undermounted tub resides under a stunning slab of marble that has been professionally cut and polished to follow its oval profile.

TIP Surveys show that showers are more popular, but a tub adds versatility. In addition to the benefits of a long soak to alleviate a sore back or muscles, tubs are also useful for cleaning small children or the family dog, and handwashing items that are too big for the sink. Many people like to shower in the morning and bathe in the evening.

An undermounted tub, like an undermounted sink, has a tile or stone edge along the top of the tub. This option is generally more expensive than a drop-in tub because the inner stone or tile edge needs to be polished smooth—a long surface with a tub. Cut the stone or tile so that an inch or more of the tub top surface is showing; that way, the bather won't be leaning back against the stone or tile, which would be uncomfortable. With this installation, it can be difficult to ensure access to plumbing, so if anything goes wrong, correcting the problem can be messy and expensive.

A freestanding tub has no abutting surfaces. The two most popular options are the old-fashioned-looking claw-foot and the soaker tub. A freestanding tub does need to be near both the incoming water pipes and the drain plumbing, which will usually be more on display, especially if freestanding plumbing is used. These tubs usually cost more, but don't require surrounding surfaces, which saves money. They certainly add style points to a room and have grown in popularity of late.

THE CLAW-FOOT OPTION. A claw-foot tub—and its plumbing—stands naked to the world, with all parts on display.

DROP-IN TUB. This drop-in tub rests on a frame that has been covered with marble slabs.

Tub materials

Enameled cast iron has long been a valued tub material. However, new and improved acrylics, resins, and composite tubs have the advantage of being lighter weight while also being durable and available in more varied molds.

A cast-iron tub coated with porcelain enamel like French casserole cookware is attractive and very durable, though it can be damaged with harsh cleaning products. On the downside, these tubs are expensive, heavy, and cumbersome to install. The subfloor structure needs to be very sturdy. However, they have a timeless appeal and many people insist they are still the best option.

Steel tubs are the least expensive and are standard issue in many new homes. Like cast iron, they are coated with porcelain enamel and look similar to cast-iron tubs. But they are lighter in weight and easier to install. On the downside, a steel tub is louder than a cast-iron tub when it's filling with water and will chip more easily. Also, it will flex if the subfloor is not solid, and it does not hold heat as well as other tub options.

Acrylic tubs are usually reinforced with fiberglass underneath the acrylic top coat. The surface has an appealing high-gloss appearance that is easy to clean. Look for a tub with a thick layer of acrylic, which is much more durable and scratch resistant than thinner models. Used for lots of different tub installations, acrylic tubs are lightweight and less expensive and—many say—keep the water hot longer than cast iron. A sturdy subfloor makes them feel as solid as cast iron. Scratches can be sanded and buffed to look like new. Look for a "green" model made with plastic that will not off-gas. Avoid cleaners with grit.

Often associated with one-piece tub/shower inserts, inexpensive gel-coated tubs are made of molded fiberglass that has been coated with a layer of polyester resin gel. They are lightweight and inexpensive but generally do not last as long. One type is fiberglass-reinforced plastic (FRP). Another is cultured marble, which has a clear plastic gel coating over a blend of materials—crushed limestone, fiberglass resin, and fillers—to produce a surface that resembles marble. Over time, as the gel wears away, these tubs may lose their shine, develop spider cracks, and be difficult to clean. To check for quality, look at the tub underside. If it looks porous or full of bubbles, steer clear.

Composite tub materials have a variety of names, depending on the manufacturer. For instance, Vikrell® is

SOLID-MATERIAL COMBO. With a composite tub and wall combo, you can get shelves that are almost tailor-made for your storage needs.

SPA FOR A CORNER. If space is tight, a corner spa may work.

WALK-IN TUB. A walk-in or gated bath makes it easy and safe for those with mobility issues to take a bath. Walk-in baths have high walls and a seat in the tub, with a door that opens on one side to allow easy access. The downside is the bather needs to stay in the tub while it fills and then while it empties. A quick drain feature is available, but it requires changing the size of the room's drainpipe. The model shown here offers an inviting air bubble massage.

Holding the Heat

Which tub holds heat the best? This debate continues. Many people swear by cast iron. Others say acrylic, composite, resin, and cultured marble tubs are better. Their reasoning is that cast-iron tubs start out cold and absorb heat from the water, reducing the water temperature; they also conduct the heat out of the water into the room, whereas acrylic (and other better-quality non-metal tubs) simply hold in the heat. All agree that freestanding metal tubs lose heat faster than drop-ins and that steel tubs are inferior to cast iron.

a "solid composite material made of resins, fiberglass, and filler that is exclusive to Kohler Company." Better composites have color that runs through the material, so a scratch or ding will be less visible. Popular in locations with high humidity, they are easy to clean.

Similar to quartz countertop material, resin tubs have a high-gloss solid surface that is more expensive. Often used for high-end soaking tubs, they hold the heat well.

Spa tubs

These tubs have higher sides to hold more water and a motor that provides electrical power for air or water jets, which supply the hydrotherapy experience. They are often made of acrylic, which is easily molded to provide a comfortable contoured shape. Here are some other considerations:

Air or water jets? Water jets are powerful, localized streams of water that you will feel hitting your body. Air jets produce a more generalized bubbling for a gentle massage effect; some people say it feels like a full body massage. Air-jet tubs do permit the use of bath products—e.g., bubble bath, etc.—whereas they are not recommended with water-jet tubs. If you prefer water jets, check out the locations of the jets (though they are usually adjustable), and see if you can find out how noisy they are. Some people find the noise detracts from the relaxing ambiance of the experience.

Heater. If you like to read or soak for a long time in the bath and want the water to stay hot, look for a tub with a heater. A water heater can be added later if you're not sure you will need one. In some cases a water heater may only work when jets are turned on. Some tubs offer a surface heater that warms the surface of the tub, so when you lean back it feels a little like a heating pad.

Size. The trend is toward smaller tubs because they're more efficient with energy and water. If you're tempted by a large tub, perhaps a two-person-size tub, check that the size of your water heater is sufficient (you may need a bigger one). Even if yours is big enough, it may use up the entire contents of the water heater and take a long time to fill, considerations that may discourage you from wanting to use it very often. If you're interested in a wider tub, be sure the sink or toilet space will not feel crowded, and be sure your subfloor is strong enough to handle the weight.

Shape. Go ahead and sit in a tub before you buy it. Stores that sell these expect you to. Make sure the molded features work for you. Options include back, arm, and foot rests, pillow, and contours. If you'll use the tub for showers too, check that it's easy to step into. If you're going to spend a chunk of time in the tub, you will probably want a ledge for a drink, glasses, book, etc. An apron tub can meet this need.

Access panel. This will be required by codes. One side of the tub will need to be removable to get at the plumbing and electrical connections. Check how many dedicated electrical circuits will be required. Some tubs will use one for the motor and a second for a heater.

The mildew issue. A long steamy bath will create a lot of moisture in the bathroom, so use high-quality paint and provide ventilation.

More features. It will take a little extra work to install, but you may enjoy chromatherapy: soothing, colored LED lights for a nighttime bath. This feature usually comes with a remote control and gets positive reviews for improving overall relaxation.

The drain assembly. This is usually sold separately. A better-quality product will have a long warranty against defects and leaks, and will ensure you don't hear the water while it's draining.

TIP Tubs with water jets need to be cleaned out after each use. Look for a tub that has a self-cleaning feature, such as an air system that automatically turns on after each bath. Manufacturers may also caution against using bath soaps or oils in order to keep the jets clean. If jets are not cleaned out, dark flecks from the previous bath may blow out the next time you take a bath.

Removing a Tub

Replacing a tub is indeed major surgery, but it can take less time and effort than you expect. First, disconnect the drain. You will probably need to chip away a row or two of tub-surround tiles, or remove tub-surround panels. If there is a pipe for the spout protruding into the room, you will probably need to remove it. You may need to remove a sink or other objects in order to make room for getting the old tub out and the new one in. Once those things are done, there may be room for the tub to tilt up, so you can carry it out of the room standing upright. Or it may be easiest to break or cut the old tub apart.

However, things are sometimes more complicated. If the framing is too tight to tilt the tub up, you may need to cut away at the studs. (Be sure to fasten "sister" studs to the sides of the cut studs later, after installing the new tub, so your framing will be strong.)

1 **DISCONNECT THE DRAIN. Most tubs are connected to only the drain plumbing; the supply plumbing is in the wall. Use a flange tool or the handles of a small pair of pliers to unscrew the drain flange in the bottom of the tub. At the overflow outlet, remove the cover plate and unscrew the mounting screws. If you have good access from behind or below the tub, you may remove the waste-and-overflow assembly (see Step 4) at this time.**

2 **REMOVE WALL PANELS OR SOME TILES.** If your old tub has solid wall panels, remove them. (If you need to remove any supply plumbing to do this, be sure to shut off the water first.) The tub and wall surround above is a single unit, which can be cut apart with a reciprocating saw and pried off the wall. If you have wall tiles, remove one or more rows, as needed. You may also need to cut away some of the greenboard or concrete backerboard, if you want to tilt the tub up and out.

BREAK APART A CAST-IRON TUB. If your existing tub is cast iron, it is extremely heavy. It may be easiest to break it apart with a sledge hammer. Wear protective clothing and eyewear, then have a bit of smashing fun.

TIP If you are removing tiles to take out the old tub, you may as well also cut away enough material to make it possible to tilt the new tub into place.

3 **REMOVE THE TUB.** Once the tub is in removable pieces, carry them out. Remove fasteners from the walls and sweep the area clean so you will not damage the new tub.

4 **REMOVE THE DRAIN.** You may be able to reuse the waste-and-overflow assembly for the new tub, but as long as you are installing a new tub, you may as well install a new drain as well. Use slip-joint pliers or a lock-nut wrench (shown on the floor) to loosen the nut, then lift the assembly out.

> **TIP** When installing a new tub, consider adding insulation to enhance heat retention and to soften noise. With a drop-in tub, you can add insulation around the base. However, if you're installing a spa-type tub, check the manufacturer's literature to be sure insulation will not interfere with the mechanical features.

Installing a Tub Faucet

When replacing a tub you may be able to reuse the old faucet and perhaps just replace the visible parts: the handles, escutcheon, spout, and shower arm and head. But if you are installing a tub in a new location, or if your walls are opened up, you may choose to install a new shower faucet. Here we show the most common type, with a single-handle control. The spout will have a lift-up diverter to direct water to the showerhead or down through the spout.

Here we show installing with copper pipe; see pp. 169–173 for cutting and sweating instructions. If you choose to use PEX or CPVC instead, see pp. 174–176 or 182–183.

1 **REMOVE THE FAUCET ASSEMBLY. Shut off water to the existing faucet (see pp. 6–8). Cap the faucet outlet to avoid drips and tape over the drain trap. Using a tube cutter, remove the faucet assembly. (Don't use a hacksaw—it can distort copper pipe.) Very likely, space will be tight; a small tube cutter (shown) comes in handy.**

2 **PLAN THE FAUCET ASSEMBLY. To avoid extra trips to the home center or hardware store, buy a range of pipe fittings. On a clean surface, work out the best arrangement for attaching supplies to the faucet.**

What's the Right Height?

Position the faucet where it is most convenient for your family. If someone likes to fiddle with the faucet handle with his or her foot while lying down in a bath, place it pretty low. If showers are far more common than baths, place it higher, so you don't have to bend over to adjust the temperature. The spout should be about 6 in. above the top of the tub.

Ideally, a showerhead should be 4 in. to 6 in. higher than the tallest person who will use it. A showerhead's fitting is commonly placed 7 ft. above the floor; the tub's floor is a few inches above the room's floor, and the showerhead itself will end up a few inches lower than the fitting, depending on the shower arm you choose.

3 **INSTALL A FAUCET SUPPORT.** Use the plaster guard attached to your faucet to establish the setback for the faucet support. Plan for the faucet to be about 6 in. above the tub. Drive screws to firmly install a 2× support. Mark for the location of the spout.

4 **DRY-FIT THE FAUCET ASSEMBLY.** Attach the faucet body to the support. Cut pipe and dry-fit your assembly. Be sure to keep the parts clean.

5 **SWEAT THE FAUCET ASSEMBLY.** Take apart and reassemble the pipe and fittings, methodically sanding or wire-brushing and applying flux to the pipe ends and the insides of the fittings. Spritz the framing with water to limit scorching. Clamp or wedge a fiber shield behind the joint you are sweating. Supply lines for this faucet slip into the threaded inlet ports of the faucet body. Sweat the connections.

TIP Consult the manufacturer's literature to install the 2× support at the correct depth in the wall so the faucet's escutcheon and handle can be neatly attached after the wall is finished. Take into account the total wall thickness, including the backerboard plus the tiles or the panels you will install. Also plan carefully so the faucet, spout, and showerhead will be centered on the tub's width.

6 INSTALL A SPOUT SUPPORT. Fasten in place a 2× support for the faucet spout. You may need to attach an additional block. Check the manufacturer's instructions for how far below the faucet body the spout should be to clear the faucet escutcheon. Cut the pipe and sweat on the drop-ear elbow before attaching it to the support. Sweat the pipe to the faucet body.

7 ADD A THREADED NIPPLE. To temporarily seal the spout, install a threaded nipple so it extends beyond the finished wall. Apply several windings of pipe tape to the threads and screw the nipple into the drop-ear elbow. Cap the nipple temporarily.

8 INSTALL THE FAUCET CARTRIDGE. Carefully line up the hot and cold chambers of the cartridge as you push it into the faucet housing.

9 ADD THE BONNET NUT. Slide the bonnet nut over the cartridge and thread it onto the faucet body. Hand-tighten it securely.

11 **SECURE THE SHOWER OUTLET AND ARM.** To safe-guard the shower arm from damage, add a pipe clamp to the riser (top). Wrap the shower arm with pipe tape and hand-tighten the shower arm into the drop-ear elbow. To be able to safely turn the water on before installing the tub—handy if you don't have stop valves on your tub faucet—add a temporary cap to the shower arm.

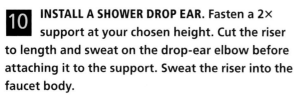

10 **INSTALL A SHOWER DROP EAR.** Fasten a 2× support at your chosen height. Cut the riser to length and sweat on the drop-ear elbow before attaching it to the support. Sweat the riser into the faucet body.

TIP After securing the shower out-let and arm, check your installation for leaks. Restore water pressure and turn on the faucet. If a joint leaks, shut off and drain the water, dry out the pipes, and repeat the sweating process.

12 **INSTALL THE FINISHING PIECES.** Install backer board and tiles or solid panels. Shut off water and remove the temporary pipes. Attach the shower arm and showerhead, the faucet escutcheon and han-dle, and the spout.

Installing a Bathtub

This section shows how to install a tub that has its drain hole in the same place as the old tub you are replacing. If the hole is in a different place, see the instructions for the spa tub (pp. 202–205). Also, carefully plan how you will attach the waste-and-overflow assembly, especially at the tub's drain hole. In the situation shown on these pages, there is easy access to a trap from below, so you can install the assembly before dropping in the sink. If you don't have such access, again see the instructions for the spa tub.

2 **INSTALL THE DRAIN STRAINER.** Position the rubber gasket on the drain-tube elbow. Apply a rope of plumber's putty to the underside of the threaded strainer body's flange. Using a strainer wrench or the handles of a small pair of pliers, tighten the strainer body into the drain-tube elbow. Attach the strainer cover.

1 **INSTALL THE WASTE ASSEMBLY.** Before setting the tub, elevate it with scraps of wood and install the waste-and-overflow tube. The tube has a rubber gasket that seals it to the outside of the tub, held in place by a retainer plate on the inside of the tub. Position the drain tube and elbow under the tub.

3 **INSTALL THE DROP CYLINDER.** Feed the drop cylinder and its linkage into the overflow opening. Adjust the linkage so the cylinder covers the drain tube when the overflow lever is up. Some units come with a handy gauge for making this adjustment. Attach the overflow plate.

4 **ADD A LEDGER.** To support the inner edge of the tub, level and attach a 2×4 ledger to the framing at the height specified by the tub manufacturer. Fasten the ledger to each wall stud with two 3-in. deck screws.

5 **CAULK ALONG THE LEDGER.** Clear the area so you can slide or tilt the tub into place. This can be tricky—you won't have much clearance between the studs. Once you are certain the tub will fit, apply a couple of beads of 100% silicone to the ledger as an adhesive and sealant.

TIP Be sure to buy a tub with either a right- or left-hand drain to match your plumbing. Most alcove tubs are 60 in. (5 ft.) long, but check to be sure; you may need to buy a 66-incher or another size. Also check the width. If the new tub is narrower than the old one, you may need to patch or redo the bathroom flooring. Also check to see that the drain hole (or outlet) is in the same position as the old tub; if not, the plumbing is much more complicated.

SUPPORT WITH MORTAR AS NEEDED. Some tubs have an integral base that stiffens the tub, but many tubs need a layer of mortar as support. (The tub should not flex at all when you stand on its floor.) To contain the mortar and keep your site clean, place about a square foot of mixed mortar in a large plastic bag, centered under the middle of the tub's floor.

6 **SET THE TUB.** Set the inside edge on the ledger and push down to spread the bagged mortar (if used). Don't stand inside the tub; that could push down too far, so the mortar will not support the tub when it dries.

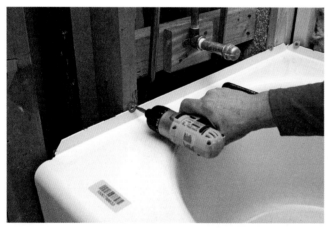

7 **FASTEN THE TUB TO THE FRAMING.** To secure the tub, install drywall screws and washers at every stud just above the flange of the tub. Be careful not to damage the flange as you drive the screws.

TIP Center the tub between the two end walls. At the back wall, install it tight to the studs. Test with scraps of backerboard to make sure the finish surface—either tiles or solid surface—will lie flat and clear the tub's flange and the fasteners you install.

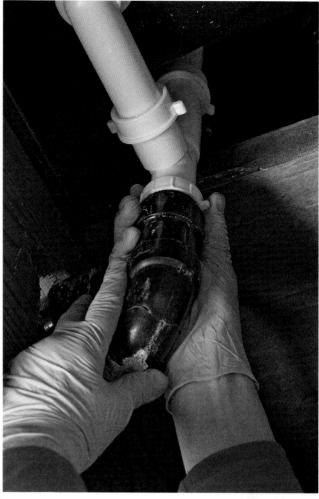

8 **CONNECT THE DRAIN TO THE TRAP.** Working from the basement or through a ceiling or wall access panel, connect the waste assembly to the trap. With luck, your waste assembly will line up with the trap. In some cases, you may need to cut a piece or add an extender to the assembly.

Installing a Spa Tub

In this section, I'll show you how to install a 60-in. alcove spa (or whirlpool) bathtub with air jets (see p. 191). The soaking area is smaller in square inches than a standard tub in order to make room for the motor, but because the tub is taller, there is plenty of room for a large adult to soak comfortably. This model is made of surprisingly hard-surfaced acrylic with fiberglass reinforcement, so it doesn't scratch easily. The tub includes a small heater, which is strongly recommended to keep the water at a great soaking temp.

A spa tub is more of a challenge to install than a standard tub, for four reasons. (1) It requires that you have access for possible repairs not only at the faucet and drain end but also at the other end, where the motor is. (2) You must install two electrical receptacles, one for the motor and one for the heater. These must be on separate 15-amp circuits; you almost certainly cannot just draw power from a nearby receptacle on an existing circuit. Depending on your electrical service, the new circuits may be as much work as installing the tub. (3) Because the tub is extra tall, it will be more difficult to tilt into place. You may need to cut away some studs and then repair them with sister studs later. (4) A spa tub is likely somewhat wider than the standard tub you will replace, which means that you will probably need to move the drain pipe an inch or three.

> **TIP** If your tub connects to a drum trap rather than a P-trap, it is generally best to replace it with a P-trap, as long as you can access the P-trap easily for augering in the future. In this example, we left the existing drum trap in place, because it is actually easier to access through the wall than a P-trap would be. With either choice, be sure to thoroughly clean out the trap before installing the tub.

Prep the Area

Before you can begin the installation, you'll need to prepare an opening for the tub. The backerboard or other substrate should be removed to ½ in. or so higher than the tub's height. Measure to see that the tub will fit between the studs. Make sure the opening is wide enough for the new tub as well. In this example, we chose to keep the existing wall tiles, so a row of tiles was removed and will be replaced after the tub is installed.

You will need two access points: the standard access to the plumbing at one end, and an opening at the back so you can reach the motor and the electrical service. If you cannot reach these from an unfinished basement below, you will need to cut one or two openings, which you will cover with access panels later.

Run electrical lines as needed into the opening. (Hire an electrician for this work unless you are skilled in wiring.) In this case, two receptacles, each on their own circuit, were required to supply power to both the motor and the heater.

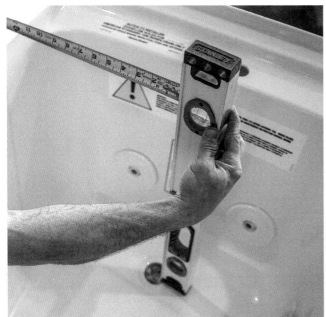

MEASURE FOR LENGTH OF PIPE.

MEASURE OVER FOR LOCATION OF DRAIN.

MEASURE AT END.

1 **MEASURE FOR THE DRAIN HOLE.** Consult the manufacturer's literature for the exact location of the drain hole, and check with a tape measure and level. Also set the tub on shims so it is level in both directions, and check how high above the floor the waste-and-overflow's drain needs to be.

> **TIP** Some tubs need to be supported with a bed of mortar, as shown on p. 200. However, most high-quality spa tubs are strong enough that they do not need the mortar bed. To be sure, stand on the bottom of the tub; if you feel it flex, then set it in mortar.

> **TIP** After dry-fitting the drain-and-waste assembly, it's a good idea to pour water into the drain and check for leaks. Repairs will be much more difficult with the tub in place.

2 **MEASURE FOR THE DRAIN LOCATION.** There's a good chance you will need to move the drain hole, because the spa tub is wider than a standard tub. If that's the case, see p. 237 for cutting old drain-pipe and attaching new. Assemble a PVC elbow onto the new tub's drain-and-waste assembly, and insert a threaded fitting into the old drain line. (In this case, an adapter with male threads is used.) Measure over from the wall in both directions to determine the location of the new drain hole, position the assembly in the correct place, and measure for the PVC piece that will fit. Dry-fit the pieces and use a level and tape measure to double-check that the drain opening will be correctly positioned, then disassemble and cement the parts together.

3 **LEVEL WITH SHIMS.** Check your bathroom floor for level in both directions. Then set the tub on a flat surface that is the same level as the bathroom floor and check the tub's rims for level. You will likely need to apply shims to the floor in order to level the tub (which is essential for good operation). Set shims on the floor where needed, using construction adhesive to hold them in place. Install a ledger or wood surfaces for attaching the tub's lip as needed (Step 8).

4 **TILT THE TUB INTO PLACE.** Move the tub into the bathroom, and slide or tilt it into place. This tub is acrylic and fiberglass, so two people can move it around without much trouble. A cast-iron model, on the other hand, is much heavier and requires very careful planning, and perhaps additional help. In this example, a stud on the left end needed to be notched; it was reinforced later with a sister stud.

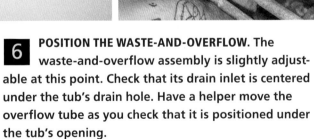

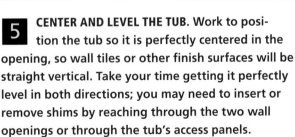

5 **CENTER AND LEVEL THE TUB.** Work to position the tub so it is perfectly centered in the opening, so wall tiles or other finish surfaces will be straight vertical. Take your time getting it perfectly level in both directions; you may need to insert or remove shims by reaching through the two wall openings or through the tub's access panels.

6 **POSITION THE WASTE-AND-OVERFLOW.** The waste-and-overflow assembly is slightly adjustable at this point. Check that its drain inlet is centered under the tub's drain hole. Have a helper move the overflow tube as you check that it is positioned under the tub's opening.

7 **ATTACH THE DRAIN AND OVERFLOW.** Place a rope of plumber's putty under the drain flange, and screw it partway into the waste-and-overflow's inlet. Screw on the washer that holds the overflow in place, then tighten the drain flange; putty should squeeze out all around the flange.

8 **ATTACH THE TUB FLANGES.** Drive screws to attach the tub's flanges to the wall framing. In this case, pilot and countersink holes were drilled first, so the screw heads sit flush and do not get in the way of tile installation.

9 **PLUG IN.** If the heater is not already installed, do so now, following the manufacturer's instructions; it is easy to attach it once you remove the tub's access panel. Plug the motor and the heater into GFCI receptacles.

10 **FINISH THE WALLS.** Test the tub by taking a nice soak or two. Install wall tiles or other finish surface material, and apply grout and caulk to ensure against leaks.

CHAPTER NINE

UTILITY REPAIRS AND UPGRADES

THIS CHAPTER DEALS WITH ITEMS YOU MAY have in your basement—or, if you don't have a basement, in utility rooms or a garage. Some are rarely seen or even thought about but are important to our comfortable lives—for instance, a hot-water heater or a whole-house water filter. This chapter also shows how to create or upgrade a laundry room with a washing machine and perhaps a utility sink.

These essential appliances are often included in lists of Things You Ought to Pay Attention to and Service Yearly, which most of us ignore. But a small amount of maintenance can save a lot of money. Consider adding these tasks to your calendar, spacing them out over the year.

• Check your sump pump, if you have one, to be sure it's operating. If it's not in working order, you can lose plenty of money through water damage to your property when a hard rain falls.

• A sediment-clogged hot-water heater heats water inefficiently, wasting expensive gas or electricity and shortening the life of the appliance. Draining a water heater and checking its anode rod can increase efficiency and make your water heater last a few years longer.

• If you don't have a whole-house water filter, installing one could save pipes, faucets, and appliances from significant corrosion. If you have one, change the filter canisters as needed, or on a regular schedule.

Installing a Sump Pump

A sump pump sucks groundwater from beneath a basement floor's surface and shoots it outside. This may not solve all of your basement moisture problems, but it can eliminate puddles and keep a basement pretty dry, even during heavy rainfalls.

If a basement has buried perforated drainage pipe or clay tile running around its perimeter a few inches below the floor surface, then the drainage pipe should be inserted into the sump pump's tank (as shown on these pages) so water can collect there. If there is no buried drainage pipe, the tank may be simply set in a hole at a low point. (Basement floors are usually slightly sloped.)

Water under the concrete floor will slowly percolate through holes in the tank.

When the tank fills to a certain level, it raises the sump pump's float, which turns on the motor. Water is directed up through a pipe, and then through a hole in the house's rim joist, and finally out onto the lawn. Most sump pumps today are the submersible type. "Pedestal" sump pumps, with motors above the floor, are less expensive but are also noisy.

> **TIP** Make sure you will be able to access the sump pump for future servicing. In the example shown here (see Step 5), the lid can be raised high enough so the pump can be reached easily.

SUMP PUMP SETUPS

A sump pump's liner may have a drainage pipe running into it, or it may be perforated so groundwater can seep in. A check valve may be installed onto the pump or in the standpipe. The water may be ejected into drainage pipes or simply routed outdoors.

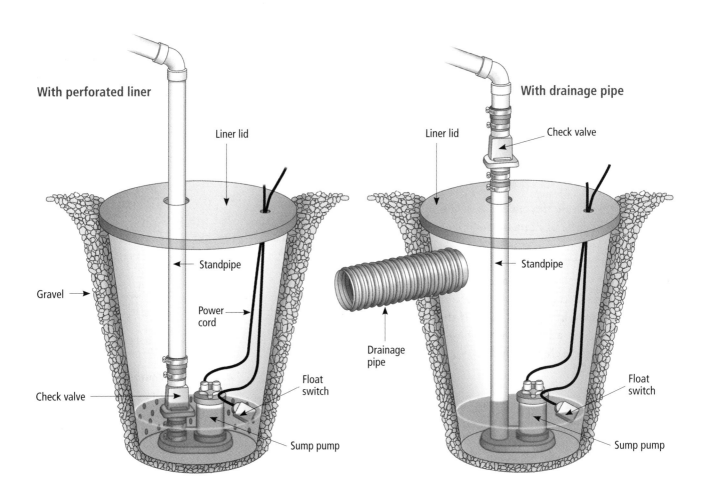

With perforated liner

Liner lid
Standpipe
Gravel
Power cord
Check valve
Float switch
Sump pump

With drainage pipe

Liner lid
Check valve
Standpipe
Drainage pipe
Float switch
Sump pump

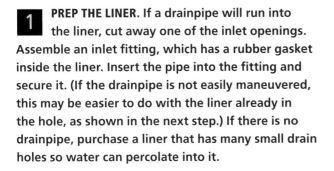

2 **SET THE LINER.** Dig a hole deep enough so that when you set in the liner, its top will be just slightly above the future concrete floor surface. It should be reasonably level, but doesn't have to be perfect. Once you are sure the pipe is secure and the top is at the correct height, fill in around it with sand or dirt. (If you have a perforated liner and no drainpipe, fill in with gravel, to keep the holes from clogging.)

1 **PREP THE LINER.** If a drainpipe will run into the liner, cut away one of the inlet openings. Assemble an inlet fitting, which has a rubber gasket inside the liner. Insert the pipe into the fitting and secure it. (If the drainpipe is not easily maneuvered, this may be easier to do with the liner already in the hole, as shown in the next step.) If there is no drainpipe, purchase a liner that has many small drain holes so water can percolate into it.

TIP In the situation shown here, much of the basement floor's concrete has been removed. If your basement floor is generally in good shape, you may choose instead to cut away and remove concrete only for the sump pump, or cut around the perimeter of the basement in order to run the drainage pipe.

3 **ADD A CHECK VALVE.** Add a check valve to the sump pump, which makes sure drain water will not back up into the pump. This check valve attaches directly to the pump; other types are installed on the drainpipe above the pump (see the sidebar on p. 210).

4   **ASSEMBLE THE STANDPIPE.** Attach a 2-in. standpipe that will rise from the pump out of the liner; make it longer than needed, so you can cut it later. Make the first connection with a flexible rubber coupling, which will effectively absorb the vibration caused by the running pump.

5   **CUT AND CONNECT THE PIPES.** Assemble the drainpipes that run to a main drain (as shown here) or outside (as shown in the sidebar below). Hold a final fitting in position to determine where to cut the pipes, and assemble. Once you are sure the pieces fit, draw reference lines, apply primer, and cement the parts together.

Another Sump Setup

SUMP PUMP WITH CHECK VALVE IN PIPE.

SUMP PUMP DRAINS OUTSIDE.

Here's another way to install a sump pump: The check valve is installed above the floor in the standpipe, and the drain line runs outside, so pumped water will flow away from the house.

Pipe Repairs

If a galvanized pipe develops leaks, it should probably be replaced; it has likely corroded and will develop additional leaks soon. However, if a copper, PEX, or CPVC pipe has been damaged by a blow or has developed a leak because water froze inside, you can make permanent repairs without much trouble as long as the pipe is easy to access. *Be sure to shut off water to the pipe before cutting into it.*

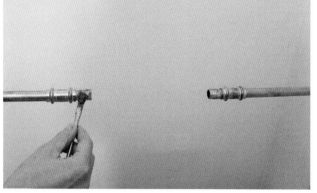

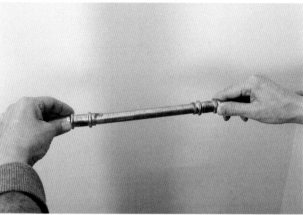

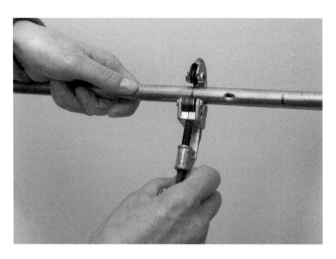

CUT OUT THE DAMAGED AREA. Cut 1 in. or 2 in. to each side of the damaged area. This is especially important for copper pipe, which could be bent out of round.

USE REPAIR COUPLINGS. This is an especially good idea for copper pipe that is held rigidly in place so you cannot move the pieces over to make room for a push-on fitting. Cut a length of pipe just slightly shorter than the gap between the two pieces. On each side, apply plenty of flux to a repair coupling, and slide it all the way onto the pipe. Apply plenty of flux to the repair piece as well, and slide the couplings over onto it. Now you can solder the joints.

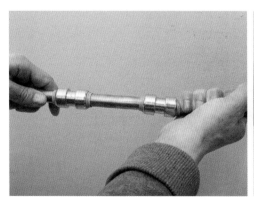

USE PUSH-ON FITTINGS. Push-on fittings are expensive but make the job mighty easy, as long as you are able to move at least one side of the cutout pipe over by an inch or two. Most push-on couplings can be used for copper (above left), PEX, or CPVC (above right). Push fittings onto each end of the damaged pipe, then measure and cut a piece to fit between. Push it on as well. If the damage is small, you can install a single long push-on fitting.

Water Heaters

Often referred to as "hot-water heaters," water heaters work silently and thanklessly for our comfort, and we rarely give them a thought. But depending on your water, a little attention could make your water heater last as much as twice as long before you have to replace it. The next two projects show how to repair and maintain either a gas unit or an electric unit; here we show some procedures that apply to both types of heater.

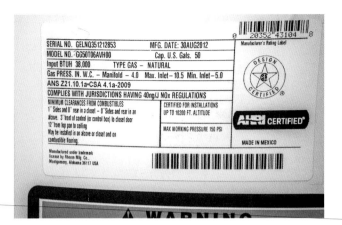

 TIP If water leaks from the tank onto the floor, the tank is almost certainly rusted out and needs to be replaced.

THE INFO STICKER. A label on the side of your water heater gives helpful information and may guide you as you decide whether to repair or replace your unit. This one heats 50 gal. of water; you may want a smaller or larger water heater, depending on your family's usage. Be sure to keep combustibles well away from the heater, as per the label.

Draining a Water Heater Tank

Depending on how hard your water is, it is usually a good idea to drain a tank every year or two, to flush out sediment that collects in the tank and limits its efficiency. *Shut off the power to an electric water heater or turn off the gas to a gas heater, and shut off the water supply.* Wait an hour or two for the water to cool a bit, then screw a garden hose onto the tank's outlet and run the other end to a floor drain. Open the drain valve—this can usually be done by hand, but you might need slip-joint pliers. After draining, remove the hose, close the valve, and turn the water back on to fill the tank. Then restore gas or electrical power. If needed, relight the pilot light on a gas tank.

T&P RELIEF VALVE. A temperature-and-pressure relief valve is seldom needed but does keep a tank from exploding in the un-likely event that water becomes dangerously hot. Test that yours is working by lifting up on the lever; water should come out.

ADD A DISCHARGE PIPE. If your water heater does not already have one, it's a good idea to hook up a discharge pipe from the T&P relief valve that directs water to the floor.

Gas Water Heater Repairs

A gas water heater may have a pilot light that stays on all the time, or it may have an electric igniter instead, which turns on each time the burner needs to fire up. If a unit suddenly stops heating water, try relighting the pilot (if there is one), following the instructions on the unit's label. If the pilot will not stay lit, then you probably need to replace the thermocouple—a very common repair. If you have an electric igniter, you may need to replace it.

If the water is not hot enough and the thermostat is turned up, try draining the tank (see the facing page). If the problem persists, look at the flame, which should be mostly blue; if it is mostly yellow, remove the burner and clean it. If you have hard water, unscrew the sacrificial anode rod and pull it out. If it is covered with minerals, replace it.

GAS WATER HEATER

Here, a thermocouple tells the control unit to keep the pilot light lit; if the pilot goes out, replace the thermocouple. Other units have electric igniters instead. A sacrificial anode ring can be removed and replaced if it is encrusted with minerals. Instructions on the side of the tank tell how to relight the pilot.

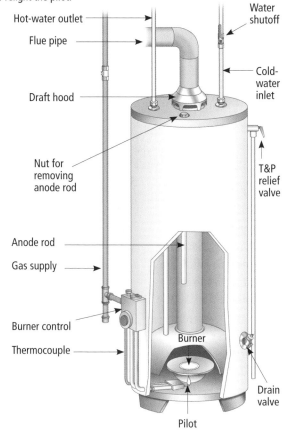

- Hot-water outlet
- Flue pipe
- Draft hood
- Nut for removing anode rod
- Anode rod
- Gas supply
- Burner control
- Thermocouple
- Water shutoff
- Cold-water inlet
- T&P relief valve
- Burner
- Drain valve
- Pilot

TEST FOR GAS LEAKS. If you suspect a gas leak (you'll probably smell it), don't waste time. Mix laundry soap with equal parts water and apply to the gas fittings. If you see bubbling, there is a leak. Tighten the joints with a pair of pipe wrenches. If that doesn't solve the problem, shut off the gas and disassemble and reassemble the pipes and fittings, using ample plumber's tape. If there is still a leak, call your gas utility company.

TEST THE FLUE. The flue should suck fumes out of the tank and to a chimney, or directly out of the house. To test that the flue is working, light a match, blow it out, and hold it under the flue's draft hood (inset). You should be able to see smoke being sucked up into the pipe. If not, check the flue pipe connections, which should be nice and tight. Check with a level to see that the flue pipe angles at least slightly upward at all points (above). Also check that it is tightly sealed at its end, where it attaches to a chimney or fitting. If you can't get the flue to operate, contact your gas utility company.

Servicing a burner and thermocouple

Work systematically, keeping track of all the screws and other parts, and perhaps taking photos to be sure you remember how things should be reassembled.

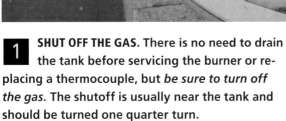

1 **SHUT OFF THE GAS.** There is no need to drain the tank before servicing the burner or replacing a thermocouple, but *be sure to turn off the gas.* The shutoff is usually near the tank and should be turned one quarter turn.

2 **REMOVE THE BURNER ASSEMBLY.** Squeeze and remove the thin metal cover below the burner control. Unscrew the nuts that hold the flexible gas line, the thermocouple, and the thermostat line to the burner control. Remove four screws, and gently pull the burner assembly out.

3 **REPLACE THE THERMOCOUPLE.** If there is a thermocouple and the pilot light does not stay on, remove it (there is a little clip at the end just above the pilot flame) and replace it with a thermocouple of the same length. Make sure the tip is in the same position, so the pilot's flame will touch it.

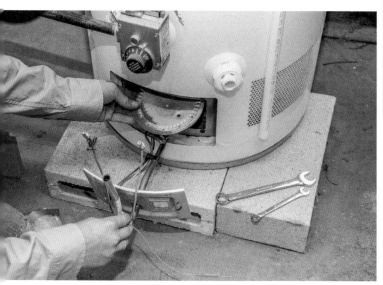

4 **CLEAN THE BURNER.** Holding the burner upside down and gently shaking it will likely loosen a good deal of debris. If any of the openings for the flame are clogged, use a wire brush or a thin wire to open them up. Hold the burner upside down and shake it again.

5 **REPLACE THE BURNER.** Carefully slip the burner assembly back in place. Tighten the four screws holding it in place, then connect the three lines and firmly tighten their nuts to the burner control. Turn the gas back on and follow the instructions on the tank for relighting the pilot or activating the electric igniter.

Electric Water Heater Repairs

A standard-size electric water heater has two heating elements. The lower element has a simple thermostat, whereas the upper element has a thermostat that is also a high-limit cutoff, which ensures that water does not get too hot in case of a malfunction of some sort.

See p. 212 for general tips on maintaining a water heater. If the tank leaks onto the floor, it probably needs to be replaced. Some problems are solved by replacing a heating element or its thermostat. It's more common for the element to go bad than the thermostat.

Caution: Very dangerous 240-volt power runs to your electric water heater. Be sure to shut off power and verify that power is off. Most repairs to an electric water heater require that you first shut off the water supply and drain the tank. Don't neglect to do this, or a disaster may ensue.

- If water dribbles out from around an element, tighten it. If that doesn't solve the problem, remove the element, clean it, and reinstall, or install a new element.

- If water is not very hot and turning up the thermostats (for both elements) does not solve the problem, you may need to replace the upper element or its thermostat.

- If water gets good and hot but the hot water runs out quickly, you may need to replace the lower element or its thermostat.

- If there is no hot water at all, check your service panel to see if the 240-volt breaker supplying the unit has flipped off. If it has, turn the breaker back on. However, this problem may repeat itself; if so, call in an electrician.

- Many electric water heaters have a reset button on the high-limit cutoff. If the unit appears to be getting power but has stopped heating water, try pushing this button. If you hear a click, wait 15 minutes or so to see if that solved the problem.

- If the unit makes a growly noise, try draining and refilling the tank. Also clean away any encrustation on the elements.

- If water gets too hot even with the thermostats turned down, one or both thermostats probably need to be replaced.

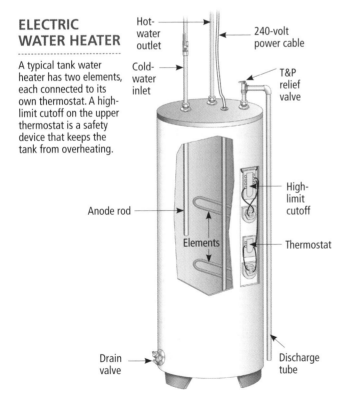

ELECTRIC WATER HEATER

A typical tank water heater has two elements, each connected to its own thermostat. A high-limit cutoff on the upper thermostat is a safety device that keeps the tank from overheating.

Hot-water outlet

Cold-water inlet

240-volt power cable

T&P relief valve

High-limit cutoff

Anode rod

Elements

Thermostat

Drain valve

Discharge tube

KEEP IT SAFE. An electric water heater has safety features that keep it from harming you and your home. Still, take care not to damage or put stress on the electrical cable that runs from the tank to the service panel, and keep combustibles well away from the unit.

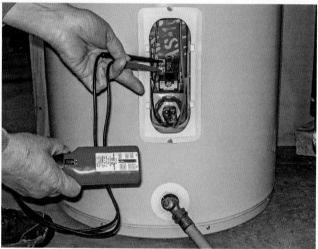

1   **SHUT OFF POWER.** Most repairs and tests should be undertaken only after power is off. Shut off the 240-volt breaker. In the case of an old fuse box, remove the fuse, which is likely in a small box that you pull out.

2   **DRAIN AND TEST FOR POWER.** Drain the tank (p. 212). Remove the cover plate for the lower element and thermostat; it's usually held in place with two screws. Then hold the prongs of an electrical tester on the two terminal screws of the thermostat to be sure power is off. Test all possible terminal combinations.

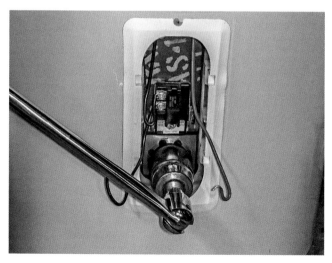

3   **UNSCREW THE ELEMENT.** Loosen the terminal screws and remove the wires from the element. If the wire ends look nicked and damaged, cut off the bare ends and restrip the insulation. Use a large socket wrench to unscrew the element. In some cases you may be able to do this with a pair of slip-joint pliers.

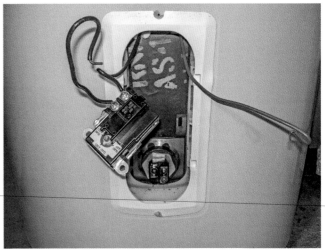

5 **REMOVE AND TEST THE THERMOSTAT.** The thermostat is held in place with two screws. Remove it, then loosen one terminal screw and remove the wire coming from the tank. Take it to a parts supply store for testing, and replace if that is indicated.

4 **REMOVE AND TEST THE ELEMENT.** Pull out the element. Take it to an appliance parts dealer, who can test it. If the element is defective, buy a replacement. To install it, first clean away the opening, and then screw it in tightly. Fill the tank and watch for leaks. Restore power and wait a half hour or so to see if it is working.

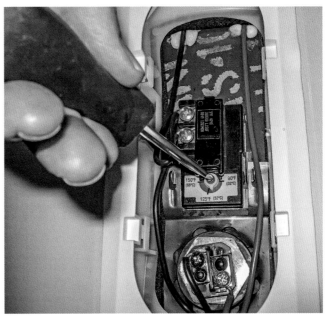

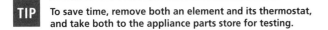

TIP To save time, remove both an element and its thermostat, and take both to the appliance parts store for testing.

6 **ADJUST THERMOSTATS.** After reinstalling, adjust the temperature to a standard 120°F. To save money, you may choose to lower the temperature. Wait a day or two between temperature adjustments to get it just how your family likes it.

Replacing a Water Heater

Replace a water heater when its tank starts leaking onto the floor. Or you may choose to replace an older inefficient unit with a new one with plenty of insulation. If you choose to install a larger or smaller water heater, check to see that your existing plumbing will match. You may need to shorten or lengthen the water lines that run in and out of the unit. If you have a gas heater, you may need to modify the black steel or other gas piping.

Here are some local codes to be aware of:

- In earthquake-prone areas, you may be required to strap your water heater firmly to wall framing. Your plumbing supplier should show you exactly how this is to be done.
- You may need to install special fittings, such as "heat-trap nipples," at the point where the water pipes connect to the water heater. These are simple to screw in, but you may also need to buy adapter fittings to connect your pipes.
- In some areas, flexible water lines, such as corrugated copper, are required to absorb the slight shaking of the tank.
- If you have PEX pipes in your house, you probably will not be allowed to run them all the way to the water heater. Be sure to install fittings of the type and length that meet local codes.
- Some local codes call for setting the tank on a galvanized pan that has a drain hose leading to a floor drain. This is a good idea, because when a tank rusts out it may leak water for weeks before you notice it.
- The old water heater may be largely recyclable. Check with your municipality or your garbage collector to learn the best way to dispose of it.

1 **DISCONNECT THE GAS OR POWER.** *Shut off the gas, or turn off electrical power at the service panel (p. 217). Drain the tank (p. 212). If you have a gas unit, use a pipe wrench (you may need two) to unscrew the nut on the gas line's union, or disconnect the flexible gas line. If you have an electric unit, unscrew the cable clamp, disconnect the wires, and pull the cable out.*

Choosing a Water Heater

- A family of four or five is usually adequately served with a 40-gal. gas or a 50-gal. electric water heater. But if you often run out of hot water, consider buying a tank with an additional 10 gal. capacity.
- A water heater with a significantly quicker "rate of recovery" may solve the problem of too little hot water.
- To save money in the long run, buy a unit with plenty of insulation. It will have lower estimated yearly energy costs.
- If you have hard water, consider a unit with two anode rings. If you remember to remove them once a year or so and either clean or replace them, your water heater will last years longer.

- If you buy a larger electric water heater, be sure your wiring can support it. As a general rule, a 4,500-watt heater must be connected to cable or conduit with 10-gauge wires, whereas a 3,500-watt unit can be connected to thinner 12-gauge wires. If your wires are too thin for the new unit, have an electrician run new wiring. You may also need to up the 240-volt breaker, perhaps from 30 to 40 amps.
- If you plan to stay in your home for a long time, or for greater resale value, consider buying a water heater that has a lifetime warrantee. These are made of materials that will not rust or corrode. Of course, they cost more than water heaters that are expected to last 10 to 15 years.

2 **DISCONNECT THE WATER. Disconnect the** water supply. In the case shown at top, this can be done simply by unscrewing union-type connections at the tank. In some instances, though, you may need to cut the pipe (above). (See pp. 169–183 for instructions on working with various types of pipe.) If you have a gas unit, disconnect the flue's draft hood; it usually just pries out.

3 **SET THE NEW WATER HEATER. Remove the old** water heater and bring in the new one. (Two people can carry a medium-size unit, but a two-wheeled cart makes the job easier.) Position it for easy connection with the water and perhaps gas lines. Check that the tank is at least close to plumb. If it is not, shim the pan or the blocks that it sits on—not the tank itself.

4 **HOOK UP THE WATER LINES.** Screw nipples or other connectors into the tank's inlets, and tighten with a pipe wrench. Connect the water supply and outlet pipes, also with a pipe wrench.

5 **ATTACH THE DRAFT HOOD** For a gas unit, insert the legs of the vent's draft hood into the slots on the top of the tank. If they do not align, you may need to remove a duct screw or two and rotate the hood. The hood has little tabs that can be bent as needed for a fairly snug fit.

6 **HOOK UP THE GAS.** Connect black pipe using gas-approved pipe tape for all connections. Use a pipe wrench or two to screw a horizontal length of black gas pipe onto the burner control. Add a T positioned in line with the gas supply pipe, and a drip leg—a short capped vertical nipple—screwed to the underside of the T. Then install a vertical nipple and a union to connect to the gas supply pipe. Turn on the gas and test for leaks, as shown on p. 213.

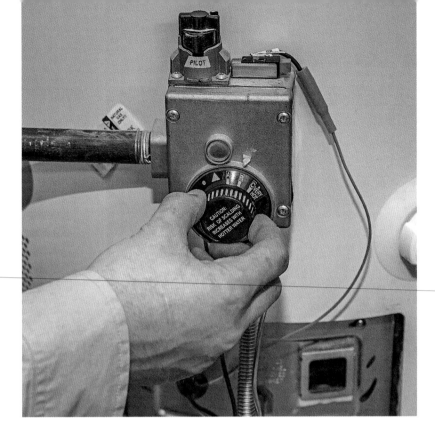

7 **RESTORE GAS OR POWER AND TEST.** If you have an electric unit, attach the cable's wires with wire nuts and attach a cable clamp. If it is gas, follow the instructions on the label for lighting the pilot. Adjust the heat to your desired temperature. After a few days, you may choose to turn the temp up or down.

Tankless Water Heaters

A tankless water heater can heat water instantly, turning on only when hot water is demanded. This saves energy costs over keeping a tank of water hot and ready. Both electric and gas tankless heaters are available, though gas is more common and more energy efficient. You can buy a whole-house tankless water heater, or a "point-of-use" unit that supplies hot water only to an individual bathroom or fixture.

Homeowners sometimes install tankless heaters, and if you have good skills you may try to do so. There are many models that install differently, so follow the instructions carefully. However, it is easy to make installation mistakes that will cause a unit to work for a while but break down sooner than it should, or to heat inefficiently. For that reason, we recommend that you hire a plumber or heating company to install yours. They should provide a solid guarantee that the unit will work as advertised.

Laundry Room Setup

A laundry room should have hot- and cold-water supplies conveniently located near the washing machine, plus a drain of some sort. Many people prefer to have a utility sink nearby, which they can use for general cleaning as well as for draining the washing machine.

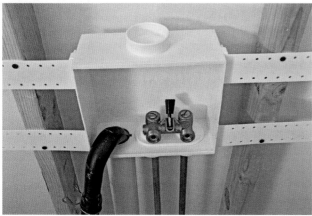

1 **BRING THE SUPPLIES.** Run a hot and cold line about 8 in. above the washing machine's control panel. Lines may be copper, PEX, or CPVC. If the wall is finished, end with drop-ear elbows (top). If the wall is concrete or masonry, attach the lines with masonry screws. If the wall is unfinished, install a washing machine supply box between studs. It can also be plumbed for a standpipe, so you can run the machine's drain hose into it (above).

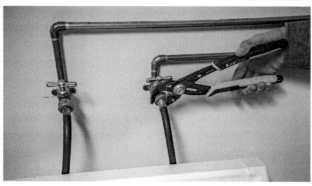

2 **ADD HOSE BIBBS AND HOSES.** Screw hose bibbs— the same kind you would use for an outdoor faucet—into the drop-ear elbows. Then screw on the hoses.

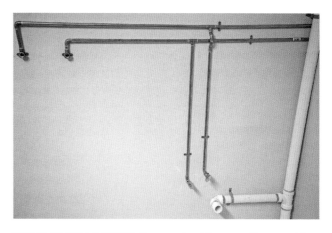

THE PLUMBING SETUP. Hot- and cold-water lines end in drop-ear elbows for the washing machine, as well as stop valves for a utility sink. A 1½-in. line drains the sink.

 TIP Allow a few inches of space between the washer, dryer, and sink, so you can easily access the machines for repairs.

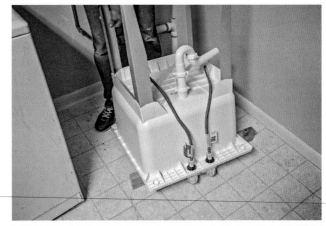

THE SINK. A plastic utility sink is inexpensive and easy to assemble. Hook up a plastic trap with large nuts so you can take it apart without tools (to clear out clogs once in a while). Install a simple faucet with flexible risers, and slip on the metal legs (top). Anchor the sink with screws driven through the legs and into the floor. Slip a hose diverter onto the side of the sink and run the drain hose into it (above).

> **TIP** If you install a utility sink, be sure the horizontal pipe running to the stack is at least 4 in. long. If it is shorter, the drain can siphon water out of the trap.

THE DRAIN. The drain line may end with a 1½-in. trap adapter behind the sink (top). Or you can install a standpipe beside the sink (above). By code, a standpipe's trap arm (the horizontal pipe running to the stack) must be between 6 in. and 18 in. above the floor, and its top must be between 18 in. and 30 in. above the bottom of the trap arm.

Whole-House Water Filter

A water filter that services the entire house is usually installed shortly after the water meter and the main shutoff. You can buy various types of filters that reduce various types of sediment and pathogens, much like those installed under a sink (see pp. 156–157). A whole-house filter should have a shutoff valve on either side, so incoming and back-flowing water can be shut off when you need to change a filter cartridge or service the unit.

Because so much water runs through it, a simple cartridge-type filter may need to be changed quite often, depending on your water supply. The unit shown here is self-cleaning, meaning that it sends sediment out through a tube and into a floor drain or other outlet, thereby saving maintenance.

 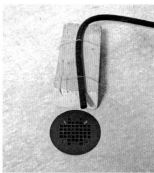

1 INSTALL THE FILTER. Shut off the main water supply. Cut into the supply pipe as needed, and attach the filter to the wall using the bracket provided. Run pipes into the filter. Install a shutoff valve on each side of the filter.

2 RUN THE DRAIN LINE. Connect the unit's drain line and run it toward a floor drain. At the drain, elevate it as shown, so there is a 1½-in. air gap between the hose end and the drain. This will ensure against blockages and water siphoning back into the filter.

Water Softeners

If the water in your area (or from your personal well) is hard, it has high levels of minerals like magnesium, calcium, and iron. Hard water is not good for rinsing soap, so you can end up with soap scum, reddish iron stains, or whitish mineral buildup. In addition to being a cleaning problem, this can actually damage appliances—for instance, it can cause a water heater to die young.

The most common solution is a water softener, which captures minerals in a brine solution. Though some newer units work without salt, most water softeners still require that you add salt periodically. The resulting water has higher-than-usual levels of sodium, though it will probably not taste salty. Still, many people with water softeners provide for good-tasting drinking water by having a line bypass the softener or by installing water filters.

You can install a water softener yourself; most come with easy-to-follow instructions. However, many people prefer to rent from a water softening company, which installs and maintains the unit for a modest fee.

Water softeners are rated by "grains." Depending on the hardness of your water, as well as the number of people in your house, you may need a softener rated anywhere from 20,000 to 50,000 grains. In most cases, you can simply install a unit of the same size as that used by your neighbors. If in doubt, have a water softener company test your water and do the calculations for you.

3 PROGRAM OR MANUALLY CLEAN. Program the filter to clean itself periodically. Or when you see the canister filling up, press the "clean now" button to expel sediment. In most cases, the screen inside the canister needs to be taken out and cleaned only yearly.

CHAPTER TEN

RUNNING PIPES FOR NEW SERVICE

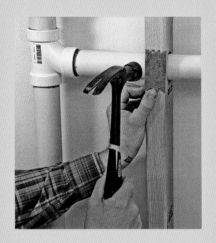

THIS CHAPTER SHOWS THE BASICS OF "roughing in": running drainpipes and water-supply pipes that extend service into new plumbing rooms. When remodeling a house, this is usually for a new or an extensively remodeled bathroom and kitchen.

Though many pipe extensions are straightforward, plumbing a new room can be a surprising mental as well as physical challenge. Here we'll show how to run pipes through walls, and we'll give some of the most common examples of pipe arrangements. But there are hundreds of possible drain and vent configurations, depending on your situation. If you are doing a major remodel, you will likely need to at least consult with a plumber or inspector—and perhaps hire a pro for at least some of the work—in order to get the drains and vents right.

As you work, always take into account the strength of your home's framing. Often, the easy way is to hack away at studs and joists until little width is left of them. But it's worth your while to work more surgically, and to reinforce notched boards after the plumbing is installed, so ceilings and floors are not compromised.

Principles of Venting and Draining

Supply pipes are usually not very complicated: Run them to the right locations, and the water will go where you want. DWV pipes, on the other hand, must be installed according to strict guidelines to ensure that waste runs at the correct slope out of the house and that there is vented air behind the outgoing waste to ensure smooth flowing, to prevent gurgling, and to keep noxious fumes from entering the house. Over decades and centuries, very precise plumbing codes have been developed to ensure those outcomes.

Drainpipes

To state the obvious, the larger the pipe diameter, the less likely it will be to clog. So use drainpipes that are large enough, or even larger than required. For instance, codes may call for 1½-in. drainpipes for sinks, but plumbers generally use 2-in. pipes instead.

And get the slope right. In the great majority of cases, horizontal pipes should slope at a rate of ¼ in. per running ft. or steeper. (The exception is when a small-diameter pipe runs horizontally for 10 ft. or longer, but that is unusual. Also, some people believe that a slope greater than ¼ in. per ft. causes solids to settle in the pipe, but most plumbers reject that idea.) Slope must be constant: There must be no part of a drainpipe that is level or upward sloping.

Venting

Before you start your project, be sure you know how you will vent each fixture, and be sure that your plan will be approved by your building department. There are six basic types of vents:

- A *stack vent,* or *true vent,* is a vertical pipe that runs all the way up through the roof. A stack vent should never be clogged with water. That means that a house's main stack (usually a 3-in. or 4-in. pipe) can certainly act as a vent for upper-story fixtures. Where the main stack is below upper-story fixtures, meaning that waste

DRAINPIPE SIZE AND SLOPE

A drainpipe that is large enough in diameter will probably not clog. A good ¼-in.-per-ft. slope will effectively wash away waste matter.

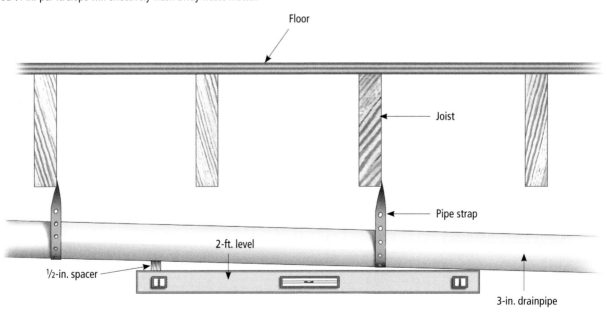

water will run through it, it can act as a vent only if it is considered large enough never to be clogged. If a new fixture is too far away from an existing stack vent (see below), you may be required to run a new vent pipe up through the roof—which can be a major job, depending on your situation.

- A *branch vent,* also called a *re-vent,* runs up and over to a stack or true vent. Very specific codes determine when and how you can run a branch vent. Consult with your building department to be sure they will approve a branch vent. Commonly, a branch vent may be 1½-in. pipe for a single fixture and 2-in. pipe if it vents two fixtures. A branch vent can travel horizontally no farther than the "critical distance," which is often 5 ft., though it may be longer or shorter, depending on vent pipe size. So if, for instance, you use 2-in. or even 3-in. pipe for a re-vent, you may be able to travel more than 5 horizontal feet to the true vent, saving you the trouble of running a new true vent through the roof.

- *Wet vent* is a somewhat imprecise term; some would say that it is not a vent at all. It refers to using a pipe that sometimes has water in it as a vent (see p. 231). If the pipe is large enough, a wet vent may be approved.

Working with a Building Department

Most building departments do not mind if you replace fixtures or run new flexible lines without an inspection, but when you start roughing in with hard pipes, they will want to oversee your project. Though inspectors may seem overly critical and picky, they are there to ensure that your installation is safe. And you can get into trouble if you do serious plumbing without inspections. Many departments will not allow you to do the work all by yourself; you may need to hire a licensed pro, at least to sign off on the job. Go to your building department with detailed plans and follow their guidelines to the letter. You will likely need to have two inspections: one for the rough-in and one for the finished plumbing.

STACK AND BRANCH VENTS

In this example, the toilet is directly hooked to the house's main stack, which acts as a true vent going through the roof. Branch vents run from the tub and the sink.

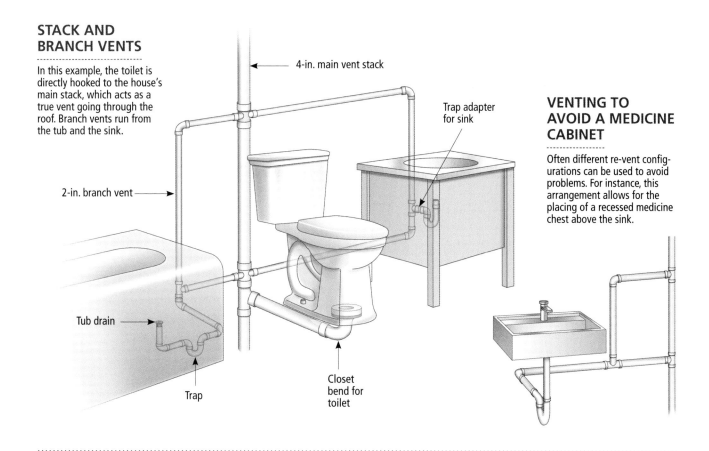

4-in. main vent stack

Trap adapter for sink

2-in. branch vent

Tub drain

Trap

Closet bend for toilet

VENTING TO AVOID A MEDICINE CABINET

Often different re-vent configurations can be used to avoid problems. For instance, this arrangement allows for the placing of a recessed medicine chest above the sink.

- A *common vent* occurs when two fixtures tie into a vent at the same point. This is often done with sinks that are back to back in opposite rooms.
- An *air-admittance valve* (AAV; sometimes called a *mechanical vent*) is a small device that is most often installed under a sink. It has a flap that allows air from the room in but does not allow gases from the drain to come out. If a pipe fills with water, it will create suction that pulls air into the pipe, so the water can flow smoothly. AAVs are approved by many building departments, usually for individual sinks but sometimes for more than one fixture. They must be accessible and not buried in a wall.
- A *loop vent* is sometimes used for a sink in the middle of a room—most often, a sink in a kitchen island. The top of the loop must be at least 6 in. above flood level.

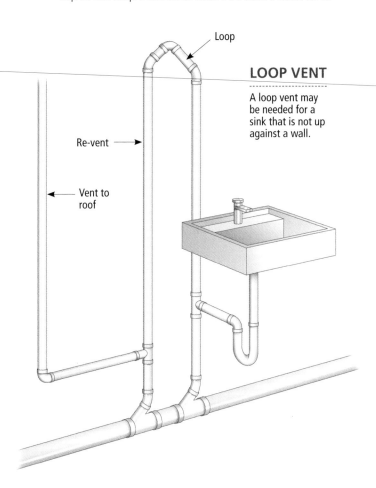

Loop

LOOP VENT

A loop vent may be needed for a sink that is not up against a wall.

Re-vent

Vent to roof

Venting Principles

As you plan and run vent pipes, work closely with your building department to be sure you do things their way. Here are some general guidelines that apply in many situations:

- Vent pipes are usually smaller than the drainpipes to which they connect; 2 in. and 1½ in. are the most common sizes.
- Horizontal vent pipes are usually sloped the same as drainpipes, pitched up toward the roof. If there is an obstacle such as a medicine chest or ductwork, it's usually OK to route the vent in a meandering way around it—but check with your inspector first.
- A single toilet or sink can usually be vented with 1½-in. pipe. Two or more toilets or sinks require a 2-in. vent pipe.
- Although "vent Ts," "vent elbows," and other special vent fittings are available, most plumbers simply use sanitary fittings instead; the vent fittings are only slightly less expensive. A vent T must be installed upside down (so the smoother flow is upward rather than downward).
- Horizontal re-vent pipes often must be run through wall studs, but if possible, run a vent line up into the attic and make the horizontal run there.

WET VENT

A "wet vent" arrangement like this may or may not be approved by your inspector. The toilet's 4-in. drainpipe and the sink's 2-in. drainpipe are unlikely to be completely filled with water, so an air vent behind the running waste water is pretty much assured.

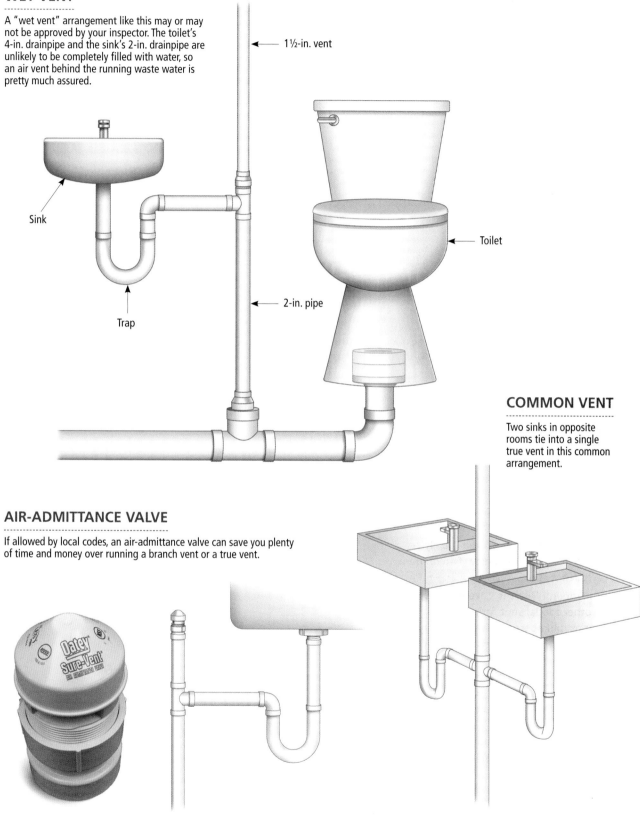

1½-in. vent

Sink

Toilet

Trap

2-in. pipe

COMMON VENT

Two sinks in opposite rooms tie into a single true vent in this common arrangement.

AIR-ADMITTANCE VALVE

If allowed by local codes, an air-admittance valve can save you plenty of time and money over running a branch vent or a true vent.

Pipe Fittings

At a home center or plumbing supply store you'll see an almost bewildering array of pipe fittings; the drain and vent fittings have the greatest variety. For a remodel job (especially a bathroom), don't be surprised if you end up buying more than 20 different fittings to enable you to make all those twists and turns and changes in pipe size. A plumbing inspector will look for very specific fittings to perform certain tasks; if you don't use the right fitting, you may have to tear out the job and repipe. Shown below are some of the most commonly used fittings. (Most of them are available for different sizes of pipes, which makes the variety even greater.)

Fittings that change direction

The terms *elbow* and *bend* are both used to name fittings that turn corners. A 90° elbow may be called a ¼ bend, a 45° elbow is a ⅛ bend, and so on. Most commonly you will use 90° and 45° elbows with a hub (the wide female part of the fitting, into which pipe fits) on each end. A sanitary elbow makes a fairly tight turn, whereas a long-sweep elbow makes for smoother water flow. A street elbow has one male end, making it useful in tight situations. Bushings insert into a fitting hub to accept a smaller-size pipe. Elbows can also reduce in size. Couplings come in handy when you want to avoid notching framing members (see p. 241).

Connection fittings

These fittings are needed when joining drainpipes and vent pipes. Ts turn 90° corners, and Ys are angled at 45°. Ts may have one or more hubs that are reduced in size: A "3-3-2," for instance, has two 3-in. openings and one 2-in. opening. Specialized fittings may have, for example, a fourth opening for a smaller-size pipe on one side. A low-heel vent 90 is often used for plumbing a toilet: Its top opening accepts a vent pipe.

Traps and flanges

For a toilet or tub you will likely need to install a flange (see p. 234), usually after the flooring is finished. An offset flange moves the flange over a couple of inches. A trap that is inaccessible inside a wall or floor should be solvent-welded, meaning it is primed and cemented like

PIPE FITTINGS

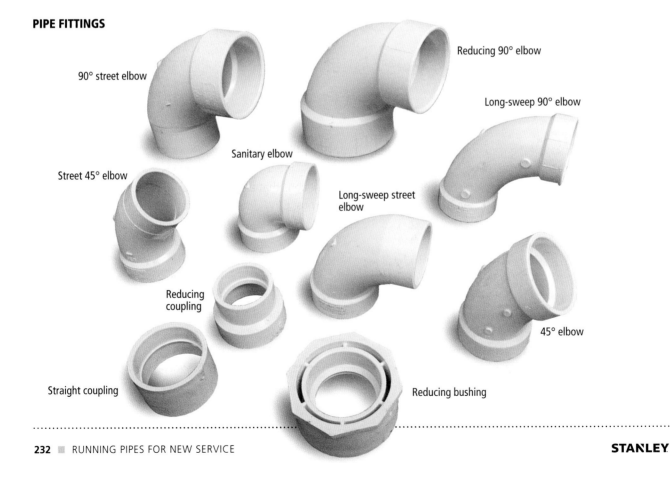

90° street elbow

Reducing 90° elbow

Long-sweep 90° elbow

Street 45° elbow

Sanitary elbow

Long-sweep street elbow

Reducing coupling

45° elbow

Straight coupling

Reducing bushing

CONNECTION FITTINGS

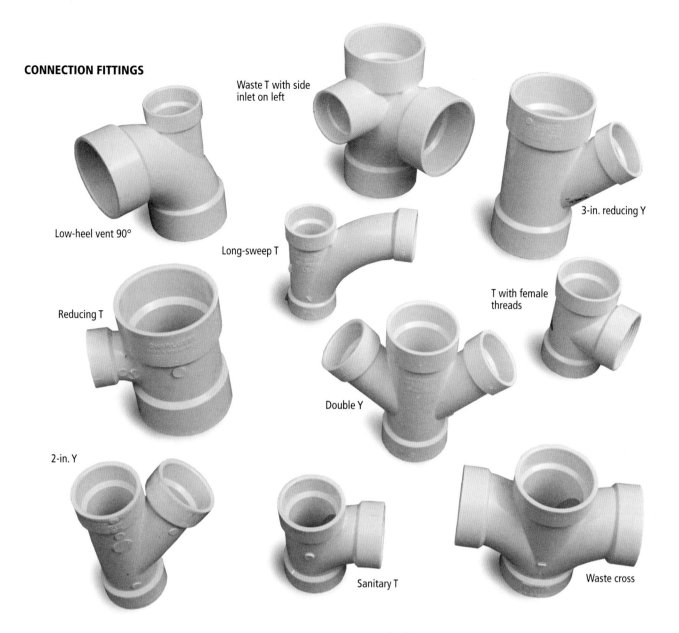

Waste T with side inlet on left

Low-heel vent 90°

Long-sweep T

3-in. reducing Y

Reducing T

T with female threads

Double Y

2-in. Y

Sanitary T

Waste cross

a standard drain fitting. If the trap is reachable, you may choose to install one with a nut, so you can disassemble it for cleaning out. A trap adapter has male threads and an opening that accepts a 1½-in. or 1¼-in. trap arm.

Flexible fittings

If plastic drain or vent pipes do not line up perfectly, it can be very difficult to make connections. Flexible fittings can make the job easier, and are often well worth their extra cost. These "rubber" fittings are actually made of flexible PVC, and so are usually considered a permanent solution. They connect firmly via hose clamps at each end (p. 234). Consult with your building department; they may not allow these fittings to be installed inside walls or floors.

Supply fittings

Supply fittings are less numerous, but there are some variations that are very useful. On p. 234, we show copper fittings; CPVC fittings are pretty much the same, and PEX pipe calls for fewer fittings. In addition to the standard 90° and 45° elbows, street elbows can make tight turns and minimize the number of joints you have to solder. A reducer T is most often used to change from ¾-in. to ½-in. pipe. A coupling with a stop automatically positions the two pipe ends in the center of the fitting; a slip coupling is sometimes needed when tapping into an existing pipe to add new service. A drop-ear elbow is most often used when installing shower plumbing, but can also be used for stubbing out into the room.

TRAPS AND FLANGES

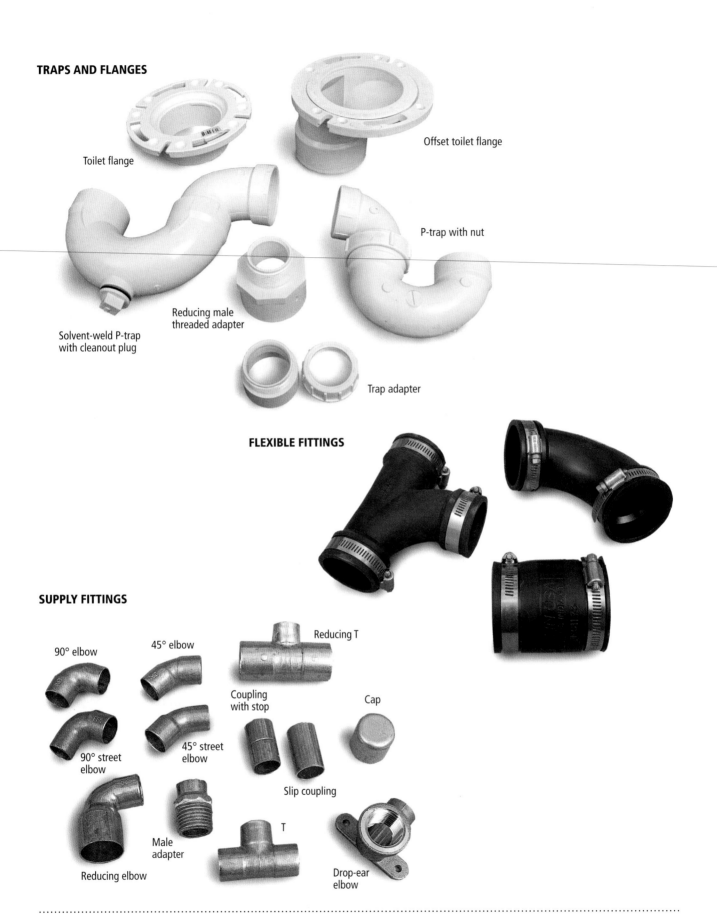

Toilet flange

Offset toilet flange

P-trap with nut

Solvent-weld P-trap
with cleanout plug

Reducing male
threaded adapter

Trap adapter

FLEXIBLE FITTINGS

SUPPLY FITTINGS

90° elbow

45° elbow

Reducing T

Coupling
with stop

Cap

90° street
elbow

45° street
elbow

Slip coupling

Reducing elbow

Male
adapter

T

Drop-ear
elbow

Tapping Drain Lines

For most modest to moderate remodel jobs, you will tap into an existing drain/vent line rather than run new pipes all the way from the main drain and out through the roof. Consult with a plumber or with your building department and read pp. 228–231 to make sure that your new project will be drained and vented properly. The next three pages show some of the main methods for tying into existing lines.

T-ing in

T fittings are commonly used to tap into an existing drain and vent pipe. If the new plumbing will use smaller pipes than the existing plumbing, you can use a reducer T or install a reducer bushing in the T. Measure for cutting into the pipe carefully, so the new lines will be at the correct heights and can be sloped correctly. An important consideration is whether there is sufficient leeway for the existing pipe to be moved up or down—or side to side—to permit you to install the T. If it is solidly in position, you may need to use flexible fittings. Flexible fittings are also often the best solution when changing materials—for example, when tapping into steel pipe with PVC.

2 **MARK FOR CUTTING THE EXISTING PIPE. Hold the new pipe section in place, making sure the drain and vent fittings are at the correct height. (A piece of tape helps keep it from moving.) Mark the pipe for cutting.**

1 **ASSEMBLE THE TIE-IN PLUMBING. In many tie-in situations you need to tap in for both the drain and the vent. If you are tapping into a stack that acts as both a drain and a vent, start by assembling a section of plumbing with a sweep T at the bottom for the drain line and a sanitary (or vent) T at the top. Note that the sanitary T for the vent is installed up-side down, to help air flow smoothly upward. Glue carefully, so both tees are facing exactly the same direction.**

3 **SUPPORT HEAVY PIPE. If the existing pipe is cast iron or steel, it will be heavy and may be in danger of falling after it is cut. Support with a piece of blocking and a tightly screwed strap.**

4 **CUT THE PIPE.** Cut steel pipe with a reciprocating saw that has a metal-cutting blade. Cast iron is more difficult to cut: Use a circular saw or a grinder equipped with a metal-cutting blade if possible; cutting with a reciprocating saw is very slow work.

5 **INSTALL THE TIE-IN SECTION.** Use flexible fittings to attach the new section. Tighten all the clamps firmly.

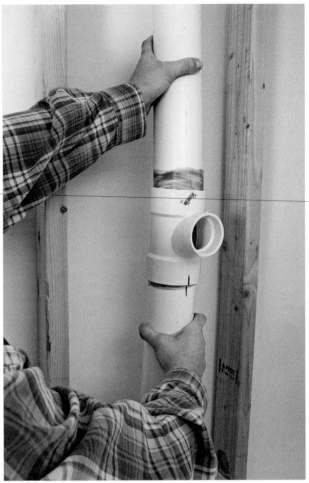

IF THERE IS ROOM TO MANEUVER. Often, especially in the case of plastic pipe, the existing pipe can be moved up and down and back and forth after it has been cut. In that case, you can simply install a T fitting. The cement hardens quickly, so first install it in a dry run, check that the Ts outlet is facing in the right direction, and make a reference mark on the pipe and the fitting. Then disassemble, apply cement, and reassemble.

Working in tight quarters

Sometimes you need to tie into a pipe that is in a tight spot, as in this case where a new drain line must be installed for a whirlpool tub (pp. 202–205). Here you may have a choice: tear open a wall, floor, or ceiling to give yourself plenty of room, or work more surgically.

1 **REMOVE THE EXISTING PIPE.** Cut the existing pipe with a reciprocating saw and then unscrew the old pipe stub using a pipe wrench.

2 **TORCH IF NEEDED.** If the pipe refuses to budge, spray with penetrating oil and wait a few minutes before unscrewing. Or, heat the joint with a torch, then unscrew.

3 **SCREW IN A NEW FITTING.** In most cases, a new threaded PVC fitting can be screwed into an old metal fitting. Here a male adapter is installed, so PVC pipe can be cemented from there on. Apply plenty of plumber's tape or TFP paste to the threads, screw on by hand, then use slip-joint pliers or a pipe wrench to tighten the fitting.

Tapping Supply Lines

When supplying water to a new fixture, you need to tap into the existing pipe, usually with a T fitting. Don't forget to shut off water to the existing pipes before cutting or unscrewing them to tap in. If the pipes are movable after cutting, you can often simply install a T fitting. But if they are solidly in place, you will need to use repair couplings as well. Here we show tapping in with copper pipe; see pp. 174–187 for working with other types of pipe.

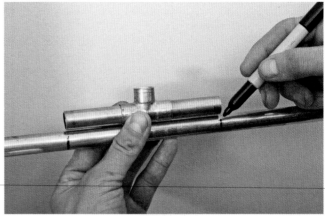

A SIMPLE T-IN. If you can move the cut pipes far enough, you can just pull them apart and then press them into each side of the T in a dry run. Pull the pieces apart, apply plenty of flux to the fitting and the pipe, and then solder.

1 **MARK AND CUT.** If the pipe will not move from side to side, assemble a T with two short nipples and hold it in place to mark for cutting the existing pipe. Cut the pipe at each end.

Dielectric Fittings

If you are transitioning from galvanized pipe to copper, codes often require that you install a dielectric union, which has plastic innards that prevent ionization that can corrode the joint.

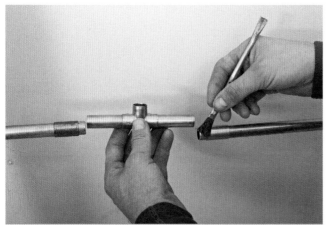

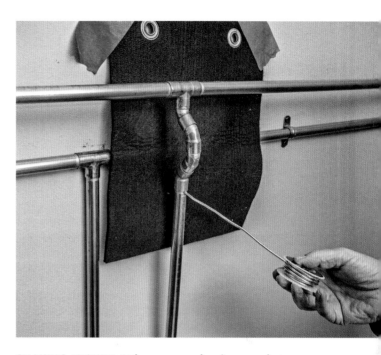

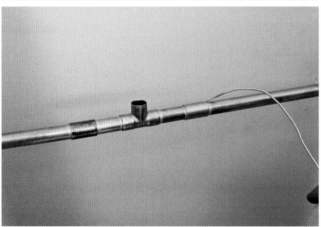

2 FLUX AND SOLDER. Apply flux to two repair couplings (which do not have stops, and so can be slid all the way onto the pipe), and slide them onto the two cut ends (top). Position the new section and slide the repair couplings over to make the joints. Make sure the T is facing in the right direction, and solder the joints (above).

SNAKING AROUND. Where a supply pipe needs to cross another pipe or other obstruction, you may need to snake it around. Use a series of fittings that make as neat a route as possible. Often you'll find that 45° street elbows (which are male at one end and female at the other) are your best friends. Assemble all the parts and check that they are facing in the right direction. Disassemble, apply flux to all the insides and outsides, reassemble, and do a bunch of soldering.

Running Pipes through Walls, Ceilings, and Floors

Once you've figured out how to tie into your plumbing system and you've installed Ts or other fittings, you need to run the pipes. It's easiest to run them in a basement or crawlspace, where they can hang below joists or inside walls, so you don't have to cut into framing to make room for them. When you do run pipes in walls and joists, take care to make your holes and notches as small as possible, so you won't seriously compromise your framing's strength. Because the holes are not much larger than the pipes, they must be drilled at precise locations for the pipe to run in a straight line.

1 **POSITION PIPES AND MARK WITH A SQUARE.** Position the pipes where they will go, on the face of the framing. Use tape to hold them in place, and check that the horizontal lines are sloped down for the drain and up for the vent at about ¼ in. per foot. Use a Speed Square® to mark a line even with the top of the pipe at each framing member.

2 **MARK FOR PIPE AND STUD CENTERS.** Measure the pipe's outside diameter and divide in half to find the pipe's center dimension. Cut a small piece of wood to that dimension and use it as a guide to mark each framing member (top). Then use a sliding square to mark the center of the stud (above); the intersection of the two lines is the center of the hole.

> **TIP** You can also mark for cutting holes using a long square, positioned at the center of the pipe diameters. The method shown on these pages takes more time but is more fail-safe, especially for do-it-yourselfers.

3 **DRILL HOLES.** Equip a right-angle drill with a hole saw that is about ½ in. wider than the outside diameter of the pipe and drill holes. The cordless drill shown here is powerful enough to drill seven or eight holes before the battery wears out, so keep an extra battery in the charger. If you have plenty of holes to drill, consider renting a corded ½-in. right-angle drill.

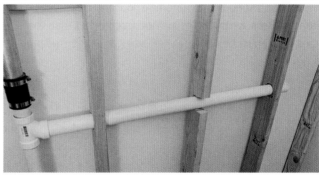

4 **RUN PIPES WITH NOTCHES.** Because you cannot bend the pipe, you will not be able to simply thread it through more than two holes in a row. There are two options: The first is to cut a notch in one or more of the studs.

OR USE COUPLINGS. The other method is to cut the pipe into sections short enough to thread through two holes, and use one or more couplings to join them together. When you do this, keep in mind that each coupling will add ½ in. or so to the length of the pipe.

5 **PROTECT THE PIPES.** Hammer on protective plates at each hole, to ensure that a nail driven through the future drywall cannot reach the pipe. If the studs are 2×6 and the framing member is at least 1½ in. thick at the hole, you are not required to do this.

Bathroom Plumbing

Plumbing for new service can sometimes get complicated, and no book can cover all the possible problems you may encounter. The rest of this chapter shows how to install common plumbing configurations for a simple bathroom and a kitchen remodel. Along the way we'll learn a good many things that can apply to other situations.

TIP For major plumbing like this, the wall framing should be 2×6 or larger, not 2×4. If you have 2×4s, you might be able to remove the drywall from the entire wall and fur out the studs with 2×2s.

ONE POSSIBLE ARRANGEMENT

If you are able to run plumbing into the room below, installing drainpipes can be a bit easier. In this arrangement, the main vent is behind the toilet on the right, and the bathtub and sink are re-vented over to it. The main drainpipe can be tied into a house drain below.

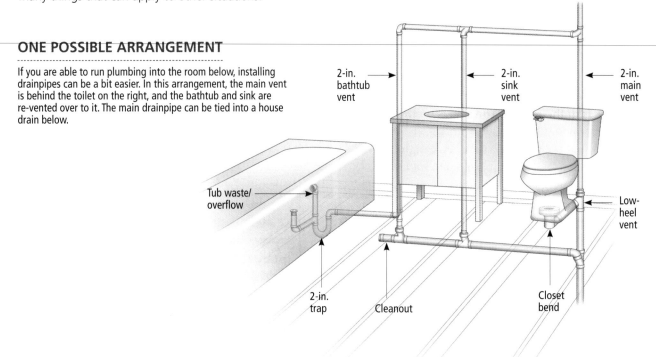

2-in. bathtub vent

2-in. sink vent

2-in. main vent

Tub waste/ overflow

Low-heel vent

2-in. trap

Cleanout

Closet bend

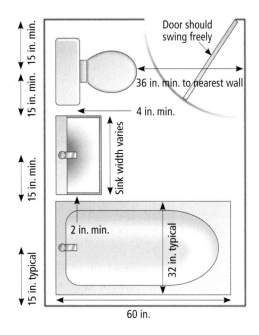

Door should swing freely

36 in. min. to nearest wall

15 in. min. 15 in. min.

15 in. min.

15 in. min.

15 in. typical

4 in. min.

Sink width varies

2 in. min.

32 in. typical

60 in.

SPACING OF BATHROOM FIXTURES

This shows the minimum clearances for a toilet, sink, and tub or shower stall. If possible, place things a few inches farther apart, to avoid feeling cramped.

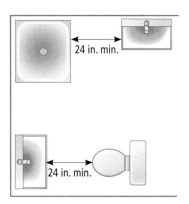

24 in. min.

24 in. min.

THE DRAINS AND VENTS. In this arrangement the main stack is in the middle. The sink is on the left, and is re-vented into the main stack, which is just behind the toilet. On the right is a drain for a shower stall. The drain plumbing fits in a floor with 2×10 or 2×12 joists; if yours are 2×8, run some of the plumbing into the room below, as shown in the drawing on the facing page, top.

2 **STACK AND A T OR LOW-HEEL VENT.** If there is a main stack in place, cut it and install a T fitting as low as possible inside the floor or under the floor. (If there is no stack, install a low-heel fitting as shown in the drawing on the facing page, top, and run 2-in. or 1½-in. vent pipe in the wall.) Attach the vent pipe to the fitting. (It is there temporarily; see Step 7.)

1 **CUT AN OPENING.** Cut an opening in the floor for running the pipes. Give yourself plenty of room; it's almost as easy to reinstall a large piece of plywood as a small one.

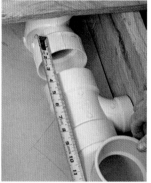

3 **INSTALL THE CLOSET BEND.** Assemble the closet bend onto a fitting with an outlet for the shower drain (to the right), and position it the correct distance from the wall for a toilet. (Most plumbers make this about 13 in. from the framing, so there is plenty of room for a 12-in. toilet.) Measure and cut the piece that goes between the fittings (top). Set the toilet flange into the closet bend, and set it atop a board that represents the finished height of the sub-floor (above).

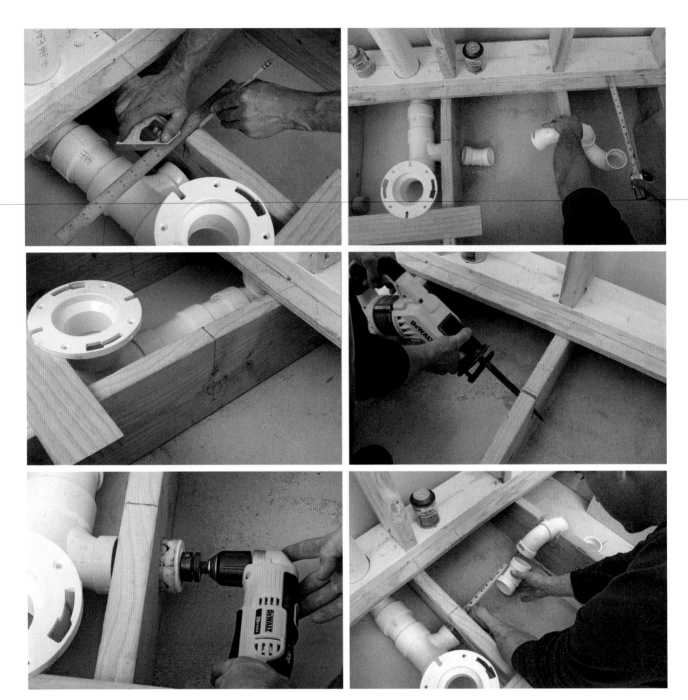

4 CUT A HOLE FOR THE SHOWER DRAIN. Mark the top of the joist at the center of the shower drainpipe, and transfer the mark to the other side of the joist. Drill a hole for the shower drainpipe.

TIP When plumbing complicated piping like this, dry-assemble all the parts, mark reference lines, and then disassemble, prime, and cement the parts. If you cement as you go, you're likely to get off line, with a pipe facing slightly in the wrong direction.

5 PIPE OVER TO THE SHOWER DRAIN. Hold the shower or bath's drain trap in the position where you want it to be, and mark for cutting a notch in a joist. Cut the notch only as deep as needed, position the fittings where they go (here, the trap plus two 45° elbows), and measure for the pipes that connect the fittings.

7 **PLUMB THE SINK DRAIN.** Remove the tall vent pipe and cut a piece that will just rise above the baseplate. Assemble a short pipe (enough to rise above the base plate by a couple of inches), a Y fitting, and a 45° street elbow, and insert into the elbow below the baseplate. For the sink vent, assemble a sweep elbow and a sanitary T fitting as shown, and measure to ensure that the T's outlet is at the right height—16 in. or 17 in. is good—when it is aligned with the 45° elbow. Eyeball this carefully.

6 **DRILL A HOLE FOR THE SHOWER VENT.** Hold the shower vent in place and carefully eyeball to place it in line with the drain fitting. Mark for the center of the pipe, then mark the center of the baseplate and drill the hole. Slip the vent pipe down, place the elbow on it, and measure and cut the pipe that runs between them.

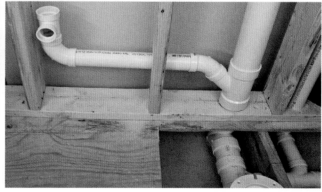

8 **ATTACH THE SINK DRAIN.** Cut a hole in a stud and assemble the sink drain. Make sure the drain slopes at a rate of ¼ in. per ft. or more.

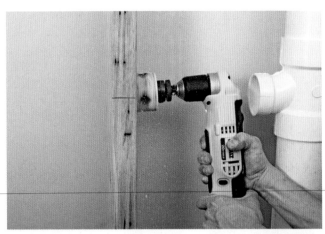

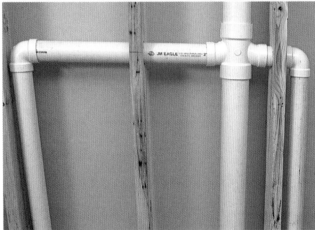

9   **DRILL THE HOLE FOR THE VENT.** Run the main vent pipe up to the correct height, so the vent pipes will be at least 6 in. above the flood level of the sink. Attach an upside-down sanitary cross. (This one reduces, for 2-in. branch vent pipes on each side.) Mark and drill centered holes, and attach the vent pipes on each side.

10   **INSTALL THE SUPPLIES.** Run supply pipes for the sink and for the shower. (To install tub and shower supply pipes, see pp. 195–198.) Here, the pipes for the sink have air arresters on top and are attached to a brace that runs between studs. Attaching a strap behind the sink's drain and vent line will keep it firm.

11   **REPLACE THE SUBFLOOR.** Before reinstalling the plywood piece you cut out (Step 1), attach 2×4 or 2×2 cleats to the sides of joists as needed to provide fastening surfaces. You'll need to cut holes for the toilet and the shower drain. Cut the shower drain-pipe to the height of the finished shower base.

Kitchen Plumbing

Rough-in kitchen plumbing (the pipes in the walls) is often surprisingly simple. For most kitchens, you need one vented drain, plus hot and cold supply lines for the sink. All the other plumbing lines—for the garbage disposal, dishwasher, sink appliances, and icemaker—are made with flexible lines running through cabinets, which can be installed after the walls are finished.

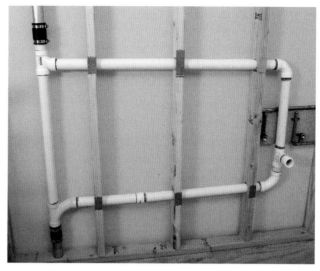

INSTALL DRAINS AND VENTS. See pp. 240–241 for running drain and vent pipes through walls. Install nail plates to protect the pipes where they are closer than 1½ in. from the edge of the stud.

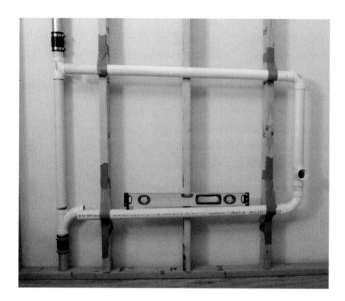

POSITION THE DRAIN AND VENT PIPES. If during a kitchen remodel you will move the sink more than a few feet, you'll need to move the sink drain. See pp. 228–231 to plan for venting. In this case, the re-vent line is slightly shorter than 5 ft., which is within most codes.

SUPPLY PIPES. Here's another way to install supply pipes. Attach a plywood brace behind the drainpipe. Run the supplies to drop-ear elbows, which can be screwed firmly to the brace. You can insert a galvanized nipple into the drop-ear's threads, or solder a male adapter to a copper pipe and screw that in.

> **TIP** In some areas you may be allowed to install an air-admittance valve under the kitchen sink. In that case, you will not need to run a branch vent line; just run the drain at a slope to tie into the existing drainpipe.

INDEX

CREDITS

All photos by Steve Cory and Diane Slavik, except as noted below:

American Standard: p. 53 (top left), 54 (top right, bottom), 55 (top left, bottom left and right), 56 (top left and right, bottom right), 128 (top left, bottom right), 130 (bottom), 145 (top left, bottom)

Aquasana, Inc.: p. 157

Blanco: p. 145 (top right), 146 (bottom right)

Pete Cory: p. 216, 217 (bottom left, top and middle right), 218 (all)

Dornbracht: p. 56 (bottom left)

Jeffrey Goulding, photo-synthesis.co: p. 60 (bottom left and right), 61 (all), 64–65 (all), 74–76 (all), 81 (all)

Joshua Griffin, Griffin Air LLC, Urbanna, VA.: p. 207

Kohler: p. 53 (middle right, bottom right), 55 (top right), 84 (all), 85 (all), 86 (all), 105 (right), 113, 128 (top right, bottom left), 129 (all), 130 (top

left and right), 131 (all), 144 (all), 146 (top left and right, middle right, bottom left), 188 (all), 189 (all), 190 (all), 191

Jeff Ross: p. 6 (bottom); 8 (both)

Shutterstock/holbox: p. 10

Speakman Company: p. 53 (top right, bottom left), 54 (top left)

Jeff Ross: p. 6 (bottom); 8 (all)

David Toht: p. 15, 57 (all), 58 (top left and right), 187, 193 (top left and right), 194–201 (all)